Professional Table Service

Professional Table Service

Sylvia Meyer
Edy Schmid
Christel Spühler

Translated by
Heinz Holtmann

JOHN WILEY & SONS, INC.

New York Chichester Weinheim Brisbane Singapore Toronto

Printed in the United States of America
Designed by Manfred Glauser, Küsnacht
Photographs by Dutoit+Hayoz, Zurich

English translation copyright © 1991 by John Wiley & Sons, Inc.
First published as *Service-Lehrbuch* by Verlag Schweizer Wirteverband,
Zurich, Switzerland, copyright © 1987

This text is printed on acid-free paper. ♾

Published simultaneously in Canada.

This publication is designed to provide accurate and authoritative information in regard to the
subject matter covered. It is sold with the understanding that the publisher is not engaged in
rendering legal, accounting, or other professional services. If legal advice or other expert
assistance is required, the services of a competent professional person should be sought.

02 01   15 14 13

Library of Congress Cataloging-in-Publication Data

Meyer, Sylvia.
   [Service Lehrbuch. English]
      Professional table service/by Sylvia Meyer, Edy Schmid, Christel
         Spühler; translated by Heinz Holtmann.
         p.   cm.
   Translation of: Service Lehrbuch.
   ISBN 0-471-28926-4
   1. Table Service.   I. Schmid, Edy.   II. Spühler, Christel.
III. Title.
TX881.M4813   1990
642'.6—dc20   89-14679
                                                                        CIP

Contents

1. The Service Profession   11

   Spheres of Activity   12
   The Service Hierarchy   14

2. Equipment and Materials   17

   Personal Equipment   18
   Restaurant Furniture   20
   Réchauds   23
   Table Linens   24
   Utensils   27
   Glassware   31
   China and Dishes   39
   Platters, Bowls, and Other Containers   41

3. Preparatory Work in the Waiters' Pantry and Dining Room   47

   Mise en Place in the Waiters' Pantry   48
   Mise en Place in the Dining Room   55

4. The Bar   59

5. Service Organization   63

   Work Schedules   64
   Service Stations   66

6. The Menu   69

   The Classical Menu Structure   70
   Short Menus   72
   Menu Design   75

7. *Mise en Place*   83

    Service *Mise en Place*   84
    The Guest Table   87
    The Basic Table Setting   91
    Extending the Basic Setting   94
    Condiments   100
    Table Decoration   102

8. Service Rules, Service Techniques,   105
    Service Styles

    Service Rules   106
    Service Techniques   111
    Service Styles   114
    Service Methods   118

9. Breakfast   121

    Breakfast Areas   122
    Breakfast *Mise en Place* and Service   123
    Breakfast Beverages   125
    The Breakfast Menu   126

10. Banquets and Functions   131

    Types of Functions   132
    Arrangements for a Special Event   133
    Preparations for a Banquet   136

11. Our Guests   141

    Guests' Expectations   142
    Guest Categories   144
    Reservations   147
    First Impressions   149

Complaints 151
Farewells 153

12. Sales Techniques 155

The Proper Approach 156
Active Behavior 158

13. Cost Control 171

Control Systems 172
Kitchen Orders and Order Writing 179

14. Methods of Payment 183

Cash Payment 184
Cash-free Methods 187

15. Working at the Guest Table 193

Basic Rules 194
Carving and Boning 196
Slicing Cakes and Pies 204
Flambéing 205
The Service of Cheese 208

16. The Study of Beverages 219

Beverage Basics 220
Wine 222
Aperitifs 239
Liquors 244
Liqueurs 255
Mixed Drinks 259
Beer 267
Alcohol-free Beverages 274

Coffee 280
Tea 285

17. The Art of Cooking 289

Basic Kitchen Knowledge 290
The Basic Preparation Methods 291

18. Wine Lexicon 299

Swiss Wines 301
French Wines 323
German Wines 353
Austrian Wines 367
Italian Wines 375
Other Wine-producing Countries 393

19. Glossary of Culinary Terms 401

French Terminology 402
Cold Appetizers 403
Warm Appetizers 404
Soups 405
Fish Dishes 410
Sauces 412
Compound Butters and Butter Preparations 418
Main Dishes 419
Potatoes 428
Desserts 432

20. Glossary of Service Terms 435

Index 455

Preface

The key to success in any profession is enjoyment: you will succeed if you like what you do and do not view it merely as a way to make money. When you are really interested in your work, you can master the most difficult situations and will become a master at whatever you do.

In the hospitality industry, as in any other, one never stops learning. Unlike most other professions, however, in the foodservice profession, progress is clearly evident to both yourself and your supervisors. In table service, not only professional knowledge counts; the personality and character of an individual play an important role. Performance is always directly attributable to the individual and visible to both your guest and your supervisor. Consequently, if you are personally committed to your work, you will be on your way to success.

In this spirit:

Welcome to this book.
Welcome to your profession.

1. The Service Profession

The quality of its service determines reputation of a foodservice establishment. The best cuisine cannot make a regular customer out of an occasional one if the waiters and waitresses do not do their share.

Good service creates an atmosphere in which the guest feels comfortable. This is the goal of every task you perform. Your guests do not see all your preparatory work, but they perceive it unconsciously and demonstrate, through repeat visits, that your efforts are worthwhile.

Spheres of Activity

The service profession comprises three spheres of activity:

· Preparatory work
· Guest service
· Sales

If you want to be successful in service, none of these areas can be neglected.

Preparatory Work
(mise en place)

Preparatory work (*mise en place*) creates the conditions that make smooth service possible. It includes every behind-the-scenes task, from setting the table for the guests to filling the salt shakers, that is performed by the service staff. In all preparatory work, order and cleanliness play a major role, to say the least. A perfect *mise en place* is essential for good service.

Guest Service

Guest service is the area that demands the most from service personnel, involving conduct, self-discipline, and an ability to empathize.

Your concern for the welfare of your guests clearly indicates your level of professionalism: to provide quality service, you must assume responsibility for your guests' enjoyment of their dining experience. You cannot provide such service by rushing through your work, expending a minimum of effort. Pleasing the guest is the primary concern in this profession, and because you are dealing directly with those who will judge your performance, the results of your efforts (or lack thereof) are immediately evident.

Sales

In foodservice, sales is actually an advisory function, an effort to satisfy your guests by making them aware of what your establishment has to offer. If you consider the organization of a restaurant, you will understand the essential role service personnel play in sales. Neither the kitchen (production) nor the management staff (administration) can influence sales directly. Only the service personnel (the sellers) reach the guests (the buyers).

In sales you can put your vast professional knowledge to good use. You can advise guests based on your knowledge of the food and beverages your establishment has to offer. You must know in which glass a specific beverage is served, what the right serving temperatures are for each beverage, and which wine to recommend with a particular dish. You must know the preparation method and time required for each item and must believe completely in the quality of the food and beverages. By actively selling, you will support the kitchen brigade in their efforts.

Even this short explanation of the three spheres of activity shows that good service involves much more than setting out food and drink.

The Service Hierarchy

The preface promised you a successful future if you never lose interest in your profession. Your training, professional experience, and knowledge will determine the rank you attain in your career. Experience abroad, knowledge of different languages, and special training, for example, being certified as a *maître d'hôtel,* will naturally help you to advance.

The chain of command for service personnel in small and large establishments may differ, but the outlines below provide an overview of the hierarchy in a typical establishment.

Hierarchy for a Medium-sized Operation

Title	Function
Headwaiter	The waitperson responsible for the overall management of service.
Captain	The waitperson responsible for a service station (approximately 15–25 guests), with the help of one front waiter or an apprentice.
Front waiter	A young, trained waitperson with 1–2 years of experience.
Apprentice	A waitperson in training.

Hierarchy for a Large Establishment	Title	Function
	Maître d'hôtel	The waitperson responsible for the overall management of service.
	Headwaiter	The waitperson responsible for service in a particular area, such as a banquet room or restaurant.
	Captain	The waitperson responsible for a service station (approximately 15–25 guests), assisted by one front waiter or an apprentice.
	Front waiter	A young, trained waitperson with 1–2 years of experience.
	Apprentice	A waitperson in training.

Specialists

Depending on the size and style of the establishment, there may be professional titles for specialists that perform particular jobs.

Title	Function
Banquet manager	Directs the catering and banquet operations.
Food-and-beverage manager	Directs the sales and purchase of food and beverages.
Wine steward or sommelier	Responsible for wines and their service.
Host or hostess	Responsible for greeting and seating the guests.
Bartender	Responsible for bar service.
Room-service waiter	Responsible for service in guest rooms.

2. Equipment and Materials

This chapter contains a wealth of information on every tool, utensil, dish, and glass you will use as a service professional, including your personal tools and utensils, restaurant furnishings, table linens, glassware, and *réchauds*. Discussions of each piece of equipment, accompanied by photographs of the items being examined, explain how to use and care for all the equipment and supplies you will encounter.

The information in this chapter focuses on theory, but it is theory that you will apply daily in your work.

Personal Equipment

Five items are indispensible to the professional waitperson — only five. Carrying such a small number of items at all times should be a simple matter, shouldn't it? So simple that it would be downright embarrassing to be missing one of them when you need it. The five items are:

A Clean Hand Towel or Napkin

The hand towel protects you from burns when you handle hot platters, plates, and the like. It must be clean not only during your first hour of duty, but also during the last. That means you must check it constantly and change it as necessary. (Your guest will certainly prefer learning what the chef has to offer by reading the menu, rather than looking at the remnants on your towel.)

Matches

Always carry matches so that you can offer a guests a light if they wish to smoke and can light candles or *réchauds*. If matches are not furnished on each guest table, you might also keep a small supply at your service station so that, after you offer a light to a guest, you give him or her the whole book. Lighters are not as practical, especially when you have to light cigars, pipes, or even a *réchaud*.

A Corkscrew

The corkscrew must include a bottle opener and a small knife to cut the foil or plastic cap on wine bottles.

Change

How much change to carry—and whether you need to carry it at all or instead deposit it in and retrieve it from a register or cash drawer—depends on the type of establishment in which you work. In most American retail foodservice establishments, however, change is not usually carried by the waitperson.

A Pen and Order Pad

These, of course, are used to take orders.

These five items should be carried by servers at all times and should always be kept in the same place so they are handy when needed.

Restaurant Furniture

How a restaurant is furnished depends almost entirely on the concept behind the establishment. A cozy restaurant in a small hotel that offers inexpensive, hearty meals and a high-priced restaurant that tries to attract gourmets are furnished quite differently. But the basic equipment in both is not that dissimilar.

The Service Table

The service table holds a selection of tableware needed for the *mise en place* of a service station, so that the server need not leave the station for additional flatware, plates, glasses, and the like when they are needed. The service table must always be immaculate and orderly, or it is of no help to the server—and is an eyesore to the guest. The service table should be cleared every evening and freshly set each morning.

The Restaurant Table for Two to Four People

This rectangular table has two decided advantages. First, it allows the server to establish eye contact with every guest, enabling the server to give each guest personal attention when taking orders.

Second, guests can see and appreciate what is being done for them by a server working at the table, whether it be arranging food on a plate, carving, or flambéing. Watching a good server working at a table should be an aesthetic pleasure.

The Round Table for Four or More Persons

The round table was once typically reserved for regular customers and was also used for dining outdoors. Today, however, it is very commonly used in all types of restaurants for all guests because it can usually accommodate five to six guests comfortably.

Tables should never rock or shake. To prevent this nuisance, a piece of cork can be placed beneath them. (Modern tables have a set screw that can be adjusted to keep them steady.)

Guéridon *or Side Table*

Commonly used in European restaurants but infrequently seen in the United States, the small side table, approximately thirty inches long and twenty inches wide, sometimes on wheels, is used by servers at tableside, especially when food is dished out and arranged at the table or for carving.

The *guéridon* should have at least four sets of carving utensils on it at all times.

Special Carts

Common in Europe but rarely used in American restaurants (except to showcase desserts and pastries), special service carts are used to highlight the specials of the day. These special service carts, or *voitures,* contain heating or cooling elements to keep the food at the proper temperature.

Voitures with heating elements are used mainly for the day's specialty or the menu for a special day. When, for instance, a large roast or ham is featured, it is placed on the *voiture* and wheeled over to the guests' table, where the meat is sliced.

Refrigerated *voitures* are used mainly for appetizers, salads, and chilled desserts. In restaurants where market availability determines the daily menu, the *voiture* actually becomes a three-dimensional menu from which the guests select their choices directly.

Some service carts are are used mainly to present already prepared foods, such as hors d'oeuvre, cold platters, sandwiches, desserts, and pastries. All of these rolling showcases should serve to stimulate the guests' appetites and make it easy for them to select an item; of course, at the same time, they should encourage sales.

Since special carts and *voitures* are showcases, two requirements must be met:

Absolute cleanliness — they must be thoroughly cleaned every day.

Beautiful presentation — the presentation should delight the guest with imaginative arrangements and appetizing colors.

Réchauds

Platter Warmers and Electric Plate Warmers

schwarz

The family of *réchauds* — hotplates, warmers, and burners — provides a source of heat outside the kitchen. They are used to warm dinner plates and serving platters so that the food remains hot after being served. To achieve a higher temperature, for example, to serve fondues or to flambé tableside, alcohol or gas burners are used; the heat from gas burners can be regulated more precisely.

Depending on the size of the establishment, different types of *réchauds* are used to heat plates and keep food warm.

Candle Réchauds, *Gas Burners, and Fondue Burners*

schwarz

Electric *réchauds* should be switched on one hour before they are needed. If you want to handle silver platters gently, cover the electric *réchaud* with a heat-resistant cloth before placing the platter on it. This also keeps the *réchaud*'s surface clean, and less maintenance is required. If using silver platters that have inserts, such as a china platter, the insert must be removed from the silver and placed directly on the *réchaud*.

Table Linens

The importance of clean table linen and a well-set table to the reputation of an establishment is obvious — as is the effect of the opposite. Naturally, the quality of the table linens and the style of the setting depend primarily on the restaurant concept.

Cleanliness and uniform appearance are essential, regardless of the type of restaurant. The tables are your responsibility; you use them for your work. Therefore, do not try to economize too much when changing table linens but avoid unnecessary changes.

Silence Cloths

In the past, a silence cloth was made of soft fabric, usually flannel; today plastic is also used. A silence cloth is placed on the table beneath the tablecloth. If it is made from flannel, it is usually has elastic corners that secure it to the table. Plastic silence cloths are generally cut to the size of the table. A silence cloth has several functions:

- It prevents the tablecloth from sliding.

- It makes the tablecloth feel softer.

- It protects the tabletop from heat and wetness.

- It muffles the noise caused by placing tableware, utensils, glassware, and the like on the table.

- It extends the life of a tablecloth.

Tablecloths

The tablecloth always deserves special attention because it is the most visible table linen. It must be absolutely spotless and ironed.

The proper method for laying a tablecloth is explained in chapter 7.

Overlays, or Napperons

An overlay, or *napperon*, is a small tablecloth, traditionally used to cover just the tablecloth. It protects the tablecloth from crumbs, ashes, and drips. It is also used decoratively, to contrast with the color of the tablecloth. Overlays are also used to cover serving carts.

Overlays should never be used to hide soiled table linens. This is not hygienic.

Napkins

Either cloth or paper napkins can be used, depending on the style of the restaurant. Obviously, every guest should receive a fresh napkin.

Placemats

Linen or paper placemats are used instead of tablecloths in diners, coffeeshops, and other small restaurants. Of course, placemats are replaced for each new guest.

Hand Towels

The hand towel, mentioned before as part of your personal equipment, is also part of a restaurant's table linens. Because you use it often and it is visible to your guests, the cleanliness and appearance of the towel are very important.

Hand towels are always changed during a shift if they are not absolutely immaculate.

Never use hand towels for jobs for which they are not intended. Carry the towel draped over your left arm, and use it as needed to serve hot plates or carry hot platters.

Wine Napkins

In some restaurants special napkins are reserved for serving wine. If special napkins are not available, regular cloth napkins are used. Napkins for wine service, folded twice lengthwise, are used to open bottles of wine and sparkling wine.

Utensils

Today's service personnel must be familiar with approximately twenty different eating and serving utensils and must know when and how to use them correctly. In the Middle Ages, servers definitely had a much easier job: they carried in only bowls and plates, and the guests used the most natural eating utensils — their hands. Knives and forks only came into use in the fifteenth century and even then were exclusively used by high-ranking individuals. By the sixteenth century, their use was spreading, but for quite some time, the average person still considered them unusual and luxurious, and many people made fun of them, especially those that trusted their hands more. The following pages show how these simple utensils have been modified for special uses and how they are used for today.

Dinner knife	For the main course.
Small knife	For breakfast, appetizers, fruit, cheese, smoked fish such as salmon and eel, bread and toast, caviar, and frogs' legs.
Fish knife	For fish dishes; also used by servers to fillet fish tableside.

Dinner fork	For main courses, certain vegetables such as asparagus and artichokes, pasta (used with a soup spoon).
Salad fork	For appetizers, desserts, cheese, fruit, salads, smoked fish such as salmon and eel, shellfish cocktails, and sometimes for cakes and pastries.
Fish fork	For fish dishes; also used by servers to fillet fish tableside.
Cake fork	For cakes, tortes, pies, and pastries.
Soup spoon	For soups served in soup bowls (rather than cups), pasta (used with a dinner fork), and for ladling sauces and serving foods.
Teaspoon	For soups served in cups (rather than bowls), desserts, snails, and melon.
Sauce spoon	A flat, wide spoon, for dishes served with sauces and gravies.

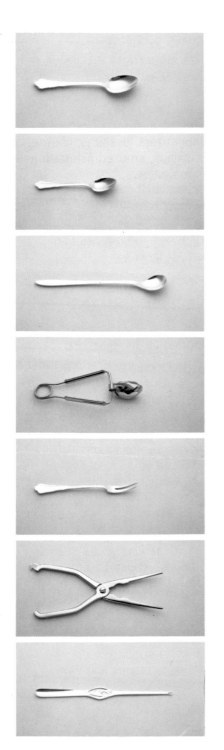

Coffee spoon

For coffee, tea, hot chocolate, shellfish cocktails and fruit cocktails, grapefruit, and ice cream.

Espresso spoon

For espresso and *ristretto,* for removing marrow (as for *osso buco*).

Sundae or iced-tea spoon

For ice-cream sundaes, iced coffee, and iced tea.

Snail tongs

For snails.

Snail forks

For snails.

Lobster tongs

For lobster.

Lobster fork

For lobster.

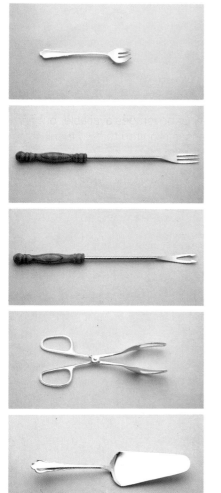

Oyster fork

For oysters, clams, and other bivalve shellfish.

Fondue fork for cheese fondue

For dipping in cheese fondue.

Fondue fork for beef fondue

For cooking and dipping beef cubes for fondue.

Pastry tongs

For serving pastries.

Cake and pie servers

For serving cakes and pies.

Glassware

Everyone knows about the wide variety of beverages available, but few stop to consider the many kinds of glasses required to hold them. That will no longer apply to you, because this section discusses thirty different glass types and their uses. You may not have or use all of these glasses in your daily work, but you should know which glass to use at all times. When it comes to wine, the glass is chosen not only because it is traditional, but also because it allows the wine's bouquet to be appreciated and helps maintain the proper temperature of the wine.

Water goblet

Large, tulip-shaped glass for water.

Red-wine glass

Tulip-shaped stemmed glass for light red wines, part of the basic table setting in *à la carte* and banquet service.

White-wine glass

Small, tulip-shaped stemmed glass for white wines.

Wine tumbler

Stemless glass used in Europe for local naturally sparkling wines.

Bordeaux glass

Large, tulip-shaped, stemmed glass for Bordeaux wines.

Red-wine snifter

A large, balloon-shaped glass for aged burgundies and aged Italian wines.

Champagne glass

A tulip-shaped, stemmed glass for Champagne and Champagne cocktails and sparkling wines.

Sparkling-wine glass

A variation of the Champagne glass, used interchangeably with it for Champagne and sparkling wines.

Champagne saucer

A once-popular wide-bowled, stemmed glass used for Champagne and sparkling wines, now seldom used because the wide mouth causes the wine to lose its effervescence too quickly.

Rhine-wine glass

A long-stemmed, nontapering glass used for German and Alsatian white wines.

Rummer

A large-bowled, heavy-stemmed glass with thick side walls used mainly to serve red or white Rhine wines by the glass.

Cognac glass

A stemmed glass for Cognac, commonly used in France.

Large snifter

A large, balloon-shaped glass with thin side walls, used to serve Cognac and brandy that has been aged in wooden casks.

Small snifter

A small, balloon-shaped glass with a short stem, for aged spirits such as Calvados, Marc, and various liqueurs.

Shot glass

A stemless glass used to serve clear spirits such as Trester, Kirsch, and other *eaux de vie*. Also used to serve individual portions of various strong liquors and to measure the liquor used in cocktails and mixed drinks.

Cocktail glass — A small-saucered glass for cocktails.

Fortified-wine glass — A small, tulip-shaped glass for fortified wines, such as sherry, port, and Madeira.

Aperitif glass — A tall, stemless glass for tall drinks and aperitifs.

Rocks glass — A cylinderical, stemless tumbler for scotch, bourbon, and other whiskeys served with only ice.

Irish-coffee glass — A tulip-shaped glass for Irish coffee (coffee with Irish whiskey and whipped cream).

Coffee glass

A heat-resistant glass for coffee; glasses today are tempered, so placing a spoon in the glass to prevent it from cracking is no longer necessary.

Tea glass

A glass cup for tea and grog, always served on a saucer with a paper doily.

Milk glass

A tall, stemless glass for cold milk and milkshakes.

Sundae glass

A thick-walled glass with a short stem for dessert and ice-cream specialties.

Carafes and pitchers

Used to serve open wines or ice water.

Decanter

For decanting red wines.

Short beer glass

For tap and bottled beer.

Pilsner beer glass

A tall, slender, slightly tapered, footed glass, for beer.

Tall beer glass

For draft beer.

Beer tulip

For draft and bottled beer.

Beer tankard

A thick-walled glass or ceramic mug or stein for draft or bottled beer; this glass goes by a variety of names, depending on its shape and the country in which it is used.

China and Dishes

The Chinese were familiar with porcelain by the seventh century B.C., but it was introduced to Europe only in the thirteenth century. Porcelain was for a long time so unaffordably expensive that it was called "white gold." The products of the world-famous china manufacturers (such as Meissen, Worcester, and Sèvres) are still considered treasures today, especially those pieces that have become antiques. It is unlikely that you will handle these precious objects in your work, but even simple hotel dishware deserves attention and care.

Soup plate (8–10 inches in diameter)

For soups, stews, mussels, snails, and Italian pasta specialties.

Dinner plate (10–12 inches in diameter)

For main courses, various appetizers, and flambéed desserts such as crêpes. Also used as a base plate, covered with a doily, for foods served in soup bowls, such as stews and pasta.

Salad plate (7–8 inches in diameter)

For breakfast foods, salads, desserts, and various appetizers. Also used as an underliner, with a doily, for fruit and shellfish cocktails, timbales, vegetable bowls, sauce boats, and ice-cream sundaes. Also used as a side plate for bones.

Bread plate

For bread. Also used as an underliner for relish and jam or jelly containers, butter dishes, sugar bowls, condiment containers, sauce boats, and finger bowls. Also used to present the check.

Bouillon or soup cup

For soups served in a cup, such as consommé or cold fruit soup.

Coffee cup

For coffee, tea, and hot milk drinks.

Espresso cup

For espresso and *ristretto*.

Platters, Bowls, and Other Containers

After finishing this section on platters and bowls, you will be familiar with all the items commonly used for table service.

Platter

Large round, oval, or rectangular plates or shallow containers, with or without lids, used mainly to serve meat and fish dishes that are prepared without a sauce.

Cocotte

A casserole dish; a round or oval bowl in which meats prepared in sauce are served.

Vegetable bowl

Also called a *légumier,* this bowl is used not only for the service of vegetables, but also for rice, pasta, and potatoes; regardless of its shape, round or rectangular, a *légumier* always has a lid and is always served on an underliner with a doily.

Oval casserole

Also sometimes called a boat, this large container can be used like a vegetable bowl, as well as for serving a roast with a lot of sauce or a side dish such as noodles; it always has a lid to retain heat.

Fish server

Also called a *poissonnière,* this vessel is used especially for the service of trout *au bleu* or poached fish; it has an insert with a perforated bottom and two handles so the fish can be removed tableside.

Soup tureen

For the service of soup.

Cloche

A bell-shaped lid that covers and preserves the heat of plated food on its way from the kitchen to the guest.

Snail plate

Because there are two different ways to prepare snails, they are served in two different dishes.

When the snails are put into shells with butter and herbs, heated, and served, a flat snail plate is used.

Ceramic snail dish

When the snails are to be served without shells, the ceramic snail dish, which has indentations in which the snails are placed with butter, is used.

Both snail dishes are served on underliners with doilies.

Sauce boat

The sauce or gravy for meat dishes is always served separately in a sauce boat, which is always placed on a small underliner with a doily, on which the spoon also rests. Sauce boats are available in all sizes and shapes.

Finger bowl

This small bowl is filled with lukewarm water and a slice of lemon and placed above the dinner fork, on an underliner with a doily. The guest uses it to cleanse his or her fingers.

Coffee server

This small coffee pot, made from silver or china, is used for individual servings of coffee.

Tea server

This small pitcher, made from silver or china, contains the hot water for individual servings of tea; a tea bag is served alongside.

Milk pitcher

This small pitcher, made from silver or china, is used for individual servings of milk or cream.

Ice bucket

For the service of white and sparkling wines, which are placed in the bucket filled with ice and water. If there is no special stand for the ice bucket, it is placed on an underliner with a doily.

Wine basket

Used to keep aged red wines that have sediment in the same position in which they were stored, to prevent the sediment from being disturbed.

45

3.   Preparatory Work in the Waiters' Pantry and the Dining Room

The preparatory work required for smooth service is the theme of this chapter. Such work is very important because it forms the basis for good service, on which the reputation of an establishment depends. Good preparation revolves around daily checking of all equipment and utensils for service and for the dining area. Whether your service during the day is excellent or mediocre depends to a large degree on how well you prepare for it in the morning, before your guests arrive.

Mise en Place *in the Waiters' Pantry*

Good service does not always begin in the waiters' pantry—but it usually does. The pantry is where everything you need for service except the food itself—such items as condiments, burners, service carts, china, glassware, and flatware—is stored and maintained.

The Condiments

Salt and Pepper Shakers	Keep these full and clean. Make sure the holes are not clogged and that the salt and pepper sprinkle freely.
Sugar Bowl or Shaker	Keep full and free of lumps. Be sure to wipe away any moisture on it so it does not become sticky.
Mustard Container	Empty this daily, clean it, and refill it; otherwise, a very unappetizing crust of dried mustard will form.
Liquid Condiments	Containers with liquid condiments, such as Worcestershire sauce, ketchup, Tabasco, and soy sauce, should always be full. Their bottlenecks and caps should be kept clean at all times.
Oil and Vinegar Cruets	Keep full; if the oil or vinegar becomes cloudy, empty the cruet and clean and refill it.
Containers of Grated Parmesan	The cheese should always look light, fluffy, and appetizing. Always keep the container full.
Toothpick Holder	Keep full, preferably with packaged toothpicks.
Bread Basket	Check constantly for cleanliness.

Réchauds

Réchauds

Clean thoroughly daily. Watch for food remnants, carbon, or wax buildup when dealing with candle *réchauds.* Check candles, and remove used matches; when necessary, replace the candles.

Alcohol and Gas Burners

Keep the burners filled with fuel, and be sure their wicks are adequate. Thoroughly clean the burners, and have matches available.

Fondue Burners

Check, clean, and refill as necessary.

Service Carts and *Voitures*

Service Wagons

Check daily and keep thoroughly clean, wiping away any food remnants or grease spatters. If the cart is equipped with a gas burner, check the gas supply and burner. Clean copper flambé pans (suzette pans) regularly with special copper cleansers. Carving forks and knives should be kept immaculate and ready for service. The same applies, of course, to the cutting boards used for carving.

China

China Dishes

China should be scraped and then washed in the dishwasher. After removing the dishes from the dishwasher, every piece must be checked for cleanliness again before being placed in the appropriate storage area. Never use scouring powder or steel wool on china: it scratches the glaze, which not only dulls the finish, but results in tiny crevices in which food and dirt can lodge. Use a soft brush instead.

When storing plates avoid stacking them too high, to prevent chipping and breakage.

▷ Damaged china should be discarded at once. Chipped plates and cracked cups damage the reputation of an establishment.

Silver and Flatware

Have you ever observed how some guests mechanically wipe their flatware with a napkin? This is a good clue as to how sensitive many people are about their utensils when dining out. You cannot be too careful in the care of your flatware. Even a harmless water spot noticed by a guest may elicit a loud complaint.

Stainless Steel

Wash with dish detergent and rinse thoroughly with hot running water.

Silverware

Because silver tarnishes easily, it requires constant care. It can be cleaned with special silver cleaners or polish. Special cleaning attention must be given to silver used to serve certain foods, including eggs, asparagus, red cabbage, mayonnaise, and tomato sauces, as these foods tarnish silver heavily. After cleaning, the silver should be sorted and stored in the appropriate boxes to save time during service.

Glassware

Glassware should be kept as fastidiously as flatware is, because both come in direct contact with the guest's mouth. Be absolutely fussy with your glasses—you can be sure your guests are.

In most cases glasses are washed in a dishwasher. Make sure the glass crates are filled correctly, to prevent damage or breakage. Check the water in the dishwasher, and make sure the correct detergent is used.

Wine, Water, and Tea Glasses

These glasses are washed in very hot water with the appropriate cleaning solution, then rinsed with hot water. When they come out of the dishwasher, they should be polished (if health statutes in your area permit) and checked for water spots. They should sparkle.

Beer Glasses

Always wash these glasses separately and rinse them with cold water. If local health statutes permit, air-dry them on a rack.

Carafes and Pitchers

If the water in your area is hard, minerals may build up on water pitchers and carafes. They should then be cleaned with a commercial cleanser until they sparkle. A mixture of vinegar and salt might serve the same purpose.

Regardless of how tableware is cleaned, it must be thoroughly rinsed with hot water so that not even a hint of detergent or fragrance remains.

Silverware should always be wiped with a soft cloth.

If local health statutes permit, all flatware should be wiped before being set. It should always be carried on a small tray or with a towel, never with the bare hands.

 Damaged glasses are dangerous; discard at once.

Washed glassware should be stored upside down (stem up).

If glassware is stored on a tray, always use a paper or cloth lining on the tray to prevent sliding.

Platters and Bowls

When platters and bowls are not as shiny as you would like them to be after normal washing, repeat the process by hand.

Silver Platters

These can be cleaned by hand with a silver paste or a silver dip. Large establishments or those that use silver frequently often have special silver-polishing machines.

Stainless Steel

The original shine of these serving dishes can be restored with a fine, soapy steel-wool pad (if local health statutes permit).

▷ In the waiters' pantry you should be most concerned about cleanliness and order. The *mise en place* will pay off with smooth service, the foundation for the good reputation of an establishment.

Mise en Place *in the Dining Room*

Cleanliness and order are as important in the dining room as they are in the waiters' pantry—perhaps even more important, because your guests can see how well or poorly the dining area is kept and will form their impressions of the restaurant accordingly. To keep the dining area as clean, orderly, and attractive as possible, try looking at it with the critical eye of a new customer.

Dining Room, Grill, and Lounge

General Cleaning

Stale odors must be ventilated from all rooms every morning, either with an air conditioner or by airing them out for at least ten minutes. Make sure the floors are spotless and all furnishings are properly dusted. Check everything with the eye of a guest.

Phone Booth

Check for cleanliness. Arrange the phone books neatly. To eliminate stale odors, leave the booth door open overnight.

Lights

Check the lighting fixtures in all rooms regularly—do not forget the rest rooms. Burned-out bulbs should be replaced immediately.

Coatroom

All items left behind by guests should be labeled with the date and location and should be locked up in a safe place.

The Interior, from Chairs to Potted Plants

Chairs and Tables

Broken or damaged chairs should be replaced immediately. Wobbling tables should be adjusted. Check under the tabletops for chewing gum, and remove with a knife. Tabletops, table legs, and chairs must be immaculate.

Check for splintered wood and jagged edges on furniture. They damage pantyhose and cause pulled threads on clothing, costing you the guest's goodwill, if not his or her business.

Newspapers

If newspapers are provided for guests, be sure they are arranged neatly and are up to date.

Menus

Always make sure the right menu is in the showcase and in the menu folders.

Plants and Flowers

Make sure the potted plants are watered and the flowers look fresh. Replace or remove any that are dead or wilted.

Room Temperature

Check the temperature of the dining room and adjust the thermostat or air conditioner accordingly if necessary.

In addition to order and cleanliness, the appearance of the dining room is a concern. Therefore, try to look at your restaurant with a fresh eye and consider what kind of impression it will make on your guests, for that is of primary importance.

4. The Bar

In many European restaurants, the bar is much more than the place where alcoholic beverages are served. Although this arrangement is uncommon in the United States, the bar in Europe is something of a central point in the waitperson's daily work. Here servers handle a good part of their organizational tasks, order food and beverages and pick them up, find what is needed for *mise en place,* and usually find the cash register. The bar in European restaurants is, so to speak, the command post for a smooth-running service, the heart of an operation.

The Bar as Distribution and Control Point

Bar with Service

In European operations, the bar is the issuing point for food and beverages. This traditional form of the bar is found in every European foodservice establishment, serving as a kind of "switching area" of the organization between the servers and the kitchen. At this bar you relay the guests' orders to the kitchen and pick them up. For both of these functions, the cash register receipt plays a role: it confirms orders in the kitchen and serves as a control for you when picking up the food. In addition to its role as a switching point, or distribution area, for service and kitchen personnel, the bar also has another function: it is where all necessary daily supplies are kept. This includes all beverages and everything needed to serve the menu offerings and the daily specials, from bread to grated cheese, milk, butter, cream, half-and-half, and the like. Responsible for stocking of supplies, delivering order receipts to the kitchen, and issuing and controlling food and beverages on the basis of the receipts, as well as preparing and dispensing beverages at the bar are the restaurant employees.

Self-Service Bars

With this system, the server helps himself after punching the order into the cash register.

5. Service Organization

Can you imagine an enterprise that can succeed without organization — without a clear concept of who does things and what, when, where, and how things are done? In the hospitality industry, *who* and *when* are of great importance, because the amount of time the personnel must be available is greater than in other professions — in some cases service is continuous, twenty-four hours a day. Work schedules that indicate which employees work at which times must be planned exactly and adhered to without exception if a smooth-running service is to be achieved. Almost as important to organization as scheduling the service staff is arranging guest tables into service stations, which determines who is responsible for each table grouping. To facilitate this, all tables are numbered. Such an arrangement also benefits the guests, who will always deal with the same personnel during their visit and so will know which staff members are responsible for their service.

Work Schedules

The basis for the work schedule for service employees is the operating hours of the restaurant. In principle, the schedule must cover the time from early morning to late evening. The available service personnel must be divided among as many shifts as needed to cover the operating hours; the schedule must also allow staff members time off. During the busiest times — lunch and dinner — shifts should overlap, so that *mise en place* for service can be completed calmly while smooth service of guests continues.

This masterpiece of planning is usually prepared by either the head-waiter or the manager. Depending on the establishment, the work schedule will cover a short or a long time span. In large establishments, planning must be done farther in advance, dictating schedules that cover long periods, such as a full month. In smaller places, schedule changes can often be handled individually by arrangements between staff members and so schedules can cover short periods, such as a week.

Consequently, work schedules cover two principal time spans.

Weekly Schedules

The weekly schedule shows the working hours for service personnel for one week.

Monthly Schedules

The monthly schedule shows the working hours for service personnel a month in advance. This provides a timely overview, allowing the individual employees to see how scheduling affects them.

Examples of both types of schedule are shown on the next page.

Weekly Schedule

	Mo/Lu	Di/Ma	Mi/Me	Do/Je	Fr/Ve	Sa/Sa	So/Di
R. Silvani							
G. Steiner							
V. Martin							
H. Moser							
E. Blanc							
E. Rossi							
A. Collin							
M. Favre							
R. Costa							
F. Sommer							
O. Wyss							

☐ Early shift	7 A.M.–11 A.M. 11:30 A.M.–5 P.M.	▨ Vo-tech for apprentices	
▨ Middle shift	10 A.M.–11 A.M. 11.30 A.M. 2 P.M. 5 P.M.–5:30 P.M. 6 P.M.–11 P.M.	▨ Off	
▨ Late shift	2 P.M.–6 P.M. 6:30 P.M.–11:30 P.M.	▨ Vacation	

Monthly Schedule

	Octobre	Oktober

(Monthly schedule grid for October, days 1–31, for R. Silvani, G. Steiner, V. Martin, H. Moser, E. Blanc, E. Rossi, A. Collin, M. Favre, R. Costa, F. Sommer, O. Wyss)

Service Stations

Every restaurant and every hotel dining room has a certain number of tables, which determines its capacity. The number of tables, of course, significantly affects the demands placed on the kitchen and service personnel, because even at the busiest time, when the dining room is full, the quality of the kitchen and service must remain at the highest standard.

For service, tables in the restaurant or dining room are divided into service stations. A service station generally has twenty to thirty seats, depending upon the service style. The service personnel are rotated among the service stations because not every station has the same number of tables that guests prefer, such as window and corner tables.

Guests, of course, do not know the boundaries of the stations. If a guest in a station would like to order and the waitperson responsible for that station is occupied, someone from another station should take the order if possible and then hand it to the person in charge of the station.

The infamous response "not my station" to a guest requesting service from a waitperson not responsible for that station is correctly perceived by the guest as a rebuff. Service stations are intended to ensure good service and should not hinder it or be used as an excuse for not providing it.

▷ Service stations are supposed to guarantee excellent service — and this applies throughout the restaurant. Therefore, any server who thinks he or she is responsible only for his or her own station does not understand the idea behind this organizing technique.

A Sample Service Station Arrangement

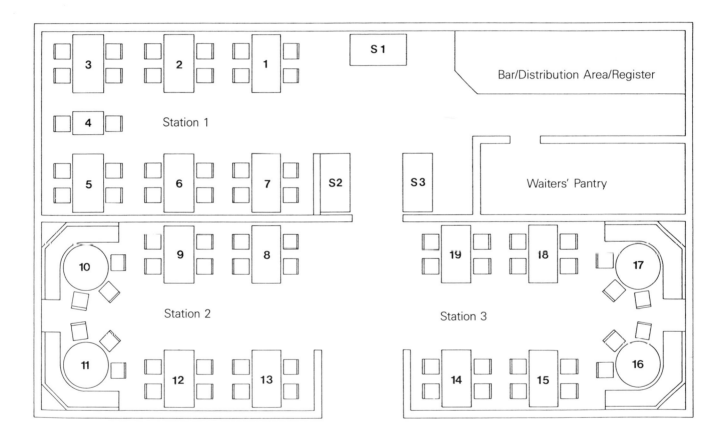

6.   *The Menu*

The first part of this chapter examines the basic structure of the menu for classical French cuisine, which consists of thirteen courses. This structure underlies every menu, even though the menus of today have far fewer courses.

The second part of this chapter discusses the grouping of food and beverages on the menu and the important role of sales in designing a menu.

The Classical Menu Structure

Offering the right varieties, combinations, and preparations of foods is a basic requirement for a restaurant's commercial success, but what will work for each restaurant, of course, differs from case to case. The concept behind the operation determines its offerings. An up-scale restaurant that tries to attract wealthy gourmets must have a menu that, in content and style, is completely different from that of a small coffeeshop that caters to the local lunch crowd. Choosing the right menu offerings, therefore, requires consideration of all the factors that shape a restaurant, including location, target markets, competing establishments, ambience, and the number and skill of the service and kitchen staffs.

Menu Composition

A successful menu depends upon composition — the right combination of foods, prepared perfectly. So claimed Antonin Carême (1784–1833), the French chef who is considered the founder of classical cuisine. A *table d'hôte* or *à part* menu is a predetermined succession of courses, offered at a set price. (Today the *à la carte* menu, from which guests choose from a variety of courses and foods at different prices, is also popular.) One can judge the skill of a chef by the menu composition: do the courses complement each other and progress from light to more substantial dishes?

The classical French menu contains thirteen courses. Today, a menu of this size is hardly ever offered. But even today's shorter menus follow the structure of the classical French menus as far as succession of courses is concerned. They always start with something light to stimulate the appetite, build up to the main course, and then become lighter toward the end of the meal.

The Thirteen Courses of the Classic Menu for French Cuisine

Course	French	English	Example	Modern Menu
1.	*Hors-d'oeuvre froid*	Cold appetizer	Melon with port ————————→	**Cold appetizer**
2.	*Potage*	Soup	Consommé brunoise ————————→	**Soup**
3.	*Hors-d'oeuvre chaud*	Hot appetizer	Morels on toast ————————→	**Warm appetizer**
4.	*Poisson*	Fish	Fillet of sole Joinville	
5.	*Relevé/Grosse pièce*	Main course	Saddle of lamb	**Main course with vegetable**
6.	*Entrée*	Intermediate course	Sweetbreads with asparagus	
7.	*Sorbet*	Sorbet	Champagne sorbet	
8.	*Rôti, salade*	Roast with salad	Guinea hen stuffed with goose liver, salad	
9.	*Rôti froid*	Cold roast	Game terrine	
10.	*Légume*	Vegetable	Braised lettuce with peas	
11.	*Entremets*	Sweet	Charlotte russe ————————→	**Sweets/cheese**
12.	*Savoury**	Savory	Cheese fritter	
13.	*Dessert*	Dessert	Jellied fruit ————————→	**Dessert**

*Today, this course is served only in Britain.

For the modern menu, the courses are chosen as needed (three to five courses) but follow the classical order.

Short Menus

The following examples of five-course, four-course, and three-course menus illustrate that even today's short menus follow the same sequence based on the classical thirteen-course French menu. The individual courses, however, have been merged in many cases. For example, the main course of the past is not identical to today's main course. The original main course consisted of an entire, uncarved poultry, meat, or game animal — a whole prime rib of beef, for example. What was known as the entrée, or intermediate course, comprised already carved pieces of fowl or organ meats. Today the entrée has merged with the main course. The vegetable, at one time a separate course, today is served as a side dish with the main course.

 Cold appetizers are always served before the soup. Hot appetizers are served after the soup.

An exception to the sequence established in the classical menu is the salad, which can be served between any two courses.

Examples of Modern Short Menus

5-course Menu

Course	Example
Cold appetizer	Melon with port
Soup	Consommé with marrow
Warm appetizer	Fillet of sole Joinville* Steamed rice
Main course	Saddle of veal Orloff Chateau potatoes Fennel Milanese
Dessert	Hazelnut cream

*Fish courses can be substituted for warm appetizers or main courses, depending on the portion size.

4-course Menu

Course	Example
Cold appetizer	—
Soup	Consommé with marrow
Warm appetizer	Gnocchi, Parisian style
Main course	Roast pheasant Williams potatoes Red cabbage with chestnuts
Dessert	Peach Melba

4-course Menu

Course	Example
Cold appetizer	Melon with port
Soup	—
Warm appetizer	Fillet of sole Joinville* Steamed rice
Main course	Chicken breast with truffles Steamed rice Braised lettuce with bacon
Dessert	Hazelnut cream

*Fish courses can be substituted for warm appetizers or main courses, depending on the portion size.

3-course Menu	
Course	Example
Cold appetizer	—
Soup	Consommé with marrow
Warm appetizer	—
Main course	Roast Pheasant Williams potatoes Red cabbage with chestnuts
Dessert	Fresh fruit

3-course Menu	
Course	Example
Cold appetizer	Melon with port
Soup	—
Warm appetizer	—
Main course	Fillet of sole Joinville* Steamed rice Mimosa salad
Dessert	Champagne sorbet

*Fish courses can be substituted for warm appetizers or main courses, depending on the portion size.

Menu Design

The Menu Format

In restaurants with *table d'hôte* service, the menu still serves the traditional role: it outlines for the guest the dishes to be served in a set number of courses (sometimes offering alternative dishes); occasionally two different menus, such as a three-course and a five-course menu, are provided to give the guest a choice as to the size of the meal.

In many cases, especially in restaurants serving haute cuisine, the *à part* or *table d'hôte* menu is beautifully handwritten to emphasize the traditional character of the restaurant. In less fancy restaurants, a modern variant that is similar but simpler is often used: the blackboard, on which are written recommendations concerning the day's specialties.

In general, however, the *table d'hôte* or *à part* menu, which changes daily or cyclically, is prepared in-house (on a typewriter or computer) and duplicated as necessary. A separate menu listing the daily specials might also be prepared.

In many restaurants the *table d'hôte* or *à part* menu and the daily specials contain only a fraction of what is offered. Often an *à la carte* menu, from which the guests can select an array of dishes that are always available, is also provided. If an *à la carte* menu is offered, the other menus are inserted in or clipped to its folder.

The daily menus may also be placed at every seat, but in most establishments they are offered by the service staff along with the regular *á la carte* menu. Any menus that are not immaculate should be discarded.

 The service staff should know every detail of the menu by heart. They should know the ingredients and the method of preparation of every dish, to be able to aid the guests in their selections and suggest the right wines.

The Menu as a Sales Tool

The *table d'hôte* menu offers a number of courses in a prearranged succession, whereas the *à la carte* menu offers the guest a selection of items that are prepared by the kitchen as they are ordered. With the *à la carte* menu, guests can create their own feasts, with the help of the service staff.

A menu that lists only what the kitchen has to offer does give information about what is available, but it is of no help in selling. When creating a restaurant menu, more than simply listing offerings and prices must be considered.

The Focal Point and the Field of View

To create a menu that is also a promotional tool, you must apply the design principles you would use for a poster. Since viewers cannot read everything at once, you must guide their vision. This is very important when positioning menu items on the menu card.

The eye naturally gravitates to a certain area of a rectangular menu, called the focal point, and then moves in a fairly standard pattern around the rest of the page.

The One-Page Menu

The Two-Page Menu

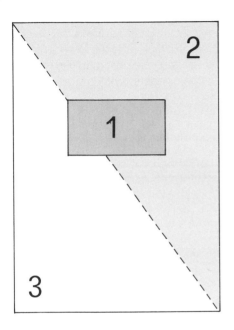

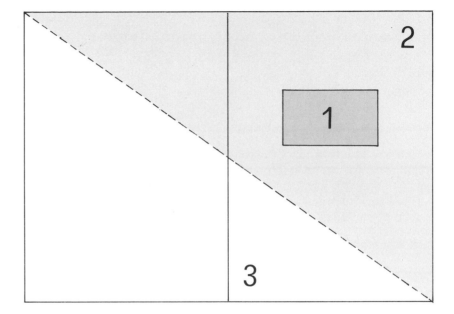

Area 1: The Focal Point

The eye naturally focuses first on this area. Therefore, it is a good sales technique to list all items with high profit margins here. This is not the place to list well-known items that sell well, which in many cases are not very profitable. Dishes listed in the focal area should be chosen to boost sales.

Area 2: The Secondary Focal Area

After viewing the focal point, the guest's eyes will naturally gravitate to this secondary area. This would be a good area to list house specialties that produce a high profit margin.

Area 3: The Neglected Menu Area

The eye moves to this part of the menu only after it has perused the rest. This is the spot where you list the standard offerings found in most restaurants, items the guest expects to find. In most cases these are low-profit items that sell themselves.

Basic Principles for Organizing a Menu

Cold and warm dishes are listed separately.

Appetizers, soups, seafood, and main courses are listed in separate groups.

In every group the lighter dishes are listed before the richer ones.

Salads should be highlighted.

If offered, low-calorie foods should be specially indicated, and the number of calories should be provided.

Every dish should be described clearly and simply, in an appetizing way, without being too flowery.

House specialties and seasonal items should correspond to the season and should change accordingly. Use a clip-on menu or special insert to attract attention to them.

The dessert selection should be listed on a separate attractive card. The menu should inform the guests that such a card is available.

The numbering of menu items can save time and confusion, especially with many of the new computerized cash registers. Numbering, however, discourages communication between guests and the service staff and thus does not help promote sales. For an easy compromise, place one numbered menu at the register or where orders are relayed to the kitchen so you can punch in the guest's order by number; the guest, however, orders the the actual foods with words, not numbers.

The Beverage List

When beverages are not included on the menu, a separate wine and beverage list is offered to the guests. When dealing with couples, it is customary to offer this list to the gentleman.

Like the menu itself, the beverage list contributes to the visual impression a restaurant conveys. Avoid making corrections by overwriting or using stickers on the printed original at all costs. In addition to being attractive, the beverage list should be clear and legible.

A few rules govern the organization of a beverage list:

The specific beverage groups are listed separately.

Every listing includes the price and the amount to be served.

Wines are listed separately by the glass and by the bottle.

Domestic wines may be listed before imported ones.

White wines are always listed before red ones.

With bottled wines the vintage year is listed, as well as, in many cases, the importer or distributor and any other important information.

The offerings of a restaurant's wine cellar are an important feature of the restaurant to gourmets. Offering good wines at reasonable prices can significantly enhance the reputation of a restaurant. A manager, therefore, should expend considerable effort in establishing an excellent wine list that includes superior wines from a variety of regions. A restaurant's knowledge and price consciousness in purchasing its wines is immediately evident. The number of regular guests will increase if the wine cellar makes a good impression.

The Structure of a Beverage List	Division by Beverage Group	Order within Beverage Groups
	Wine	White domestic wines by the bottle
		Red domestic wines by the bottle
		White imported wines by the bottle
		Red imported wines by the bottle
		Sparkling wines and Champagne
		White wines by the glass
		Red wines by the glass
	Aperitifs	Fortified wines
		Vermouths
		Bitters
		Anise-based liqueurs
	Liquors and Liqueurs	Clear spirits, such as gin and vodka
		Whiskey
		Brandies
		(Cognac, Calvados, etc.)
		Liqueurs
	Beer	Domestic beers
		Imported beers
	Mixed Drinks	Tall drinks
		Cocktails
	Alcohol-free Beverages	Mineral water
		Soda pop
		Fruit and vegetable juices
		Iced tea and coffee
		Cold milk and milkshakes
	Warm drinks	Coffee
		Tea
		Hot chocolate

7.   Mise en Place

Previous chapters discussed preparatory work quite a bit. All work not performed directly in response to a guest is considered *mise en place* — for instance, the maintenance of equipment and of all public rooms.

This chapter discusses two particular areas of *mise en place:*

• Service *mise en place:* how to prepare a service table or side stand to guarantee a smooth service.

• Guest *mise en place:* how to set a table so a customer feels comfortable and the service staff can concentrate on customer assistance and sales.

Service Mise en Place

You have already learned that all utensils needed for service can be found in the waiters' pantry. But from there to the guest's table may be quite a distance — too far in any case to fetch them during service. Therefore, between the waiters' pantry and the service station is the service table, also known as a side stand. This is where all service and table utensils for lunch and dinner are kept, ready for use. All utensils are brought from the waiters' pantry and arranged in an orderly fashion on the service table so they are at hand and easy to find.

The Service Table

The service table greatly assists in keeping service smooth because:

- The distance between the guests and the tableware is shortened.
- All utensils needed for service, including service of daily specials, is together in one place.

In larger restaurants each service station has its own service table so that service personnel do not get in each other's way and to keep the *mise en place* organized.

The service table is always set for the appropriate meal being served, so that at breakfast the setup will be different than it is, for example, at dinner.

The service table should be set with everything you need for the next service:

Linens

Tablecloths
Overlays
Napkins
Hand towels

China

Plates for cold foods (dinner, salad, and bread plates), stacked by size. If the plates have a logo or emblem, it should be at 12 o'clock.

Plates for hot food and tea and coffee cups should be kept in a warmer.

Glassware

Water goblets
Red-wine glasses
White-wine glasses

Flatware

Spoons and forks should be positioned in pairs, on their sides, with the fork nestled in the curve of the spoon; the fork should be to the left of the spoon to facilitate setting.

Condiments

Salt
Pepper, peppermills
Sugar and artificial sweeteners
Sauces (Worcestershire, ketchup, steak, soy, and the like)
Mustard
Oil and vinegar
Grated cheese, if served

Menus	Have an adequate number of menus, beverage lists, and dessert cards available.
Ashtrays	Have enough clean ashtrays ready, so that those on the guests' tables can be changed as soon as they are dirty.
Réchauds	Plate warmers and candle *réchauds* should be properly maintained and ready for use.
Service Trays	Have a variety of trays in different sizes available.
Miscellaneous	Guest checks Matches Finger bowls and water pitchers Crumbers

▷ The more conscientiously you prepare your *mise en place,* the less you will waste time and feel stressed during service. Being cordial to your guests will be that much easier.

The Guest Table

The guest table is the place where your guests want to relax and have their needs met. Here the accomplishments of the house are literally dished up for the guests. If the tables are set without care, guests will not expect much from what follows. A sloppy table will dampen their enjoyment, and they may not order as much as they would have otherwise. A carefully set table shows your guests that you appreciate their patronage, giving them the feeling that they are welcome.

When you understand this natural reaction of your guest, you will set all tables as you would in your home for a private party.

The importance of immaculate linen was already mentioned in chapter 2. That chapter also described the different table linens. Here you will learn how to set the table.

Setting the Linens

Silence Cloth

The silence cloth, when cut to the size of the tabletop, should align exactly with the edges of the tabletop.

Tablecloth

The most visible and so most important of the linens, the tablecloth must be laid very carefully. On large tables it should be laid (and later, removed) by two people.

Ironing and folding create horizontal and vertical creases in the tablecloth that must be considered and used when it is laid.

First, lay the tablecloth on the table so that the center crease is on top, facing you, with the two edges underneath.

Now hold the center crease between your thumb and index finger and the cloth edge beneath between your index finger and middle finger.

Now lift the tablecloth and let its lowest edge hang over the opposite side of the table.

Then release the center crease, and with the index finger and middle finger, pull the tablecloth over the rest of the table.

The tablecloth must hang evenly on all four sides. With some practice, you will be able to lay the cloth correctly on your first attempt. Correcting the fall of the tablecloth once it is on the silence cloth can be very difficult and time consuming; moreover, the cloth may lose some of its crispness.

With a round table, you must be sure the cloth's corners align exactly with the table legs and that all creases in the room run in the same direction.

Removing a Clean Tablecloth

A clean tablecloth should be removed so that it can be folded exactly along the original creases. The right method is to lift it at the center crease, letting the sides hang free. See the photo at left.

First, pick up the center crease at the right side of the table with the thumb and index finger of your right hand.

Spread your arms, and with your left hand, pick up the left side of the crease in the same manner.

Then lift your arms so the edges of the cloth meet above the table.

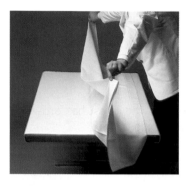

Lay the folded cloth on the table with the center crease farthest from you.

In the same way, lift the cloth at the center crease and fold it back along the next-closest crease; then fold along the final crease.

Now put both index fingers under the center vertical crease, lift your arms, and fold over.

The cloth should now have only the last two creases open.

Repeat the procedure, putting your fingers beneath the crease on each side, lifting, and folding along the remaining creases.

The Overlay

The overlay is laid like the tablecloth, either diagonal to or aligned with the tablecloth. If aligned with the tablecloth, the creases of each must align exactly. Most important, the overlay must hang evenly on all sides.

The Basic Table Setting

Regardless of whether service is *table d'hôte, à part,* or *à la carte,* always start with the basic table setting. After the guest has ordered, the tableware can be extended or removed accordingly.

 Before setting a table, check to be sure the tablecloth has been correctly laid, and make sure the chairs are in their proper positions.

To Set the Table

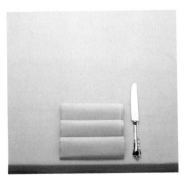

In recent years fancy napkin folding has become quite popular. A simple napkin fold is preferable, however, because the napkin is not touched as much and is therefore more hygienic.

The napkin as shown here is folded very simply and placed approximately one-quarter inch from the edge of the table. This is the center of the basic setting.

The dinner knife is always placed to the right of the napkin, with the blade facing in.

The dinner fork is always placed to the left of the napkin. The distance between the knife and fork should be wide enough to fit a dinner plate between them.

The glass, usually a red-wine glass, is placed about one-half inch above the tip of the knife. A second glass, for white wine, for example, is set to the right of the red-wine glass, slightly closer to the table edge.

Salt and pepper shakers should be on the table. All other condiments are kept ready on the service table and are presented when appropriate.

Ashtrays, one for every two people, should also be set, except in the nonsmoking section, of course. Have clean ashtrays ready on the service table so you can change used ashtrays as necessary.

The bread plate, with a small knife, is placed left of the fork; the blade of the knife should face left.

A carefully prepared basic table setting is an important part of your *mise en place* and will make your service much easier.

Extending the Basic Setting

The number of utensils on the table depends on the number of courses to be served, and the order in which they are placed is determined by the order in which the food is served. Never preset more than three glasses, and never set more than three pairs of flatware. The exception is the dessert silver. When dessert is planned, the silver for it can be placed above the napkin. If more utensils than can be preset are needed, they should be brought during service, always before the course arrives. The same applies if more glasses are needed.

A second knife, for instance, a fish knife, is placed to the right of the dinner knife.

A second fork will be placed to the left of the dinner fork and slightly above it.

The spoon always goes to the right. Use a teaspoon for soups served in a cup, a soup spoon for soups served in a soup plate or bowl.

Since the sequence of courses determines the setup, the spoon can be placed differently (see photo). For example, when a soup is served after a cold appetizer, it is placed to the left of the knife for the appetizer.

The dessert silver is placed on the table only when the menu includes desserts. It is placed above the napkin and is moved down by the service staff just before the dessert is served.

For most desserts a small fork, such as a salad or cake fork, and a small spoon, such as a teaspoon, are set. The fork is placed with its tines to the right; the spoon is placed above with its bowl to the left.

For crèmes, mousses, and ice creams, a coffee spoon is sufficient.

For fresh fruit set a small knife and a small fork. The knife is placed with the handle to the right, blade facing down, and the fork is placed below with the handle to the left. Shortly before serving the fruit, serve a finger bowl filled with cold water and a slice of lemon.

For cheese set the same utensils as for fresh fruit, but do not bring the finger bowl.

Three glasses are set as follows. The red-wine glass is placed about one-half inch above the tip of the knife. The white-wine glass is then placed below the red-wine glass at a slight angle, and the water goblet is placed above the red-wine glass at the same angle.

Special Flatware for Special Main Courses

When special flatware is needed for the main course, utensils are not added to the basic setting; rather, the required utensils are set instead of unnecessary flatware in the basic setting.

Food	Utensil	Additional Tableware
Fish	Fish fork and knife	Plate for bones when the fish is not a fillet
Lobster	Lobster fork Lobster tongs Small knife	Toast and butter Finger bowl Plate for shells

Beef fondue

Fondue fork for beef
   fondue
Dinner fork
Dinner knife

Cheese fondue

Fondue fork for cheese   Bread cubes
   fondue

Which Flatware for Which Appetizer?

Imagine the guest orders an appetizer in addition to the main course. You must extend the basic setting with the correct utensils for that appetizer. If the guest orders only an appetizer and no main course, the basic setting is not extended but exchanged.

The following pages show several appetizers and the flatware used to extend the basic setting.

Flatware and Additional Tableware for Cold Appetizers

Food	Utensil	Additional Tableware
Smoked salmon Goose liver pâté Smoked eel	Small knife Salad fork	Toast and butter
Prosciutto or other cured meats	Small knife Salad fork	
Shellfish cocktail (crabmeat, shrimp, lobster)	Salad fork Teaspoon	Toast and butter
Oysters, clams	Oyster fork	Buttered crackers Finger bowl
Asparagus Artichokes	Dinner fork Dinner knife	Finger bowl Small plate for leaves

Flatware and Additional Tableware for Hot Appetizers

Food	Utensil	Additional Tableware
Snails in shells	Teaspoon Snail fork Snail tongs	Snail plate on a larger flat plate
Snails in a ceramic dish	Coffee spoon Snail fork	Bread cut in strips
Mussels	Fish fork and knife Teaspoon	Finger bowl Small plate for shells
Omelettes Scrambled eggs	Dinner fork	
Pasta	Dinner fork	Some guests may want a soup spoon for twirling long noodles, such as spaghetti

Condiments

Of course, salt and pepper belong on every table, and they are removed only before the dessert is served. Depending upon what the customer orders, additional condiments should be offered. The following pages suggest a few.

Food	Condiment
Grapefruit half, melon, fruit tart, berries, fresh fruit juices	Granulated sugar
Prosciutto, smoked meats, smoked salmon, cheese fondue, quiche	Freshly ground pepper
Tomato juice	Freshly ground pepper, Worcestershire sauce
Oysters	Tabasco sauce, freshly ground pepper, lemon halves, cocktail sauce
Risotto, minestrone, pasta	Grated Parmesan cheese
Grilled beef that is not served with herb butter or butter sauce	Worcestershire sauce
Hamburger	Ketchup

Brisket of beef	Mustard, horseradish
Frankfurters and other sausages	Mustard
Saddle of venison	Cranberry relish
Saddle of hare	Lingonberry relish
Curry dishes	Mango chutney
Cheese	Mustard

▷ An exactly set table, immaculate china and silver, sparkling glasses, and well-kept condiments will definitely make a good impression on guests, enabling service personnel to concentrate on their most important tasks, fulfilling the guests' wishes.

Table Decoration

Even the most beautifully set table can be improved. Flowers and candles are simple but very effective means of creating ambience in a restaurant. They give the tables an elegant finishing touch and tell guests that they can expect friendly and courteous service.

During the day, only flowers should be used on the tables. Candles are reserved for the evening, unless it is a special occasion.

There are several points to consider when flowers are used.

The Style of the Restaurant

A high-class elegant restaurant, the corner coffeeshop, and the rustic country inn should, of course, each choose different flowers for decoration. For instance, in a country inn, a bunch of dried flowers would be very pretty. In an elegant restaurant, a single rose would be just right. A coffeeshop might use blooming African violets in charming flowerpots for a friendly touch. Whatever the type the flowers must be appropriate to the restaurant's style and decor.

The China and Table Linens

When china and table linens are color coordinated, the flowers should be chosen accordingly. An elegant arrangement of salmon-colored carnations will not harmonize with gray-blue dishes on rustic hemp placemats.

The Table Shape

A round table should have a round arrangement, whereas a long table should have a long one.

The Special Occasion

For festive occasions, such as weddings, baptisms, and birthday celebrations, dark-colored flowers should be avoided. An arrangement of striking autumn flowers might be perfect when game is featured as a specialty or for a hunt dinner.

To keep flowers fresh for as long as possible, store them after service in a cool room or walk-in refrigerator. Before placing them on the table in the morning, change the water and trim the stems.

 Never choose flowers that are very fragrant. Also, be sure the height of the flowers is below eye level, so that they do not obstruct the guests' views of each other. The container should be one-third and the flowers two-thirds of the height of the arrangement.

Whatever is chosen for the floral decorations, it should always be in total harmony with the restaurant's style, furnishings, and concept.

Candles in the Evening

Candles not only give a table a special glow, but they may also help to disguise tobacco smoke. Candles can be very decorative if they are perfectly coordinated with table linens and floral arrangements. If candles are used, they should be on every table, even the smallest table for two. They should be lit as soon as a party sits down. The candleholders should be designed to prevent wax from dripping onto the table and to be easily cleaned. Candlelight loses a lot of its romance when it illuminates a dirty candleholder.

8. Service Rules, Service Techniques, Service Styles

This chapter discusses the basic knowledge and skills of your profession. Perhaps you are thinking, at last. If so, you grossly underestimated the importance of all the preparatory work discussed in the previous chapters. What good will it do you to know how to handle serving equipment in the most elegant mannor, if your china and silver are dull? Take heed of what has already been taught, as well as what you will soon learn: that table service is an art in itself.

Service Rules

Every profession has rules, more or less. Table service has more. There are personal rules dealing with you as an individual and rules for working directly with guests. This should not scare you — in fact, the rules should make you feel more secure. All these rules are based on common sense and are designed to make your work easier.

Personal Rules

Gum chewing and smoking during working hours are forbidden.

A noisy service station is a sign that the service personnel are neglecting their main task, which is creating a relaxing environment in which guests can enjoy their meals. All utensils should be handled carefully and silently, and orders should be called calmly, so that even during your busiest time, the atmosphere will not become hectic.

Collisions with colleagues are easily avoided if you obey the following two rules:

1. Never stop abruptly.

2. In a restaurant, as on the road, there is right-hand traffic. Always keep to the right.

Always move forward, never backward. You will soon learn that service is much easier this way. Moreover, you will appear more graceful and elegant.

Wasted motions mean more work, and they are a sign of inattentiveness. Always think about what you are doing and plan ahead — make every move count.

 If you need a hand towel, carry it, neatly folded, over your left forearm.

Carrying Plates, Glassware, Flatware, and Other Utensils

During service the right and left hands have distinct functions. The left hand carries while the right hand works.

Flatware, glasses, cups, and the like are always carried on a tray, never in your hands.

For safety and to prevent clattering, this tray should always be covered with a paper or cloth napkin.

When bringing platters to the side table or guest table, always carry them with both hands. The hand towel should be draped lengthwise over the cloche so you can hold the platter on both ends. If several plates or serving dishes are carried at the same time, place them on the towel so they will not slide.

Serving bowls and sauce boats are always placed on a small plate with a paper doily.

The Carrying of Plates

A Stack of Plates

A stack of plates is always carried with both hands. Wrap your hand towel around the plates, as shown in the photo, so that you do not touch the plates with your bare hands. Do not hold the plates against your body.

One Plate

Always hold a plate between the thumb and index finger. Your thumb should be flat on the rim of the plate, pointing toward the rim, never into the plate.

Two Plates, Held from Below

Hold the first plate between the thumb and index finger. The index finger is placed slightly behind the lower rim. Slide the second plate against the index finger and support it with the other fingers from beneath.

Two Plates, Held from Above

The first plate is held with the thumb and index finger. With that hand turned slightly upward, balance the second plate on the lower forearm and the ball of the thumb. Support the upper plate with the other fingers.

The Clearing of Plates

The basic technique is the same as carrying two plates from above.

After picking up the first plate, arrange the flatware on it. The handle of the first fork is under your thumb; this will secure the remaining flatware. Then slide the knife in at a right angle under the fork.

Now pick up the second plate with the flatware, and place the flatware on the first plate, fork beneath the thumb and knife below.

The remaining plates are stacked on the second plate, while the flatware is arranged on the first plate.

 In an elegant service no more than four plates are cleared at once.

Small food remnants on the plates can be pushed to the lower plate; be sure to turn away from the guest when doing this. When the plates contain a lot of leftovers, they must be scraped away from the table. Clear only two plates at a time and sort in the waiters' pantry.

Rules for Service at the Guest Table

Women are usually served first. If it is an honorary dinner, of course, the guest of honor is served first. Otherwise, age and status of the guest determine the sequence, with older or more distinguished guests served first. The host is always served after his or her guests. When children are present at the table, serve them as quickly as possible to maintain peace.

During service your movements should always flow naturally. The following rules therefore should become second nature.

Left of the Guest

- Present platters

- Serve from platters with a spoon and fork

- Hold platters when the guests help themselves

- Serve salad, when it is served as a side dish

- Serve bread for the bread plates

- Clean the table of breadcrumbs with a folded napkin or crumber

- Clear anything served from the left

Right of the Guest

- Set and clear plates

- Replenish or change flatware

- Pour beverages and present bottles

Every Rule Has Exceptions

At corner tables, for instance, it is not always possible to observe the service rules. In this case the guests are served so as to disturb them as little as possible.

At a rectangular table, stand at the head of the table:

- To work at a side table, so the guest can see what and how you serve

- To open wine

- To speak with the guests, when assisting them with the menu or taking orders

Service Techniques

Once you understand the principles behind the service techniques discussed in this section, elegance is only a matter of time and training. Practice makes perfect—that old cliché is nonetheless true. Just relax. With time and practice you will master these techniques.

The Service of Food with One Hand

This service technique is used only for platter service and involves the so-called tong grip.

In the tong grip, the utensils are held in the right hand. Hold the spoon between the index and middle finger and the fork between the index finger and thumb. The curves of the spoon and fork should align. Gently slide the spoon under the item to be served, so that it is held between the fork and spoon. Remove your index finger, apply light pressure to the fork, and lift.

The Service of Food with Both Hands

This technique is used when working at a side table or a buffet.

When serving with both hands, hold the spoon in your right hand and the fork in your left hand.

If the food you serve is prepared in a sauce, always scrape the bottom of the spoon with the fork, to prevent drips and to keep the plate you are preparing clean and neat.

Arranging Food on the Plate

To the uninitiated, it might seem very simple to arrange food nicely on a plate. Actually, in a refined service, food is arranged according to particular rules that are followed the world over.

Meat is always placed at the lower part of the plate, at 6 o'clock.

Sauces are served separately in a sauce boat, or they are served to the left of the meat or fish.

When a dish is cooked in a sauce, such as a curry or stews, the sauce is served over the meat.

Compound, or flavored, butters, such as maître d'hôtel butter or herb butter, are placed directly on the meat.

Side dishes are arranged to achieve color harmony.

A piece of cake or pie should be served with the point facing toward the guest.

Plates with a logo or other graphic decoration should be arranged so that the decoration is at 12 o'clock when placed in front of the guest.

 Plates should never appear overloaded; the rims must always be free of food and without drips.

Hot food is always served on hot plates; cold food, on cold plates.

Pouring Beverages

This topic will be discussed in chapter 16 in detail. Here, however, are a few ground rules.

Hold glasses by the foot or stem only, to avoid fingerprints. All glasses are always placed to the right of the guest with the right hand. If the glass has a logo, it should face the guest.

Beverages are always poured from the right side of the guest. When serving heavy red wines that have been decanted or are in a wine basket, hold the glass, slightly slanted, on the table with the left hand and slowly pour the wine with the right hand, so that the wine sediment is not disturbed.

A bottle of wine is first presented to the host. Then the bottle is opened, and a small amount is poured for the host. After the host approves, the guests are served; the host's glass is filled last.

The Sequence of Clearing

When an aperitif has been served, the empty glasses are cleared only after the wine is served.

If a white wine is served with the appetizer, the empty glasses are removed only after the red wine has been poured. The red-wine glasses are cleared after the coffee or after-dinner drinks are served.

When guests are smoking, ashtrays are always changed before a new course is served.

After the guests have finished the main course, any platters or serving dishes on the table are removed first. Then the dinner plates are cleared, along with the flatware. Finally, any smaller plates, bread plates, and finger bowls are removed.

Before dessert is served, the table is totally cleared, except for flowers or other decorations. With a folded napkin or a crumber, clean the table-cloth of crumbs.

Service Styles

Five service styles are internationally recognized:

French service

Platter service

Side-table service

Plate service

Self-service

Because all service styles are not suitable for all occasions or all foods, few restaurants employ only one service style exclusively. For example, for a small *à la carte* item at one table, the staff will use plate service, while a large *à la carte* item at the next will be served from a side table. Not only will you learn about the different service types in theory here, but you will likely encounter them all in your daily routine.

French Service

In French, or butler, service the guests help themselves from a platter.

In this service style, the platter is either placed on the table (hot platters on a warmer) or offered to each guest by the server. In the latter case, the server holds the platter on the left hand and presents it to the guest from the left side. The handles of the service utensils point toward the guest.

This service is suitable for:

Banquets

Table d'hôte service

A part service

Room service

Platter Service

In this service style, hot plates are placed in front of the guest first.

The platter is carried on the left forearm. The waitperson, holding the serving spoon and fork in the right hand with a tong grip, serves the guests from the left.

This service style is suitable for:

Banquets

Table d'hôte service

A part service

The Side-Table Service

When using this service style, the platters are first presented to the guest and then placed on *réchauds* on the side table.

Hot plates are already on the side table.

When preparing a plate, always use both hands, not the tong grip. The finished plate is placed in front of the guest from the right side.

Very often, only part of the food is served to avoid overloading the plates. In this case, fresh plates are used for second helpings.

The side-table service is the most elegant and is suitable for:

A la carte service

Small banquets (up to twenty people)

A part service

Plate Service

In this style of service, the food is plated in the kitchen. The service staff picks it up and brings it directly to the table. In this service, the plates are always served from the right.

This service is suitable for:

A la carte service

Small and medium banquets (up to fifty people)

Parts of a menu, such as:
• appetizers
• soups
• desserts

Self-Service

In self-service, the tables are set by the service staff. All food is arranged as a buffet, where the guests help themselves.

A self-service buffet can offer hot and cold food at the same time, as at a banquet, or only part of a meal, such as a salad or dessert bar. Some restaurants offer a buffet at lunchtime to keep prices low.

At a buffet, guests should move in only one direction. Always locate the cold items at the beginning and hot items at the end so guests can sit down and eat as soon as the hot food has been chosen.

Self-service is very versatile and can be used in a wide range of circumstances, from simple to very festive, including:

Cold buffets

Cold and hot buffets

Salad buffets

Dessert buffets

Breakfast buffets

Self-service is suitable for:

Large banquets

Parts of a menu, such as the salad or dessert

Service Methods

Service methods are not to be confused with service styles. The service method signifies the organization of a meal; it does not determine the service style. The service method therefore can combine several styles of service.

The four most important service methods are:

Table d'hôte

Banquet

A part

A la carte

Table d'hôte

Table d'hôte is the simultaneous service of the same menu at an established price to all guests, even if they do not belong to the same group. This is most commonly used at spas and in institutional settings, such as schools and nursing homes.

The best service styles for this method are:

French service

Platter service

Plate service

Banquet

Banquets are always prepared for private parties (these are discussed in detail in chapter 10).

With this method of service, a predetermined number of guests are served the same menu at the same time. A banquet is very much like *table d'hôte* service except that the number of guests is known in advance and all the guests are affiliated in some way. The following service styles are most suitable:

French service

Platter service

Side-table service (small banquets only)

Plate service

Self-service (large banquets)

A part

With *à part* service, all guests are served the same menu, but they do not have to appear for the meal at the same time.

The service styles most suitable for *à part* service are:

French service

Platter service

Side-table service

Plate service

A la carte

With *à la carte* service, each guest chooses his or her meal from a variety of menu selections, each of which is priced separately. This free choice does not mean that the menu should not highlight certain offerings or that the service staff need not suggest particular items.

The service styles most suitable for this method are:

Side-table service

Plate service

9. Breakfast

Breakfast time offers a good opportunity to contemplate human nature.

The spectrum ranges from the early bird to the morning grouch, from those who eat on the run to those who take their time and really enjoy breakfast — and you will find a thousand variants in between. During the early shift, you will get all kinds of requests, from the mundane to the nearly impossible. Guests will ask for some odd things — three-minute eggs that are firm or raisin bran without the raisins, for example. If you want to contribute to humanity, try to fulfill as many of these requests as possible — after a satisfying breakfast, most people are much nicer for the rest of the day.

Breakfast Areas

Where breakfast is served depends mainly on custom and the capabilities of the establishment. Hotels usually have a special breakfast room or reserve part of the restaurant for breakfast. Many hotels also offer room service.

In restaurants breakfast is often served only at specified times, at tables set up for it. The role of breakfast in a restaurant depends very much on its style and location. For example, a resort area would be more likely to serve a themed breakfast than a city hotel would, as the latter is frequented mainly by businesspeople who have less time and less desire for a substantial breakfast.

Breakfast Mise en Place *and Service*

In a restaurant with a busy breakfast trade and in a hotel with a special breakfast room, much of the preparatory work is begun the night before. This also applies for room service, though the preparations differ somewhat.

In a Restaurant or a Hotel Breakfast Room

The Night Before

First the tablecloth or placemats are put on the table. Then small plates, small knives, saucers, teaspoons, and napkins are set.

In the Morning, before the Guests Arrive

Now the setting is extended. Individual packages of jam and honey on a small plate are added, along with packets of sugar and artificial sweetener. When possible, decorate the table with a small floral arrangement, to say "Good morning" in a nice way.

When the Guests Sit Down

Now the order is taken and bread or rolls and butter are served. Prewarmed coffee cups are brought and placed on the saucers, and the ordered beverage is served. For everything additionally ordered, the setting is extended accordingly. For example, a soft-boiled egg requires an eggcup, small spoon, and salt and pepper.

123

Room Service

When breakfast is served in the guest's room, work is done in three phases.

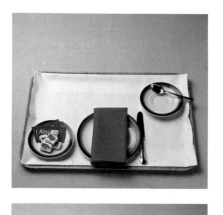

The Night Before

A tray is prepared. First it is covered with a cloth. Then, according to the number of people in the room, small plates with napkins, small knives, saucers with teaspoons, and sugar packets are set.

In the Morning

After checking the order, butter, jams, bread, the ordered beverages, prewarmed cups, and all desired extras are added. On a control sheet, the desired service time is noted.

If more than two people are in the room for breakfast, make sure they have enough table space.

The tray is carried on the left hand so that the right hand is free to open and close doors and to knock. Enter only after the guest has acknowledged your knock. After entering, wish the guests a good morning.

Ninety Minutes after the Service

Use the control sheet to determine when to remove the breakfast tray — ninety minutes after it was served. All foods that have not been consumed must be discarded, even if individually packaged, such as jellies or butter.

Breakfast Beverages

The standard morning beverages are coffee, tea, and hot chocolate. Juices, milk, mineral water, and other drinks are extras, specially ordered by the guest, which require no special preparation for breakfast.

Breakfast Coffee

In most hotels and restaurants, even if coffee is made cup by cup during the day, in the morning an automatic coffee maker is used to brew the quantity needed. Most machines work with filters.

The necessary amount of coffee is put in the filter. Then hot water (about 205°F) is added, either automatically or by hand, depending on the coffee machine. Depending on the desired strength of the coffee, 1½ to 3 ounces of coffee are used for every quart of water. The coffee is kept warm either in the coffee urn or on some kind of hotplate or burner built right into the coffee machine. Coffee should never be kept longer than forty-five minutes after brewing or it will become bitter and overcooked. The proper warming temperature is about 175°F.

For breakfast, coffee is generally served in a small, prewarmed metal coffee server, which is placed to the right of the guest, above the coffee cups, with the handle pointing to the right.

Tea and Hot Chocolate

In most houses, these beverages are served in individual pots. The hot water for tea is always served on the side so the guest can brew the tea to the desired strength.

Further discussion on preparing coffee (in a coffee machine), tea, and hot chocolate can be found in chapter 16.

The Breakfast Menu

The breakfast styles of different nations often engender long discussions among world travelers. A commonly known breakfast "border" runs between Great Britain and the European continent. The British (as well as Americans and Canadians) like to indulge in the morning, and their breakfast is often a substantial meal. The French eat much less in the early morning because, they say, they want a good reason to look forward to lunch. Small breakfasts are also common in the rest of Europe. The Italians have only an espresso on the run. The Swiss and the Germans eat fresh bread, coffee, and jam.

Internationally, four breakfast types can be distinguished:

Continental breakfast

American or English breakfast

Breakfast buffet

Brunch

The Continental Breakfast

On the European mainland, this is the most common breakfast style. Depending upon the country, it is also called a Swiss breakfast, *petit déjeuner* or *complet.* This breakfast consists of:

Hot beverages	Coffee, tea, cocoa, milk
Breads	The selection depends on the region—bread specialties, rolls, zwieback, and toast
Butter	Today, in most cases, served in individual packages
Jams and jellies	Like butter, also served in individual portions; a selection of different flavors is offered, sometimes along with honey
Extras	Fruit juices, eggs, cheeses, sausages, and the like are common extras, for which there is an additional charge

The American or English Breakfast

The British, Americans, and Canadians—indeed, anyone who likes to make breakfast a substantial meal—prefer this type. It consists of:

Hot beverages	Coffee, tea, cocoa, as in the continental breakfast

Breads	Bread, toast, rolls, and specialty breads
Butter, jams, honey	Individually packaged, as for the continental breakfast
Fresh fruit	Grapefruit, apples, pears, bananas, oranges, and others
Juices	Orange, grapefruit, and tomato are most popular
Stewed fruit	Prunes, apricots, pears, peaches
Cereal	Both hot (oatmeal) and cold (such as corn flakes)
Eggs	Fried, scrambled, poached, soft-boiled, omelettes, often accompanied by bacon, ham, or sausage
Meats	Mostly served cold, such as roast beef and cold cuts, but sometimes small steaks, lamb chops, and veal kidneys are offered
Fish	Such as kippers and haddock
Dairy products	Such as cottage cheese and yogurt

The Breakfast Buffet

The foods offered at the breakfast buffet are very similar to those in the American breakfast. The main difference here is the type of service. At the breakfast buffet, the guests help themselves. Only hot beverages are served by the staff.

All foods and beverages are arranged appetizingly on the buffet table. Hot foods are kept in chafing dishes, while cold items such as butter and fruit juices are kept cool, usually on ice.

For this type of breakfast, the staff's primary job is to keep the buffet neat and replenished, so the guest who arrives at 10:30 A.M. finds everything as appetizing as it was at 7:00 A.M.

The Brunch

The brunch is a combination of breakfast and lunch, and the menu offers items from both meals. In principle, the brunch is an extended breakfast buffet or American breakfast. In addition, salads, clear soups, cold fruit soups, smoked fish, and cakes, pies, and custards are also offered. One could call brunch a late breakfast or an early lunch; in any case it is becoming more and more popular.

10. Banquets and Functions

A function or banquet is an organized event in the broadest sense, at which all guests eat the same meal at the same time. The spectrum of events ranges from the joyous to the educational, from baptism to sales seminar, from the very intimate private affair to the very official public ceremony.

Service, therefore, can comprise anything from cocktails and snacks to the booking of a folk-dance group that will entertain guests after a five-course meal. Of course, your facilities determine what kinds of parties and how many guests you can accommodate.

Types of Functions

Three basic types of functions are held:

- Private family events, such as baptisms, bar mitzvahs, weddings, and the like

- Business functions, such as corporate anniversaries, office parties, seminars, and meetings

- Community or group events, such as club dances and proms, and public events, such as inaugurations and holiday celebrations

Arrangements for a Special Event

Every function requires preliminary planning. All agreements should be in writing. The customer will discuss with the banquet manager, banquet chef, or maître d' the services required.

The ideal starting point for these discussions is a printed checklist on which all available services are listed, so nothing can be overlooked.

Even for small functions that do not require elaborate preparations, three points should be clear from the start:

- Date and time of the planned event, so you can check immediately if the facility is available. If the desired time slot is already booked, further discussion would be a waste of time for both parties.

- Number of guests and the nature of the event.

- Name, address, and phone number of the customer.

With this information the caterer can make suggestions concerning price, menu, beverages, and other services.

Sample of a Function Checklist

Function Checklist

Organization _____ Time _____
Type of function _____ Date _____
Person to contact _____ Day _____
Address _____
Telephone   Bus. _____ Home _____ Place _____
Bill to _____ Room _____
Deposit _____

Beverages		**Accompaniments** (Nuts, chips, etc.)	**Guaranteed number of guests:**
Bar	_____		
Wine	_____		
Type and cost	_____		Room cost:
Liquor	_____		
Price per bottle	_____		Menu cost:
Price per drink	_____		

Furnishings   Floor Plan Sketch   **Menu**
Dais table   ☐   Starting time _____ Ending Time _____
Individual tables   ☐   After-dinner speeches? _____
Conference room   ☐
Theater   ☐
U shape   ☐
T shape   ☐
E shape   ☐
Other   ☐
_____
Cigarettes/cigars   ☐
Tablecloth color   ☐
Place cards   ☐
Media coverage   ☐
Photographs   ☐
Music   ☐
Meals (musicians)   ☐
Flowers   ☐
Candles   ☐
Printed matter
(menus)   ☐

Welcome sign in lobby: _____
_____

Special arrangements
(taxis, buses, etc.)

Additional equipment			**Copies to:**	
Podium	☐	Paper/pencils ☐	Guest	☐
Lectern	☐	Blackboard ☐	Chef	☐
Microphone	☐	Easel ☐	Maître d'	☐
Spotlights	☐	Film projector ☐	Hostess	☐
Ashtrays	☐	Screen ☐	Office	☐
Water	☐	Slide Projector ☐	File	☐
Glasses	☐	Pointer ☐	Other	☐
Matches	☐	Coatroom ☐		

Date reserved _____ Signature of approval:
Reserved through _____

The final arrangements with the function's organizer are confirmed in writing. The event is then entered on the banquet reservation calendar and the work schedule for servers is prepared.

All department heads — the chef, headwaiter, banquet manager, and the like — receive a copy of the written agreement.

Sample of In-house Instructions for Functions

Internal Memo for Functions

To:	Manager	☐		F & B Manager	☐
	Chef	☐		Maître d'	☐
	Hostess	☐		Bookeeping	☐
	_____	☐		_____	☐

Date _____

Type of Function _____
Date _____ Time from _____ to _____
Host/Hostess _____
Address _____
Telephone Bus. _____ Home _____
Number of guests _____
Rooms to Be Used:

_____   _____
_____   _____
_____   _____
_____   _____

Decorations and Special Equipment

Flowers	☐		Coatroom	☐
Candles	☐		Music	☐
Podium	☐		Dance floor	☐
Lectern	☐		Spotlights	☐
Microphone	☐		Place cards	☐
Paper	☐		Name tags	☐
Overhead projector	☐		_____	☐
Screen	☐		_____	☐
Slide projector	☐		_____	☐

Banquet Specifications

Guest Arrival

Time	Parking	Coatroom

Cocktails

Time	Room	Table shape/furnishings

Cocktails: *Mise en place*

___	___	___	___
___	___	___	___
___	___	___	___
___	___	___	___

Banquet

Time	Room	Table shape/furnishings

No.	Beverage	Food	Service	Speeches
___	___	___	___	___
___	___	___	___	___
___	___	___	___	___
___	___	___	___	___
___	___	___	___	___
___	___	___	___	___
___	___	___	___	___
___	___	___	___	___

Preparations for a Banquet

The arrangement of furniture in a restaurant usually does not change. That is not the case in a banquet room, where the tables and chairs are arranged however the customer desires.

The most common arrangements are:

Block Shape

Rectangular or oval for small banquets or meetings

Ideal for up to thirty guests

U Shape

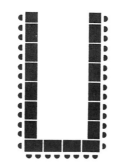

For medium-size banquets from twenty to fifty guests

For larger events

For special lectures and seminars

136

Individual Table Arrangements

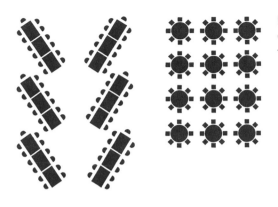

For bigger events
(round or rectangular
tables)

For seminars

Mise en Place for a Banquet

For events at which a menu of several courses is served, a sample place setting is provided by the supervisor so the service personnel can set the whole room accordingly.

All items that will be needed must be prepared in advance to guarantee smooth service. Plates, coffee cups and saucers, glasses, and spare flatware must be ready in the waiters' pantry.

 The most important moment of a banquet is when the guests arrive. You only have one chance to make a good first impression. The coordination of the table settings, furniture, and decorations is thus quite important. Therefore, check everything carefully after setting up to make sure the impression your customer receives is one of tender loving care.

The Assignment of Service Personnel

The proper coordination of the service staff is one of the most important requirements for a successful function and is therefore a major consideration in organizing a banquet.

Before the event an orientation meeting should be held to inform the staff about the table assignments and every detail of the service. For large functions, a floor plan on which every station is marked should be distributed.

Especially for a large event, marking all tables with a legible number will make the work of the service staff much easier. At the entrance, a floor plan and place cards with the table numbers should be provided to aid the guests in finding their seats.

Needless to say, the service staff should know every detail of the menu. Who will serve the meat, side dishes, and drinks to each station should be decided in advance so all guests at all tables are served at the same time and all tables are cleared simultaneously.

11. Our Guests

This chapter deals with the expectation of your target audience. What do your guests expect from your establishment? What do they expect from you? Which expectations can you anticipate? Which expectations must you probe for? This is the most interesting part of the job for most service personnel, because here you can use your experience and because turning a customer into a satisfied guost is quite gratifying.

Guests' Expectations

Fyodor Dostoyevsky once defined human beings as ungrateful two-legged creatures. Maybe you will agree with Mr. Dostoyevsky one day — and begin looking for a new profession. That would be a pity. If you want to avoid feeling this way — and you surely must — there is only one solution: learn to be observant.

If you learn how to judge guest types and expectations during your daily work, you will save yourself a lot of disappointment. Good observers can put their expertise to good use because they can pinpoint the needs of their guests. For example, they will know right away when a guest wants menu suggestions, or if he has just enough time to eat a quick breakfast. Both guests will be pleased if you help them to get what they want and, therefore, fulfill their expectations.

Maybe Dostoyevsky would call the hurried customer ungrateful because he cannot appreciate your ability to prepare a small quick menu for him. But perhaps you understand this guest better, knowing that the ground rule of better too much attention than too little does not apply if the guest signals you otherwise.

The businessman who entertains clients in your restaurant expects that you will support him in his role as a host. He correctly expects you to consider him the head of the table. All questions should be directed to him so he can control the orders (and the size of the bill). His choices cue his guest on what to order. If you lack sensitivity in this situation and, for instance, encourage an expensive "chain reaction" among his guests, you may have achieved a big sale for the moment but you will have lost return business, which is a big loss for the restaurant over the long run.

The situation may be totally different when the same businessman meets a circle of his friends for dinner in your restaurant. Now he may want to appear to be a generous connoiseur and will not mind suggestions in the higher price range. In this situation (use your own judgment), you may want to encourage an expensive "chain reaction" among the guests, which is so important to sales.

These examples demonstrate that it is your job to determine how your guests see themselves. This perceptiveness is important not only with guests whose different roles you know but for all guests. An elegantly dressed gentleman with a companion will appreciate your confirming his view of himself as a gourmet. Another person may simply be hungry and want a snack. A retired person on a fixed income might welcome an inexpensive recommendation whereas a young manager might be insulted by the same recommendation, believing you underestimated his social status. A vacationer who comes to lunch is in a totally different mood than a guest who has to be back in the office in an hour.

As you can see, guests' expectations vary greatly. Naturally, nobody expects you to have the sensitivity of a trained psychologist, but if you want to be successful in the service profession and be considered the best, you must sharpen your observational skills. For most service personnel, this is the most fascinating part of their profession.

Guest Categories

Every business pays special attention to its regular customers because they form the base for predictable future sales. This is especially true for regular restaurant customers. They definitely deserve attention. But every guest, even the person who stopped in by chance, is a potential regular. Therefore, the regular should enjoy special treatment, but the walk-in should not feel neglected.

Regular Guests

Regulars like to be greeted by name. A friendly "How are you" that is not too familiar is also appreciated. If a guest now and then makes a personal remark, you can respond with a few words, as long as your other guests will not be neglected while you chat. If a regular has not been in for a while, make it a point to tell him how glad you are to see him. To show your concern for them, it is very important that you remember the preference of your regular guests—their favorite drinks and the special foods they prefer. For example, if she likes game, make sure you call its availability to her attention. To sum up, it is important that regular guests feel they are receiving personal, preferential treatment.

Occasional Guests

Occasional guests, of course, cannot be treated like regulars because you do not know them personally. You do not know their names or preferences, and you cannot really ask them much without seeming intrusive. The only way to show these guests how much you appreciate their patronage is by providing attentive and friendly service. They should never have the impression that you are doing less for them or that they must wait longer than regular guests. Only with first-class service can you hope to make a regular out of an occasional guest. You will not always be successful, but you can always try. When suggesting menu items to such guests, always recommend the house specialties so that they receive the best impression of your kitchen.

Tourists

Put yourself in the place of a tourist, and you can imagine how important it is to find friendly cooperation when dining away from home. Help with the menu is in most cases greatly appreciated. Assist with the selection of food and beverages and explain them as well as you can, especially when there is a language barrier. Recommend local delicacies and the proper beverages to enhance them. If a guest orders a beverage that does not complement the food and insists on it, serve it without further comment (even if it is a lemonade with filet mignon). When dealing with tourists, always keep in mind that the quality of your service affects the reputation your region enjoys in other parts of the country — and abroad.

Handicapped Guests

When dealing with physically or mentally handicapped guests, you must sensitively offer as much help as is needed without being patronizing or showing pity.

Do not forget that a temporarily handicapped guest needs your help as well. A guest with an arm or a leg in a cast may be very grateful if you cater to his needs. For instance, offer a chair so he can put his leg up; if his arm is in a cast, ask if he needs assistance in cutting his food.

Guests in wheelchairs should be seated so that they can easily reach the exit without having to maneuver between the furniture.

Blind guests without escorts should be asked if they may be led to a table. When the guest wishes to order, ask if she would like menu suggestions. Always mention the house specialties. Also ask if she needs any special dishes or utensils or if she would like the food prepared in a particular way, such as precut.

You can be of great help to a guest with a speech problem if you take your time and do not interrupt, even when your intention is to help.

Mentally handicapped guests are usually escorted. If you feel they need special attention, ask the escort how you can be of assistance.

The best help for handicapped guests is to treat them as normally as possible.

Older Guests

Older guests are always grateful when you help them with their coats. They appreciate being seated at a quiet table. Older guests should never be seated near the air conditioner or in a draft. When making menu suggestions, recommend lighter dishes and avoid spicy foods.

Small Children

Provide small children with high chairs, booster seats, or pillows if they cannot reach the table. Give them the smallest flatware possible. Do not give knives to children under four. Glasses should be sturdy; replace stemware with tumblers.

When taking the order, call the parents' attention to the children's menu. The parents have the final authority over what the children order, and their wishes overrule those of the children.

Impatient children often become noisy and fidget, which makes their parents nervous and disturbs guests at other tables. To avoid this problem, serve the children as quickly as possible.

The basic rule is: if you satisfy the children, you will satisfy the parents, as well as all the other guests. The extra effort pays off.

Reservations

In many restaurants guests must reserve a table in advance. Reservations are usually made by phone and should be taken very carefully. It is embarrassing for the restaurant and, at best, disappointing for the guest when no table is available after a reservation was made.

When answering the phone, always mention the name of the restaurant first, then give your name and greet the caller.

Be accurate and write down the following details:

• The date and time of the desired reservation

• The number of people in the party

• The name of the party

Check your reservation book to see if a table is available. If so, confirm this with the guest and repeat all the information that you received.

If no table is available at the desired time, check to see if an appropriate table is available earlier or later, and if it is, suggest that time to the caller.

Thank your caller for the reservation or express your regret that you could not accommodate the party at the desired time.

When taking reservations, you should also note, in writing, if:

• Special dishes that need to be ordered in advance are desired

• Special tables are requested

• Special table decorations are desired

Guests with reservations should be greeted by name. If reserved tables are marked with the guest's name, confirm the spelling when you take the reservation on the phone and be sure the reserve sign has the correct spelling.

First Impressions

Your guests' first impression of your establishment affects how much they order and, ultimately, if they return (because the first impression lasts the longest). Two factors determine whether a guest will judge your restaurant positively or negatively after a quick glance:

- The overall impression the facilities make

- The impression the service staff makes

The Facility

Details concerning both the dining area and the staff have already been discussed earlier in this book. But because these two factors are so important, they are worth reviewing quickly.

Guests immediately judge:

Cleanliness	Are floors, furniture, curtains, rest rooms, and phone booths immaculate?
Lighting	Is the light too harsh? Too dim? Or is it cozy?
Decoration	Do flowers, pictures, and the like complement the rest of the decor?

Noise level	Is the room noisy or quiet?
Smell	Is the odor in the restaurant appetizing, or is there an unpleasant smell?
Food	Is the food presented in showcases and on display carts appetizing or not?
Informational material	Are the menus clean and up to date, or are they worn and outdated?

The Staff

Guests expect from the staff:

Cleanliness	Both the individuals themselves and their clothes must be clean.
Good appearance	Here a number of factors play a role, such as hairstyle, color of clothes, and other characteristics.
Personal attention	This involves how you greet the guests, take their coats, seat them, and serve them. Do you make eye contact when you take their order? Do you bid a friendly farewell?

 If you pay close attention to the facility aspect and the staff factors, you can rest assured that your guests' first impression will be positive—and that they will come back.

Complaints

Complaints are unavoidable, regardless of your efforts. Everyone makes mistakes, and now and then (hopefully not too often), your guests might therefore have cause for complaint.

Excusable and Inexcusable Mistakes

Excusable mistakes are technical failures, that is, for example, too long a wait for the food, the spilling of soup, and other problems. Such incidents understandably upset the guests, but in most cases they will respond reasonably when the rest of the service is satisfactory. What do you do when a guest complains?

• Let the guest talk.

• Listen very carefully to what the guest has to say.

• Apologize and do not try to make excuses, even when the mistake was not yours.

• Try to resolve the situation immediately; if the problem is serious, call your supervisor.

• Afterwards, ask the guest if he or she is satisfied with the resolution of the problem and if he accepts your apology. Only if the guest answers "yes" can you be satisfied.

The inexcusable mistakes are cases of misconduct: insolence, ill treatment, or deliberate indifference toward the guest.

Inexcusable mistakes do not even have to be discussed. They are personal insults to the guests. Such complaints cannot be resolved with explanations, as such behavior is completely unjustifiable. The guests will certainly never return.

A Small Gesture Can
Be a Great Help

A very effective response to a legitimate complaint is to offer the guest something on the house (of course, this must first be approved by your supervisor). A friendly offering of coffee or Cognac can repair some of the damage.

This also applies when, in response to your inquiry about the guest's meal, you receive concrete, credible criticism — for instance, the vegetables were undercooked or the meat was tough. When you accept the criticism graciously, express your regrets in a friendly manner, promise to inform the kitchen, and offer something on the house to make amends, the guest will feel he or she has been taken seriously. This response will often appease the guest and encourage him or her to return, because the criticism was not ignored or taken as an insult. The guests will come back even if the steak was so tough that they inevitably bit off more than they could chew.

Farewells

Just as it is important to greet the guest properly, it is also important to bid farewell properly. This is the last impression the guests take home with them, and it will influence their decision on whether to repeat the visit.

Good Service Does Not Stop after the Check Is Paid

To bid your guests a proper farewell:

• Help them with their coats, and perhaps escort them to the proper exit.

• Thank them for their visit.

• Say good-bye.

12. *Sales Techniques*

Perhaps you find the idea of sales techniques in connection with such basic human pleasures as eating and drinking a bit cold. Perhaps you envision trying to sell a bloody Mary to the nice old lady who comes in every day for a cup of coffee because it yields a better profit. You probably do not like this idea. Do not worry. Sales techniques do not require recommending something against your better judgment just to make more profit. Sales techniques are actually exactly the opposite. They help you learn to judge customers and approximately how much they are willing to spend and to make your recommendations accordingly. Sales techniques are obviously tools to increase profits. Using these tools requires sensitivity. If your efforts ring false to the guests, you will always lose them forever. If you hit the right note with your guests, they will perceive your efforts as nothing more than sympathetic, acceptable consideration.

The Proper Approach

Unlike most other retail operations, restaurants operate with a major handicap: the customers cannot see, taste, or sample the product being purchased. They can only hope that whatever they order meets their expectations. In this situation your recommendation and advice will give your guests a good idea about the quality they can expect. Your guests will accept your advice if they are convinced of your competence.

It is entirely up to you if and how your sales techniques work.

Right or Wrong—That Depends on When

In the service profession, as in most activities, there is a difference between passive and active behavior.

Passive Behavior

The waitperson hands the menus and wine list to the guests. Then he or she takes the order without offering suggestions or special recommendations. Only the guests are actively involved in selecting the meal.

Appropriate Circumstances for Passive Behavior

Passive behavior is correct at a banquet where the menu and beverages have been chosen in advance, as well as in a small restaurant with a very limited number of selections.

Active Behavior

The server recommends the house specialties and the daily specials to the guests when handing over the menus. He or she also asks if cocktails are desired. The important difference between passive and active behavior is that the waitperson does not simply hand out the menus but actively approaches the guest.

Appropriate Circumstances for Active Behavior

Active behavior is correct in any restaurant with an *à la carte* menu, where choices and recommendations are possible.

Active Behavior

You can sell only with active behavior. This does not mean that you force or push a guest to order something. Active sales techniques require much more — your aim is to fulfill the guest's every wish, even those he is unaware of. You cannot accomplish this goal simply by making a lot of suggestions. First you have to create an atmosphere in which your guests are inclined to follow your suggestions.

Show Clearly That You Care

Show your guests that you appreciate their patronage during your first contact with them, when they call for reservations or enter your restaurant. Nothing dampens the mood of guests more than the feeling that you are not interested in them. If they get this feeling, be very attentive and double your efforts.

Be Attentive When Greeting

The first contact with your guests is often decisive.

Always take a step in their direction.

Smile at them.

Greet them warmly, by name if possible.

Be Attentive by Providing Special Care

Feeling pampered enhances the positive attitude of your guests.

For every "thank you" that you receive from guests in the first few minutes because you were attentive, you gain importance. Your competence grows in their eyes, which will help you when making suggestions about food and beverages. Therefore, use every opportunity to have guests say thank you. For instance:

· Help them with their coats.

· Seat them at the table they desire if possible.

· Ask them if everything is satisfactory.

Show Attentiveness through Cleanliness and Order

When the entrance and interior of your restaurant are attractive and seem friendly, you please your guests. Any sloppiness indicates a lack of concern. Make it your business to be attentive to such details. Before your guests arrive, ask yourself the following questions:

Are the entrance and the parking lot clean?

Is the lighting, both indoors and out, in order?

Is the menu in the showcase clean and up to date and does it look enticing?

Is the restaurant spotless?

Is it necessary to air out the rooms?

Is the heating or the air conditioning adjusted correctly?

Now You Must Create Interest

All waitpeople know the importance of the *mise en place* to their tools and utensils. But your mental *mise en place* is just as important. Make sure that you know everything the house has to offer. Only then can you advise the guests properly and create interest. Interest leads to desire. But you must know which desires the kitchen can fulfill on a given day.

Therefore you must always know:

• What to recommend especially

• What is unavailable

• What the characteristics of the different foods and beverages are

• What the different preparation styles mean

You should never forget:

Taking an order is one of the most important aspects of your job. You should:

Always stand in front of the table.

Look at your guests when you talk to them. Eye contact is very important.

Remember, the one who asks, leads. When offering the menu, ask your guests if they have any special wishes or would like you to offer recommendations.

Think about interesting cocktails, and make an appropriate recommendation.

Describe food appetizingly. Strawberries are not just strawberries, but very fresh strawberries.

Listen attentively and do not get nervous.

Make sure that you have alternative suggestions for every course.

Answer your guests' questions correctly and, of course, politely.

Make sure you have your guests' attention, and try to create a chain reaction when taking the order. That is, try to have all the guests in a party follow the lead of one who takes your suggestions.

Know what is unavailable at the moment.

Stimulating the Appetite Is the Best Sales Technique

Sometimes you have to stimulate or increase the appetites of your guests. Certain foods, beverages, and sensory stimulants will encourage your guests to place larger orders.

Cocktails, White Wines, Fruit Juices

These drinks contain acids, which stimulate gastric juices and increase the appetite.

Pretzels, Potato Chips,
Peanuts, Olives

These snacks contain fat and salt. In small amounts they increase the appetite because they also stimulate the gastric juices.

An Appetizing Presentation
of Delicacies

A tempting display in showcases or on rolling carts should not be underestimated.

Appetizing Aromas

Pleasant odors that linger in the air promise good things to come.

But you are the one that can do the most to increase the appetites of your guests.

Describe Appetizingly

Guests cannot test what they order in advance; therefore, they order by imagining the food. The stronger and more positive their imaginations, the better their appetites. Ask yourself how you would react to the following recommendations.

We have prime ribs with potatoes

or

Today I can recommend our tender, juicy roast prime rib of beef and our oven-baked Idaho potatoes.

Your imagination of a good meal was surely reinforced by the second recommendation. In addition, it also said something about the method of preparation.

To describe food appetizingly is extremely important — so important that you should train yourself to do it.

This also applies to foods that you do not particularly like or would not eat yourself.

The following words and phrases can be used to provide appetizing descriptions of food and wine.

For Wine

19XX was an excellent year; this wine goes well with _____ ; it comes from the _____ region; dry, fresh, lively, delicate, charming, strong, elegant, delicious, substantial, fine, lovely bouquet

For Food

Fresh, picant, mild, light, fine, homemade, aromatic, tender, juicy, luscious, creamy, airy, silken, crisp, spicy, hearty

The prerequisite for an appetizing description, of course, is that you know exactly what your establishment has to offer. Only then can you correctly describe the special taste and quality of the food. Do not exaggerate, and try to be as exact as possible. You want to stimulate the guests' appetites, not create an overrepresentation that ultimately disappoints the guests.

Always Offer Alternatives

Imagine that you ask your guest, "Would you like to try our very delicate homemade game terrine as an appetizer?" You have given an appetizing description, but your chances of a sale are only fifty-fifty, because you allow the guest to respond negatively when you make a suggestion in this way.

If you add to your recommendation a second choice, your chances for a successful sale are much better. For example, you might say, "Would you like to try our delicate homemade game terrine, or would you prefer something lighter, perhaps a mélange of fresh fruit?" In this case the guest has three choices, two of which are positive and will generate a sale. Your chances of selling an appetizer are now two to one.

The Three Rules of Offering Alternatives

When making alternative suggestions, you must observe three points:

- Never offer more than two, at the most, three alternative suggestions.

- When making alternative suggestions, always stay in the same group. Always separately offer different appetizers, different main courses, different wines; appetizers and main courses, for example, should not be presented alternatively (nor should wines and coffees).

- The alternative should always differ in taste, method of preparation, and price.

Taste Alternatives

When recommending main courses, always have something that has proven popular as an alternative to a specialty item. There is naturally no surefire alternative, because the tastes of your guests and the offerings of each restaurant are so different. But some types of foods are commonly enjoyed by many people, whereas as others are considered less appealing specialties, as the following chart indicates:

Popular Items	Examples
Meat, poultry, and commonly served fish	Beef
	Veal
	Pork
	Chicken
	Common fish such as trout or sole

Specialties	Examples
Meat, fish, and fowl that require a specific taste	Organ meats such as liver, kidneys, sweetbreads
	Lamb and mutton
	Fish specialties and some shellfish
	Game, such as venison and rabbit
	Fowl, such as pheasant and guinea hen
	Spicy foods such as curry

Price Alternatives

Just as alternative suggestions should differ in taste, they should also differ in price. Suggesting only the most expensive dishes would not be correct and might anger your guests. On the other hand, it would be equally wrong to offer hamburgers as the alternative to filet mignon; the difference here would be too great. It is your function to find a happy medium based on what your establishment has to offer. Every menu and wine list has high-, medium-, and low-price offerings from which to choose.

Begin by recommending something in the medium price range; then, use your judgment to determine if these guests might prefer a less or a more expensive alternative and make your second suggestion accordingly.

Very important to the viability of your suggestions is your estimate of how much a guest is apparently willing to spend. Of course, this is a matter of experience. As important as it is that you do not underestimate your guests, it is even more important that you do not oversell.

Whatever the cost of the meal your guests order, it should never influence the quality of your service. Your main goal is to have the guests return. In this way, you gain the most in the long run.

Preparation Alternatives

Not everybody likes grilled, roasted, or sautéed items equally well. Since there are fourteen basic methods of preparation, it should not be a problem to offer your guests a range of preparation methods. The fourteen basic cooking methods are discussed in chapter 17 in detail. Below are listed a few that are important when making recommendations:

Poaching

Simmering

Gratinéing

Baking

Grilling

Sautéing

Roasting

Your alternative suggestions should not be prepared using the same cooking method. Therefore, you must devise appropriate combinations.

Example 1

a. Tender grilled tournedos accompanied by fresh seasonal vegetables and a light béarnaise sauce

b. Fresh calf's liver sautéed English style with crisp home-fried potatoes

Example 2

a. Fresh brook trout *meunière* with parsley potatoes

b. Tender grilled lamb chops *provençale* with fresh green beans and roasted potatoes

 Your challenge:

To combine different tastes, prices, and methods of preparation so that you offer real alternatives.

The two examples cited on the previous page are successful combinations;

Example 1	Taste	Price	Cooking Method
a.	Popular item: beef (tournedos)	Expensive	Grilling
b.	Specialty: organ meat (liver)	Medium	Sautéing

Example 2			
a.	Popular item: common fish (trout)	Medium	Sautéing
b.	Specialty: lamb (chops)	Expensive	Grilling

Additional Sales

As mentioned earlier, you have to take the initiative to tempt your guests to order. This also holds true for additional sales. You have to awaken a desire in them. But be very careful not to appear pushy. Rather, your guests should feel you want them to enjoy themselves. The possibilities for additional sales differ from house to house, but the few hints given here are useful in any restaurant.

Cocktail

The best time to ask guests if they would like a drink is when handing them the menus.

Appetizer	If the guests order *à la carte,* ask if they would like a salad or soup to start, or mention a house specialty that you can especially recommend today as an appetizer.
Side dishes	Where side dishes are not included, you can offer the fresh vegetable of the day or homemade noodles or whatever delicacy the kitchen has to offer.
Cheese and dessert	When a cheese selection is available, bring it to your guests' attention when they finish the main course. Also offer the dessert menu and point out the house specialties.
Coffee and spirits	Inquiring if the guests would like coffee after dinner is a must. This is also a good time to ask if they would like an after-dinner drink as well.

Sales Techniques—The Possibilities Are Endless

You can never learn enough about sales techniques, because success depends not only on what you do but on when and how you do it. Naturally, it takes much experience to think of so many things during a long workday. But with practice your experience will grow, and your repertoire of sales skills will increase. Confidence in yourself is your best asset for success. With it, you will truly understand the old maxim, nothing succeeds like success.

13. Cost Control

A few years ago, a popular phrase during discussions of world peace among international leaders was "Trust but verify." This saying applies to the hospitality industry as well as it does to politics. Whether a business operates with a profit or a loss depends first on a good control system. Today computers are a huge help to management and staff alike. Thanks to modern technology, the time once spent on accounting tasks such as tallying sales and balancing a cash drawer has been cut to a minimum. And, given the increasing sophistication of computers, cost control will likely be even easier in the future.

Control Systems

Naturally there are a number of different control systems, which are chosen according to the nature of the establishment. But the five purposes of every system are:

- To keep track of the daily receipts

- To find accounting mistakes and losses

- To provide sales data

- To serve as a base for bookkeeping

- To allow for a quick and accurate settlement of accounts

The Five Control Systems

In the foodservice industry, you will find one of the following control systems in use, depending upon the type and size of the establishment:

• The order pad with carbons

• The cash register at the bar/distribution area (see chapter 4)

• The cash register at a service bar

• A single cash register near the exit

• The cash register at the end of a cafeteria line

The Order Pad

This control system is used only in very small operations, as well as in hotel dining rooms and for banquets. It is used only when there is no cash register available.

The servers write their orders on an order pad with carbons; each order ticket has a control number. Only the original is perforated; the copy stays in the pad as a control.

This system can also be used as a backup in case of a power failure or a malfunction of electronic equipment.

The written original order form is torn out and brought to the bar or kitchen, where it is checked for accuracy and then filled.

When purchases are to be charged against a guest's account (as in a hotel, for example), an order pad with multiple copies is used. The original order goes to the bar or kitchen. The first copy goes to the front desk or the accounting department to be charged against the guest's account, while the second copy stays on the pad as a control.

Orders charged against a guest's account should always carry the room number or the name of the guest, preferably both. Without this information, the purchase cannot be charged, resulting in a loss.

Such an order would look like this:

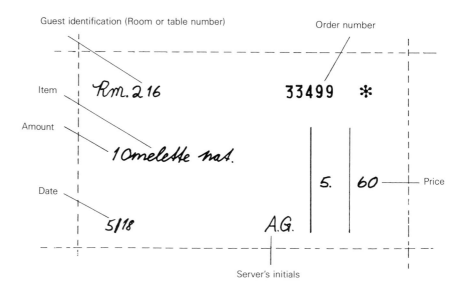

The Cash Register at a Bar/Distribution Area

With this system every order is entered into the cash register. The information is printed onto a control tape and onto a receipt. With the receipt the server can obtain the food or beverages needed.

Of the many cash register systems, the following three are most popular.

- Mechanical cash registers that total all sales and total the sales by category, with or without a guest-check printer

- Electronic cash registers that total all sales, which are programmed for individual articles and print guest checks

- Electronic cash registers that are programmed for individual articles and automatically print kitchen orders and guest checks, including such details as information about the desired doneness of red meat; provides detailed data on sales and guest frequency as well as food and beverage inventories and other comprehensive reports and statistics

Sales Totals

Every server can call up his or her individual sales totals on the register by using an individual key or punching in a personal code. All the orders that he or she has entered on the machine will be automatically totaled. The total sales for a single evening can be learned with a touch of a button, making account reconciliation very simple.

Sales Category Totals

Most cash registers have keys to record sales by category, so that sales in each category can be totaled automatically and analyzed. The keys are marked with category abbreviations similar to the following.

Abbreviation	Meaning	Items Included
Ki	Kitchen	All foods
Wi	Wine	All wines
Co	Coffee	Coffee, tea, milk
Be	Beer	Beer
Bev	Beverage	All nonalcoholic beverages that are not entered with Co
Li	Liquor	All alcoholic drinks, liquors, and spirits
Su	Sundry	Nonfood items such as cigarettes, postcards

When, for example, coffee is ordered, the price and the key Co are punched and "1 coffee" is written on the order/check. If you take an order that falls into two categories, for example, Irish coffee (Li and Co), use the key predetermined by management.

Sales category totals serve as a control and provide a statistical overview of sales. Totals by category give you a quick picture of the sales in each product group.

*Cash Registers with
Guest-Check Printers*

Some mechanical and most electronic cash registers, in addition to the features already listed, offer another advantage: they print out guest checks. With this system the guest check is inserted into the cash register, and the order is punched in. The kitchen receipt, the register tape, and the guest check are all printed simultaneously.

With every new order made by the guest, the last total must be punched in before the new purchase can be added, so that the register can calculate the new total. Modern electronic cash registers have a memory, which eliminates this task of manually inserting the last total.

*The Electronic Cash Register
with Programming*

Significantly different from the above-mentioned cash registers, this system features a preprogrammed calculator. The price of each item is already part of the program. Service personnel need only punch the key assigned to a particular item. Punching in the price and category is unnecessary. The newer models also eliminate handwritten orders, as the register automatically prints them out.

Cash Registers for a Service Bar

With this system the service staff member punches all orders into the cash register and then picks up the necessary items from the bar. The order tickets remain at the bar. After the service the missing beverages are restocked according to the tickets. This system can also be used when restaurant beverages are sold by the glass. In this case, the cash register must be hooked up to the beverage dispenser. Every service staff member can operate the beverage dispenser with the cash register key. Here the amount of the beverage sold is automatically added to the sales totals of the appropriate service staff member.

A Single Cash Register near the Exit

With this system the kitchen order and the guest check are prepared simultaneously; they are written in duplicate. The duplicate serves as the kitchen order, while the original stays at the guest's table. When leaving the restaurant the guest passes by the cashier and pays the bill. This system is quite advantageous for the guest as well as the service staff. The guest does not have to wait for the check, and the service personnel need not spend time collecting money. In Europe this system is mainly found in places where minutes count, for example, airports and railroad stations. In the United States, it is used extensively, even in elegant restaurants.

A Cash Register at the End of a Cafeteria Line

Here guests help themselves to their choice of food, place it on a tray, and go to the cashier at the end of the counter.

Kitchen Orders and Order Writing

In many foodservice operations, the cash register is used to prepare the kitchen order, and the printed order is the most important means of communication between the kitchen and service staff. Unfortunately, this communication sometimes goes awry, for example, when keys are incorrectly punched or orders are illegibly written. This creates tension among staff and with management.

 Only kitchen orders that are complete and accurate lead to good communication. The smallest mistake can result in huge misunderstandings.

 Therefore, be sure that your orders are brief, clear, and understandable.

The printout of an order by a mechanical (nonelectronic) cash register contains the following:

The following information must be written by service personnel:

a. Order for food

b. Order for beverages

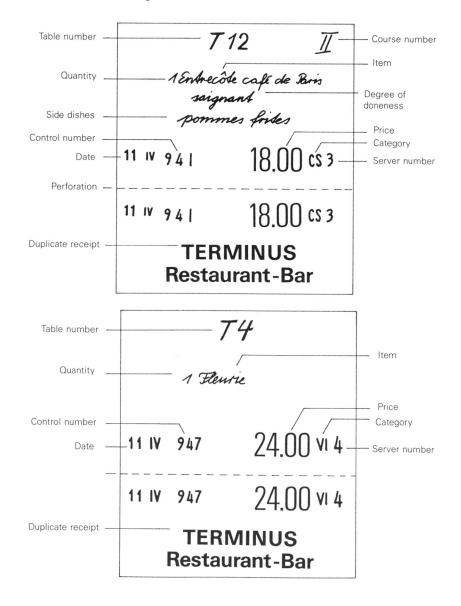

Quantity and item must match the printed price and category. Because time is money, abbreviations may be used for frequently sold items such as coffee, tea, beer, and the like. Decoding these abbreviations should not be difficult. Be brief but clear and distinct.

The printout of an order by an electronic cash register contains the following:

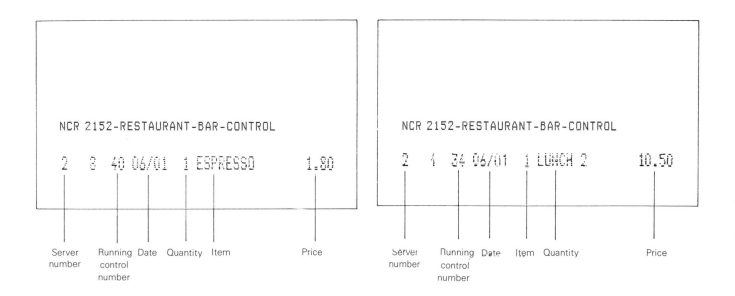

14. *Methods of Payment*

May I have the check please?
Check please!
Check!
Where the Heck Is My Check?!

Perhaps psychologists know why people who spend several hours comfortably seated in a restaurant become frantic with haste when they decide they want their check. As a member of the service staff, be prepared for calls for checks to haunt you even in your dreams. To reduce stress, on yourself and on your guests, prepare and present the check as quickly as possible when it is requested. How payment can be made, from cash to credit cards, will be discussed in this chapter.

Cash Payment

Today guests have many options to choose from when paying their checks, and for the beginning waitperson, the variety of methods can be confusing. But, in principal, there are actually only two methods of payment.

a. Direct payment with cash
b. Cash-free systems

Cash Payment without a Guest Check

With small purchases, such as a single beverage or a small snack, a check is not prepared unless the guest requests it. The server simply names the price of the served item and collects the amount due right at the table.

 When making change, do not put the money the guest hands you into the cash drawer (or wherever the cash is kept) until handing back the right amount of change. This practice prevents any disputes about the amount of the payment or the change, and you need not worry about loss.

Cash Payment with a Guest Check

Restaurant management determines the amounts a guest is charged for each item. This is then recorded on the guest check. Every check, whether prepared by machine or handwritten, acts as a control and as a receipt for the guest, but it is also something of calling card for the establishment. As such, guest checks must be accurate, easy to understand, clean, and legible. The illustrations that follow show what a guest check should always include.

Example of a handwritten guest check:

Beispiel für eine handgeschriebene Rechnung

Example of a guest check from an electronic cash register:

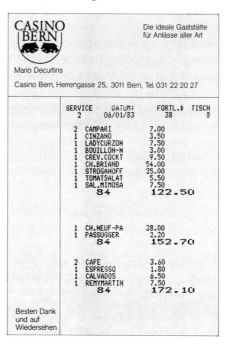

In a restaurant the check is presented as follows. The check, placed face down on a small tray or plate, is placed on the table. The waitperson then leaves the table until the guest has put money on the tray or plate. Then he or she picks it up and brings back any change as quickly as possible. At this point, the guests are also thanked for their visit.

Immediate Payment with Guest Checks

For special occasions such as private-club parties or dances, the ground rule is normally that you serve and collect right on the spot. When working such an event make sure that you have plenty of change.

Cash-free Methods

Every service staff member should know the most common noncash methods of payment and how to handle them. When a method accepted by the house creates confusion and has to be handled by two or three people, guests often become impatient and annoyed. Most restaurants post signs at the entrance listing the methods of payment they accept.

The most common noncash methods are:

Gift certificates

Meal tickets/lunch checks

House accounts

Checks

Credit cards

Gift Certificates

In recent years gift certificates have become increasingly popular. These are made out for a certain amount or are blank and can be used as payment in the issuing restaurant. When you accept a gift certificate, be sure it is from your restaurant, and check the amount. If the certificate is blank, make sure that it has an address where the bill can be sent.

Meal Tickets/Lunch Checks

In some areas companies have arrangements with local restaurants where lunch tickets given as a bonus to employees can be redeemed at the restaurants. You must check to be sure these tickets are accepted at your restaurant. They are handled like cash, but change is not returned if the ticket is for more than the cost of the meal.

House Accounts

Many businesspeople prefer this form of payment. Checks are not presented immediately but are mailed to the guest's company, usually on a monthly basis. Naturally, such an arrangement must be agreed upon in advance by the parties involved. With an unknown guest, such an arrangement would be allowed only under exceptional circumstances. With this method of payment, be sure to record the correct address of the responsible party, as well as the date and the guest's signature, on the check.

Eurochecks

The Eurocheck system is used only in European establishments. The Eurocheck is legal tender issued by many European banks that is valid only in conjunction with a personal check-cashing card. All Eurochecks are red, white, and blue and cannot be written for more than 300 Deutschmarks or the equivalent. The great advantage of the Eurocheck is that it can be made out in any European currency. When you accept a Eurocheck in payment, verify that, on the front of the check, the amount is written in both words and figures, that the location, date, and payor lines are filled in, and that the guest has signed it. On the back, the Eurocheck must always have the number of the check-cashing card. Using the check-cashing card, which must be presented to you along with the Eurocheck, verify the check's validity by checking the number and the signature; also check the card's expiration date.

Traveler's Checks

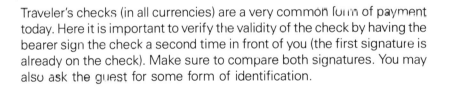

Traveler's checks (in all currencies) are a very common form of payment today. Here it is important to verify the validity of the check by having the bearer sign the check a second time in front of you (the first signature is already on the check). Make sure to compare both signatures. You may also ask the guest for some form of identification.

Credit Cards

Credit cards are one of the most common methods of payment world-wide. When the guest pays with a credit card, the restaurant sends the bill to the card company, which in turn sends the card holder a monthly bill.

Every month all credit card companies send out lists with the numbers of all invalid credit cards. This list should be placed right at the cash register so every member of the service staff can verify that a presented card is valid. (In most establishments today, these lists are electronically programmed into a validating machine, which will automatically indicate if a card is invalid. Thus, it is no longer necessary to search through lists of numbers to ensure a card is valid.) Make sure the bill does not exceed the house limit for that credit card. If it does, you have to verify the amount with the card company and obtain an approval code.

 If an invalid credit card is presented to you, notify your supervisor immediately.

The most common credit cards are:

American Express	MasterCard
Diners Club	Carte Blanche
Visa	

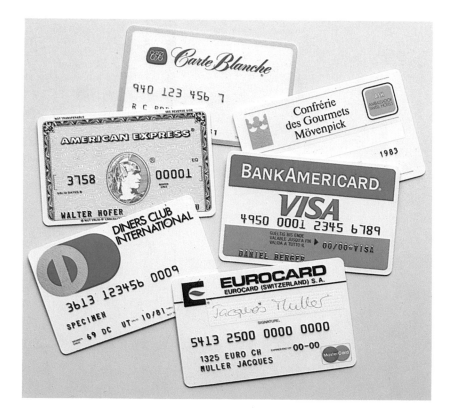

Filling Out the Billing Form

All credit card companies have different billing forms, but the cards themselves are all of the same size and made from the same material. Therefore, one imprinter can accommodate all cards. The imprinter transfers the card number and expiration date and the name of the guest onto the billing form. When paying, the guest will give you his or her credit card. You accept it, imprint it, fill out the billing form for that card, and check the validity of the card. When filling out the form, be sure to write in the correct amount and to check the expiration date. Then bring the form to the guest for his or her signature. Always provide a pen. Once the form is signed, give the guest his or her copy. The original is handled like cash.

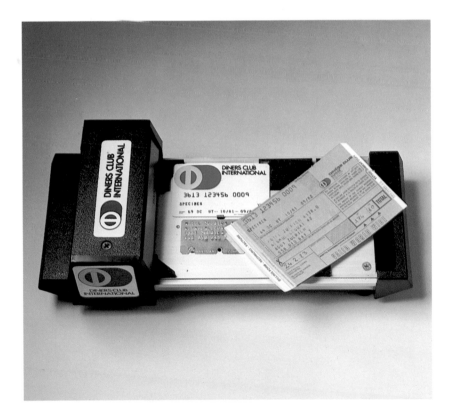

15. Working at the Guest Table

This chapter discusses working in front of the guest, which can be considered the epitome of fine service—the carving, flambéing, and boning of food right before the guests' eyes. Naturally, the following pages can provide only a theoretical foundation, which, of course, you cannot do without. That you cannot learn these skills by studying a book is obvious. After studying the theory here, there is only one way to become a master in this field: practice.

Basic Rules

After the handling of food and pouring of beverages, it is mainly carving, boning, and flambéing that give service personnel an opportunity to demonstrate their expertise and their knowledge. There are three ground rules to follow when working before the guest.

Absolute Cleanliness

Everything you use when working at the guest table should be carefully inspected beforehand. Cleanliness alone is not enough. All utensils that your guest will see should be spotless and sparkling. Not even the smallest water spot should mar the picture.

Perfect Organization

When working at the guests' table, your time is very limited. Once you begin carving or flambéing, your work cannot be interrupted under any circumstances, not even to hand something to another guest or to fetch missing materials. That means you must:

- Check your flambéing or carving *mise en place* for completeness before you begin

- Organize the service at all your tables so that none of your other guests feels neglected

Proper Stance and Poise

The guest will probably enjoy watching all tableside preparations, but only if you produce a dish that looks appetizing. To do this, your movements must be smooth and elegant, and every visible sign of physical effort must be eliminated. Your hands must not touch the food. If you then can control your nervousness (understandable in the beginning) and your facial expression, your guests will enjoy your performance.

Carving and Boning

The presentation of a whole fish, duck, or even a suckling pig is always an event for guests which stimulates their appetites and increases their enjoyment of the dinner. With a big piece of meat, it is also sensible to slice it tableside, because the meat is more decorative whole than sliced, and it is juicier and appears fresher when it reaches the guest.

The Carving Tools

A wooden or plastic carving board with a groove to catch juices.

A slicer with a straight edge. This is a long, thin, flexible knife approximately sixteen inches long. It is ideal for cutting large, thin slices, from smoked salmon or ham, for example.

A pointed knife with straight edge, approximately ten inches long. This is suitable for carving saddle of venison, poultry, leg of lamb, double sirloin, and chateaubriand.

A clean napkin for smoked salmon.

The carving utensils have to be ready on your side table, to transfer the piece to be carved from the platter to the carving board. A dinner fork is used to hold the piece in place. Important: never poke your fork into a medium or rare piece of meat, because too much of the juices will be lost. These pieces of meat are always held down with the back of the fork.

A platter warmer will keep the food warm while carving.

Typical Examples

As mentioned earlier, carving can be mastered only with practice. The examples that follow, therefore, are intended to provide only basic guidelines.

Poultry: Roast Chicken

For all types of poultry, use a short, strong knife, not a slicer. During carving and serving, poultry can be pierced with the fork. Almost every kind of poultry requires its own carving technique; the roast chicken has been chosen as an example because it is served most often.

Lay the chicken sideways on the carving board, with the breast facing the guest. Insert the fork under the joint between the drumstick and thigh.

With the knife, cut through the skin beneath the leg, and then remove the leg with the fork.

Cut the leg into two pieces at the joint. Then turn the chicken and remove the second leg in the same fashion.

Lay the chicken on its back; hold it steady on the carving board with the fork by piercing it from the side through the backbone. Sever the wing parallel to the breast with a short cut through the wing joint. A portion of the breast meat should remain attached to the wing, as the photos show. The second wing is removed in the same fashion.

With the tip of the knife, carefully loosen the breast meat from the bone. Then, using the knife to hold the carcass, the breast meat is removed with the fork.

With bigger roasters, the breast meat is cut into two pieces.

Arrange all the pieces of chicken on a platter.

If possible, serve every guest a piece of dark and a piece of light meat.

Boneless Meat: The Entrecôte Double (Double Sirloin)

To carve an *entrecôte double,* use a pointed knife and a dinner fork.

The steak is placed on the carving board. With the back of the fork, press lightly on the meat. Make sure not to pierce it, or you will lose the juices. Slice the steak on a bias so the slices appear bigger. Cut from the right to the left into slices about one-half inch thick.

Once the meat is carved, return it to the platter. Place your knife under all the pieces and hold them in place with your fork. In this way, the entire steak is returned to the platter.

▷ It is important that each guest receives the same number of slices. When possible, serve each guest a middle and an end cut.

Meat on the Bone: Leg of Lamb

A leg of lamb contains two bones, one in the upper thigh and the other in the lower leg. Half of the lower bone is normally cut off before cooking, and the remainder protrudes approximately four inches from the meat. When carving, this bone is used as a handle and is held with a napkin.

For the classical style of carving from the bone, the leg of lamb is a perfect example.

Alongside the bone, at the so-called seam (where the two pieces of muscle come together), make an incision.

Beginning at the shank, start slicing the top round, at a slight angle. The slices should be about one-half inch thick.

Once the top round is carved, turn the leg around and slice the bottom round in the same fashion.

Each portion is then arranged on a plate for service.

Three Examples of Fish: Smoked Salmon, Poached Trout (truite au bleu), and Sole

The salmon is already divided into halves before smoking. When slicing salmon you will always have one half before you.

The deboned salmon half is placed on a special salmon board.

Beginning at the tail end, carve slices as thin as possible with a slicer. The salmon is held with a cloth napkin.

The skin on the bottom should not be cut.

Poached Trout

The poached trout (*truit au bleu*) is normally brought to the table in the container in which it was cooked. Because this vessel has a special insert, the trout can be easily lifted out.

If the guest wishes, the trout is filleted as shown on page 202, with a fish knife and fork.

To keep the fish knife clean, dip it regularly into the court bouillon in the cooking vessel.

The trout is lifted out of the liquid with the insert and prepared in the insert to prevent the fish from cooling off.

201

With the fish knife, carefully remove the skin.

Remove the two upper fillets. Start at the head, and let your knife glide between the bones and the meat.

Turn the trout and repeat the procedure. Then arrange the fillets carefully on a warm plate.

The prepared trout is carefully arranged on a plate.

Sole

Sole is one of the most popular fishes. It can be served grilled, *à la meunière,* fried, or poached. To fillet sole, use a fish knife and a fish fork.

First, remove the side fins by applying light pressure.

Then make an incision along the backbone, and lift the two upper fillets. Turn the sole, and remove the other two fillets.

Arrange the sole on the plate.

Slicing Cakes and Pies

The most important aspect of slicing cakes and pies is the knife: it should always have a serrated edge so you do not squash the cake when cutting. When cutting ice-cream cakes and frozen desserts, the knife should be frequently dipped in hot water.

When slicing round cakes and pies, first lightly mark the wedges before cutting, so all pieces are of the same size. Mark the cake first in half, then in quarters, then in eighths. Cut only as many pieces as are needed, so the rest does not dry out. The cut piece is placed on a small plate and is always served from the right, with the tip pointing toward the guest.

Long cakes and pastries, such as logs and jelly rolls, cut in equal-size slices.

Flambéing

Simply explained, flambéing is cooking or final cooking at the guest's table. But the visual pleasure in watching the flame plays a major role in the guest's dining enjoyment. The flame itself has no influence on the taste of the food. The principle of flambéing is very simple: the heating of the spirits in a flambé pan develops alcohol vapors, which, when brought into contact with an open flame, will ignite. The excess alcohol is burned off, and through reduction of the spirits, the sauce is enhanced.

 Since flambéing affects the normal flow of service, only items with short preparation times should be flambóed. Only foods and ingredients that produce a pleasant aroma when cooking should be used.

Classical Flambé Items

Shrimp

Beef stroganoff

Veal kidneys dijonaise

Crêpes Suzette

Flaming fruits

Two Flambéing Methods

First Flambé, Then Prepare the Sauce

With this method, the food is placed in the pan and sautéed till done. Then it is flambéed with the appropriate liquor. The food is then removed from the pan and kept warm. The remaining liquids are mixed with the required ingredients to create the sauce. This flambéing method is suitable for delicate items that should not be cooked in a sauce because they will toughen, for example, veal cutlets, beef tenderloin, and veal kidneys.

First Prepare the Sauce, Then Flambé

With this method of preparation, first combine all the ingredients to make the sauce. The food is then placed in the sauce, heated or cooked, and then flambéed at the end. This method is suitable for various desserts, such as crêpes Suzette and fruits.

Flambéing Demands a Perfect Mise en Place

As already mentioned in the ground rules for cooking at the table, all tools and utensils to be used must be perfectly clean. Since you cannot be interrupted once you begin to flambé — for example, to fetch a missing item — everything has to be on hand before starting. The basic *mise en place* on your side table should include:

Condiments

Salt
Peppermill
Mustard
Ketchup
Tabasco sauce
Worcestershire sauce
Herbs (when needed)
Granulated sugar
Oil

Spirits

Cognac
Grand Marnier
Additional spirits based on the menu items and recipes

Tools and Equipment

Serving utensils
Dinner and salad plates
Matches
Flambé pan
Flambé utensils

Additional ingredients, such as sauces, butter, and cream, as needed in the recipe, must also be at hand before you start to work.

 When flambéing, you create a jet of flame that is pretty but could have unpleasant side effects. Fat or oil can splatter out of the pan. To protect your guests and their clothes, stand at least one yard away from them when flambéing. When igniting the alcohol, hold your face back. Also make sure to stay at a safe distance from all flammable materials, such as drapes and decorations. Avoid flaming directly under a sprinkler, or the fire department may be your unexpected guests. When working with gas burners, make sure the safety valves are closed when the service is completed.

The Service of Cheese

Every country is proud of its cheese specialties, and many restaurants will offer both local specialties and international cheeses.

The service of cheese demands some basic knowledge and some practice, so that every cheese is cut with the right tools, according to its form and shape. The rind is always left on the cheese. The two pointed ends of the cheese knife are used to serve.

Extra-hard cheeses, for example, Sbrinz, are excellent for the use of a cheese plane. Wedge-shaped cheeses can be held easily while thin slices are shaved off; wedges are shaved more easily than blocks. The slices are eaten by hand.

Sbrinz or Parmesan can also be broken and crumbled with a blunt knife. The cheese chunks are eaten by hand.

If the cheese is cut in blocks, the best way to cut it is by slicing parallel to the narrow side, into slices about one-quarter inch thick. Slices that are too big can be cut in half again.

Wedges are cut crosswise from the tip to about two-thirds in; the rest is portioned lengthwise.

The cutting of a round of tête de moine involves a special technique because the cheese must be shaved to release the full aroma. First cut off one-quarter inch from the flat side. From the remaining cheese, remove part of the rind. Then, by steadily turning the cheese, shave the top with the back of a knife. After some practice, you will be able to form pretty rosettes.

Of course, it is much easier and faster to use the shaving tool designed for tête de moine.

Cheese balls are cut in half and then portioned out in wedges. The paraffin coating that covers the cheese is left on the cheese.

Round or half-round cheeses are cut in wedges.

Wedge-shaped cheeses are cut crosswise from the tip to about two-thirds in; the rest is portioned lengthwise.

Oval cheeses are cut into slices across the narrow length.

Reblochon is a Swiss specialty. The red mold is removed, and the remaining thin rind is left on the cheese to be eaten.

Block-shaped cheeses are cut into slices down the length of the block.

Vacherin Mont d'Or is cut in wedges. The cut is covered with plastic, glass, or wood slats to keep the cheese from running out. Only if the cheese is very ripe and runny can it be served with a small spoon.

Cheeses	Fat Content	Aroma	Origin
Extra-hard Cheeses			
Sbrinz	50%	Aromatic	Switz.
Parmesan	37%	Fragrant	Italy
Hard Cheeses			
Emmentaler	37%	Mild	Switz.
Greyerzer	48%	Fragrant to pungent	Switz.
Comté	45%	Fragrant to pungent	France
Beaufort	45%	Fragrant to pungent	France
Alpkäse	27%	Aromatic to fragrant	Switz.
Bergkäse	27%	Mild to fragrant	Switz., Austria, Germany
Mischlingkäse	35%	Slightly sour to aromatic	Austria

Cheeses	Fat Content	Aroma	Origin
Semi-hard Cheeses			
Appenzeller	28%	Fragrant	Switz.
Tilsiter	10–30%	Mild to aromatic	Switz., Austria
Tête de Moine	22%	Fragrant	Switz.
Edam	25%	Mild	Holland
Fontina	39%	Mild to fragrant	Italy
Geheim-ratskäse	25–30%	Mild	Germany
Glarner Herb Cheese	10–15%	Fragrant, very pungent	Switz.
Gouda	30%	Mild to pungent	Holland
Trappisten-käse	24–26%	Mild to pungent	Germany
Steppenkäse	25%	Mild	Germany
Wilster-marschkäse	45%	Mild to pungent	Germany
Raclette	50%	Mild, lightly fragrant	Switz.
Provolone	35%	Mild to pungent	Italy
Semisoft Cheeses			
Freiburger Vacherin	45%	Creamy, mild	Switz.
St. Paulin	45%	Mild	France
Bel Paese	45%	Mild	Italy
Roquefort	32–36%	Fragrant, sharp, pungent	France
Danish Blue	45%	Fragrant, sharp, pungent	Denmark
Azzurro	45%	Fragrant, sharp, pungent	Switz.

Cheeses	Fat Content	Aroma	Origin
Soft Cheeses			
Camembert	21%	Mild to earthy, pungent	France
Brie	30%	Fragrant, pungent	France
Tomme	45%	Mild, herblike	Switz.
Vacherin Mont d'Or	45%	Mild, piny rind flavor	Switz.
Reblochon	45%	Mild to pungent	France, Switz.
Munster	45%	Mild to sharp	France, Switz., Germany
Gorgonzola	45%	Fragrant, sharp, pungent	Italy
Sour-milk Cheeses			
Mainzerkäse	2%	Mild to pungent	Germany
Harzerkäse	2%	Mild to pungent	Germany
Handkäse	2%	Mild to aromatic	Germany
Korbkäse	2%	Mild to aromatic	Germany
Fresh Cheeses			
Mozzarella	18–22%	Mild, slightly sour	Italy
Various fresh cheeses (cottage cheese, etc.)	very lean to very fat	Mild, slightly sour	France, Switz, Germany

The Cheese Platter

The type of restaurant and the different foods offered, as well as the desires of the guests, determine if cheese is offered and how wide a selection of domestic and imported cheeses the cheese platter should contain. The cheeses should be served at room temperature, approximately 65° to 68°F. Two cheese knives, each with two points at the end, one for hard and one for soft cheese, are used to arrange the portioned cheese on the plate.

A small cheese platter should contain at least one cheese from each group (extra-hard, hard, semi-soft, etc.). The cheese board selected and the arrangement of the cheeses on the board should enable the cheese to be cut into the desired portions.

The large cheese assortment on this cheese platter makes the portioning of the cheese impossible; therefore, an additional board is supplied to cut the desired amount of an individual cheese. The remainder of the cheese is then returned to its original place on the cheese platter.

When the cheese is served after the main course, the portion should be about two to three ounces. Make sure the cut pieces are arranged neatly. If the guests wish, butter, fruit, and different breads may accompany the cheeses. With Vacherin, Reblochon, and Munster, caraway seeds should be offered as well.

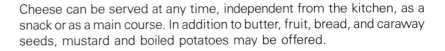

Cheese can be served at any time, independent from the kitchen, as a snack or as a main course. In addition to butter, fruit, bread, and caraway seeds, mustard and boiled potatoes may be offered.

At large banquets, the cheese is already cut in portions and arranged on platters or cheese boards. A spoon and fork are used to serve it.

The cheese buffet is an epicurean delight.

There are two buffet types. The self-service buffet has eight to ten different cheeses. Big pieces of cheese are placed on cheese boards as focal points, and the portioned pieces with the appropriate garnishes surround them for a nice presentation.

The buffet with a server has twenty to forty cheeses. Here the cheeses are presented whole or cut but not portioned. Every cheese is then cut fresh as the guest requests it. Butter curls and an ample choice of breads and fruits belong on the buffet. The buffet can be extended if desired, with, for example, more cheese varieties, quiches, fresh vegetables, and boiled or roasted potatoes. Normally, allow seven ounces of cheese per person.

Formaggini in Oil

Formaggini are small cheeses made from cows', goats', or mixed milk. This cheese specialty from the Tessin area of Switzerland can be served fresh or ripened in olive oil with herbs, white wine, or grappa. Formaggini are always served with oil, vinegar, salt, freshly ground pepper, and bread.

Fromage Frais

Fromage frais is a creamy, light, runny fresh cheese. It is served cool, with heavy cream and sugar.

Fondue

Fondue, the famous Swiss cheese specialty, is always served with bread cut into cubes or strips and never without freshly ground pepper. Recommended beverages are a dry white wine (not too cold) or black tea, and Kirsch or other distilled spirits.

Important: with fondue, use only perfectly functioning burners.

Raclette

With raclette, potatoes, pearl onions, cornichons, or gherkins are served; for seasoning, paprika and freshly ground pepper are musts.

Important: when serving raclette, the plates must be very hot so the cheese keeps its runny consistency.

16. The Study of Beverages

You might find this a very dry title for a chapter that deals with liquids. But once you examine the subject in depth, you will see that the title fits the subject. Even the jargon describing that most noble liquid, wine, is not flowery at all but rather technical. Experts and wine lovers alike, however, appreciate such technical details, because they can imagine the sensual pleasures such language defines. So, if the dry definitions and the laws that are so important in this chapter seem dull and uninspiring, perhaps you should detour from theory into practice for a bit . . . and have a drink.

Beverage Basics

In many foodservice operations, beverages are the most important profit center. (Specialized establishments, such as bars and night clubs, are supported exclusively by beverage sales.) Beverages increase sales because they can be served at any time, have a fairly high markup, and do not require much labor.

Basically, beverages can be divided into two categories: alcoholic and nonalcoholic. These, in turn, are distinguished as ready-to-drink and prepared beverages.

Ready-to-drink beverages can be served and consumed just as they are delivered from the supplier, without additional ingredients or preparation.

Prepared beverages are made on the premises, for example, coffee, tea, and cocktails. The service of these beverages does not require standard-measure-glasses or cups.

Ready-to-drink Beverages

Alcoholic

Wines
Sparkling wines
Beers
Spirits
Liqueurs
Aperitifs

Nonalcoholic

Mineral water
Lemonade
Milk
Alcohol-free beer
Fruit juices
Soda pops

Prepared Drinks

Alcoholic

Cocktails
Punches
Toddies
Mulled wine

Nonalcoholic

Coffee
Tea
Cocoa
Milk shakes
Fruit-juice cocktails

Wine

Many good books on the cultural and historical significance of wine are available. This chapter, however, contains the practical information you will need as a member of the service staff.

Definition

Wine is a beverage made exclusively from totally or partially fermented fresh grape juice.

The Principles of Wine Making

All wine-making methods are based on the phenomenon of alcoholic fermentation. Through fermentation, the sugar contained in the grape must (juice) changes into alcohol (ethyl alcohol) and into carbon dioxide (CO_2).

The Five Basic Wine Types

Red wine

Rosé

Blush wine

White wine

Sparkling wine

Wine Making

Red Wine

Red wine is always made from purple (also called red) grapes. The grape solids are retained in the must during all or part of the fermentation to extract the pigment from the grapes, giving the wine its red color.

Rosé

Purple grapes are used exclusively for rosé wine, never a mixture of purple and white grapes, as is commonly thought. The solids are kept in the must for only a very short time (between twelve and thirty-six hours); thus, the light pink color.

Blush Wine

For blush wine, purple and white grapes are used. The purple grapes must be mostly from the same growing region.

White Wine

White wine is made mostly from white grapes. In rare cases white wine is also made from purple grapes. To make white wine a mash fermentation, in which the grape must and solids ferment together, is not necessary. After destemming, the grapes are pressed immediately and the must alone is fermented.

Sparkling Wines

Sparkling wines, the best known of which is Champagne, are made from white, purple, or mixed grapes. Making sparkling wine is a complicated process. First, the wine is made; it is then saturated with carbon dioxide (CO_2). This saturation can be achieved using one of three methods.

Impregnation

By adding carbon dioxide, the wine is carbonated, just like soda. Gas added in this way forms big bubbles in the sparkling wine.

Closed Container

Here a second fermentation results from adding a solution of sugar and yeast to the wine, which is kept in a huge, hermetically sealed container. The second fermentation takes place under great pressure, which causes carbonation to occur. After filtration the wine is bottled.

Champagne

Here the second fermentation does not take place in a pressurized container but directly in the bottles. The wine, which first undergoes normal fermentation, is then blended with wines from different vintages to achieve an equal quality (*cuvée*). A small amount of sugar dissolved in old wine, together with a special yeast, is now added to the wine.

This wine mixture is poured into bottles. After the second fermentation in horizontally stacked bottles has started, the bottles are placed head down in racks. The bottles are then turned at certain intervals and shaken at the same time so that the dead yeast will settle around the cork. This cycle is completed with the decorking (degorgement). When the cork is removed, the dead yeast that has collected around the cork is also removed. At the same time, the so-called *dosage* is added. The dosage is a sugar and wine solution with which the different Champagne styles are achieved. The best-known styles are:

brut   No dosage is added; extra dry

sec   Very little dosage is added; dry (about ⅔ ounce of sugar per bottle)

demi-sec   Little dosage is added; half sweet or mild (about 1 to 1½ ounces of sugar per bottle)

doux   A large dosage is added; sweet (more than 1½ ounces of sugar per bottle)

How Wine Is Sold

Open Wines

In the past these wines were delivered in barrels and then poured into wine jugs or carafes, thus, the expression open wine. Today, the so-called open wines are always delivered in bottles. This method of serving wine is common in Europe; it is similar to service in carafes or by the half-bottle in the United States. In the foodservice industry, the following bottle sizes for open wines are standard:

1-liter bottles
½-liter bottles
20-centiliter bottles

The measurement should be marked on the bottle. If the wine from a one-liter bottle is to be served in a carafe or by the glass, then the carafe and the glasses must be of a standard measure. Bottles of open wines are opened at the bar, not in front of the guest. Naturally these wines are not vintage but a blend of different years, so quality can be maintained consistently. As a rule, these wines are generally good everyday wines but not especially high-quality products.

Vintage Wines
(Bottled Wines)

These wines are always delivered and stored in bottles and are always opened at the table in front of the guest. The glasses must be appropriate for the wine. Vintage wines are generally of a higher quality than open wines. These wines are from one particular year, which is noted on the label.

Common Bottle Sizes

¼ bottle	About six to seven fluid ounces
½ bottle	About twelve to fourteen fluid ounces
1 bottle	About twenty-four to twenty-seven fluid ounces
Magnum	About forty-eight to fifty-one fluid ounces

Wine Service

To serve wine correctly it is necessary to observe various rules. The first rule, true for all beverages, is that wine is always served from the right of the guest, which is also where the glasses are placed.

The Service of Open Wines

If the wine is served by the glass, it is placed at the right of the guest. If open wines are served from the bottle, the bottles are opened at the bar and are presented to the guest before pouring. When presenting the bottle, it is held, with two hands, in front of the guest so the guest can read the label and verify that this is the wine that he or she ordered. After the guest approves the wine, it is poured from the right side. Otherwise, the same rules used for serving food apply, that is, the women are served before the men. Refilling the glasses is the job of the service staff, and guests should never have to do it themselves.

The Service of Vintage or Bottled Wines

A vintage wine has to be handled very carefully. Even the slightest shake should be avoided. The ordered bottle is held with both hands and is presented to the guest who ordered it. Vintage wines are always opened in front of the guest. This must be done as gently as possible, with elegance and with no visible force or effort. It is advantageous to rest the bottle on the side table or, if there is enough space, right on the guest table.

With the blade of the corkscrew, cut the foil at the bottle neck at least one-quarter inch from the top. Be sure to cut the foil without turning the bottle.

Once the foil has been removed, the spiral of the corkscrew can be placed exactly in the center of the cork and screwed in. Do not allow the spiral tip to penetrate the cork completely or small bits of cork may fall into the wine.

Then the cork is slowly pulled out. If necessary, turn the corkscrew in a bit more to avoid breaking the cork.

The bottle mouth is now cleaned with a napkin. The bottle is not to be corked again.

Red wines, heavy white wines, and sparkling wines are poured directly over the glass. Two methods are customarily used to pour. In Switzerland, when pouring wine, the label is on top so it is practically covered by the hand, because this is the way the bottle was stored in the wine cellar.

In Germany and France, the label is never covered, and the bottle is held so that the guest can see the label at all times.

A small taste is poured for the guest who ordered the wine so that he or she can check the quality. After the guest approves, the rest of the party is served. The glass of the host is filled last. If the guest objects to the wine, the bottle should be changed without comment; it is better to lose a bottle of wine than a guest. (If a regular guest makes this a habit, the headwaiter should be informed.) When a new bottle is ordered, a fresh glass must be provided for the tasting.

Fizzy white wines are poured from a little higher above the glass than red wines are. The glasses should be filled approximately three-quarters full.

Old red wines that have sediment are served in a wine basket. To present a young wine in this way to a guest would be rather ludicrous. The only reason for the wine basket is to avoid a disturbance of the sediments. With the basket the wine can be presented and served in the same position as it was stored. To avoid spills when opening a bottle, the front part of the basket can be elevated. Heavy old red wines that are served in baskets should be poured into the glass very slowly. The glass is held with the hand at an angle, and it is filled only one-third full.

Opening Sparkling Wines

Place the bottle in an ice bucket. As soon as the bottle is chilled, remove it from the bucket and wrap it in a napkin.

Holding the bottle in the left hand, with your thumb on the cork, remove the foil and the wire with the right hand.

Point the bottle away from the guest when removing the cork. Holding the bottle with your left hand on an angle, turn the cork with your right hand till it loosens. The napkin should prevent the cork from popping. The Champagne should be served at once.

Serving Temperatures

Every wine has its own typical bouquet, and each wine has an optimal serving temperature at which this bouquet is developed fully. The following serving temperatures for the different wines are ideal:

Heavy red wines Bordeaux, Burgundy, Barolo	16°–18°C (61°–64°F)
Medium-heavy red wines Dôle, Côtes du Rhône, Chianti Classico	13°–15°C (55°–59°F)
Light red wines East Swiss red wines, Beaujolais, rosés	10°–13°C (50°–55°F)
White wines	9°–10°C (48°–50°F)
Sparkling wines	6°–8°C (43°–46°F)

Decanting

With this delicate procedure, a very old red wine is poured into a decanting carafe in such a way that the wine sediment remains in the bottle, separate from the wine. Through decanting the wine is also exposed to oxygen, which allows its bouquet to develop fully. Only high-quality red wine should be decanted.

The Mise en Place *for Decanting*

The following tools and materials are needed for decanting:

• Decanting carafe

• Candleholder with candle

• Matches

• Corkscrew

• Wine bottle in wine basket

• Saucer

• Paper napkin

• Additional wine glass for tasting

These are placed on a service tray on the side table.

Decanting

Present the ordered bottle in the basket to the guest.

Light the candle.

Elevate the front of the basket with an inverted saucer.

With the tip of the corkscrew blade, cut the metal cap on the bottle lengthwise.

Carefully remove the cap.

Cautiously decork the bottle and present the cork to the guest so he or she can check the print on the cork.

Clean the bottle opening with a paper napkin.

Pour a taste into a glass so the guest can taste the wine. When he or she approves, decanting can be started.

Hold the bottle with the right hand and the neck of the decanter with the left.

Touch the opening of the decanter and the bottle together. The candle should be behind the bottle neck so the light shines through the wine as it flows out.

Pour the wine slowly and smoothly into the carafe.

When the first traces of sediment appear in the lighted bottle neck, the decanting should stop.

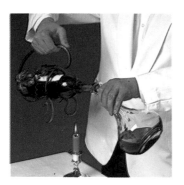

Replace the empty wine bottle in the basket and place on the table so the guest can look at the bottle.

The wine is now carefully poured from the decanter into glasses. As is usual with old wines, the glass is held with the left hand on an angle and filled to about one-third.

The candle, tasting glass, saucer, and paper napkin are now removed, together with the tray.

Chambrer

Chambrer means to temper, or bring a cold red wine from the cellar to the right temperature before serving. The best method for tempering a wine is to keep it for several hours in the place where it is to be drunk. Another method is to pour the wine into a warm decanter or wrap the bottle in warm moist towels to obtain the desired temperature. A cold red wine should never be put in a hot water bath. This means of warming would cause too rapid a temperature change, which would destroy the bouquet of the wine.

Wine should be tempered only when absolutely necessary.

Chilling

The opposite procedure is used to bring wines (white or sparkling) quickly to a lower temperature of approximately 43° to 48°F. The bottle is placed in an ice bucket that contains ice, water, and salt. After approximately five to ten minutes, the desired temperature will be reached.

Wine Labels

Because service personnel cannot possibly have tasted every wine available, they must make use of all the information on the wine labels in order to advise the guest. The following four primary details are always immediately recognizable on every label:

- Wine name
- Appellation
- Producer's name
- Vintage year

The Wine Name

Wine can be named in three ways: by grape variety, by region of production, or using a trademark name created by the grower or distributor.

Grape Variety

Examples:

Gamay
Gewürztraminer
Merlot
Pinot Noir
Riesling X Sylvaner
Cabernet

Region of Production

Examples:

Chianti
Dürnsteiner
Gevrey-Chambertin
Rüdesheimer
Maienfelder
Yvorne

A name based on place of origin gives a clue to the wine's quality. The larger the growing region after which the wine is named, the lower the wine quality.

Examples:

Large growing area
e.g., a country

"Vin rouge français"
This name translates as French red wine. This is a table wine whose grapes come from all areas of France but certainly not from the top wine-producing regions.

235

Medium-large growing area
e.g., a region

"Bourgogne"
Bourgogne is the French region known in English as Burgundy. Wines named for regions are of better quality than those named for countries. The wine region of Burgundy produces better wines than the wines as a group throughout the country. Nevertheless, quality can still vary throughout a wine region. Some villages are able to produce better wines than others thanks to their particular geography and climate.

Medium-size growing area
e.g., north Burgundy

"Bourgogne
Hautes Côtes de Nuits"
The upper part of Burgundy produces even better wines than the entire region because, in the Hautes Côtes de Nuits, the Pinot Noir grape is grown exclusively, whereas in lower Burgundy, the Gamay grape is more common.

Small growing area
e.g., a village or *commune*

"Gevrey-Chambertin"
The wine from this *commune* is of even higher quality. This name has achieved such worldwide fame that an additional regional or country name is unnecessary. A further classification is only the location in the *commune,* because the different slopes vary in quality and renown.

Smallest growing area
e.g., a vineyard

"Chambertin"
This is unmistakably a top wine of the highest quality. When a wine of an individual vineyard is of a higher quality and renown than the wines of the village, region, or country, the name of the vineyard, logically, is used on the label.

Fantasy or Trademark Names

Today fantasy names are more and more common. Many wine merchants carry such brand names. In addition to the trademark name, the grape variety or the place of origin is also printed on the label. Of course, top wines are never sold under a fantasy name.

Appellations

Appellations are legal designations that protect the quality of the wine and keep it constant. They also guarantee the origin, name, quality of the grapes with regard to sugar content, and the wine-making method. Appellations differ from country to country and are listed in the next chapter.

Producer's Name

This is the name of the vintner, the wine merchant, or the wine importer. The name and location of the company must always be listed. Top wines are always bottled where they are produced. To check if a particular wine is produced and bottled in the same place, compare the location of the company with the origin of the wine. If identical, it can be assumed that the wine is made and bottled in the same place.

Vintage

When a year is printed on the wine label or on a small label at the bottle neck, the wine is a vintage wine. As mentioned before, vintage wines are of better quality than nonvintage wines, because the quality of the different years varies for each wine. A nonvintage wine may be a mixture of many vintages. The service staff should always know which years were good for which wines; only then can they make recommendations.

Aperitifs

The word *aperitif* comes from the French, originally from the Latin *aperire,* meaning "to open." An aperitif is thus a prelude, an opening to the meal, a before-dinner drink.

Aperitifs not only provide welcome additional sales, but they also have an appetite-stimulating effect.

A variety of beverages can be drunk either as an aperitif or for other occasions, such as white wine, Champagne, mixed drinks, beer, and fruit juice. In addition, certain drinks are served exclusively as aperitifs:

- Vermouths

- Bitters

- Anise-based liqueurs

- Fortified wines

All aperitifs except fortified wines should always be served chilled. Salted nuts, potato chips, olives, or celery stalks usually accompany them.

Vermouths

Vermouths are made from white wine and are fortified and flavored with herbs (primarily artemisia, also known as wormwood; the German *wermut,* "wormwood," gives this aperitif its name). Taste variations are introduced by adding pure wine alcohol or other spirits made from wine. The alcohol content is between 16 and 18 percent. Vermouth may be sweet or dry, and it may be red or white.

The Service of Vermouth Aperitifs

Vermouth can be served in two ways:

- Sec: The vermouth is served in an aperitif glass without the addition of seltzer, soda, or mineral water, with or without ice.

- Spritzer: The vermouth is served in an aperitif glass and is diluted with seltzer, soda, or mineral water. Ice is added if desired.

Vermouths are served cool (50°), often with a lemon or orange twist.

Popular Brands of Vermouth

Brand	Color	Taste	Origin
Bellardi	Red or white	Sweet	Italy
Carpano	Red or white	Sweet	Italy
Cinzano	Red or white	Sweet	Italy
Cinzano Dry	White	Dry	Italy
Cora	Red or white	Sweet	Italy
Dubonnet	Red or white	Sweet	France
Gancia	Red or white	Sweet	Italy
Isotta	Red or white	Sweet	Italy
Martini	Red or white	Sweet	Italy
Martini Dry	White	Dry	Italy
Noilly Prat	White	Dry	France

Bitters

Bitters are made of pure alcohol, water, extracts of bitter and aromatic plants, natural flavorings, and sugar. Bitters can be artificially colored.

The Service of Bitters

Bitters are served in the same way as vermouth aperitifs.

Popular Brands of Bitters

Brand	Origin
Amaro Cora	Italy
Amer Picon	France
Alpenbitter	Switzerland
Appenzeller	Switzerland
Campari	Italy
Cynar	Italy
Ramazotti	Italy
Rossi	Italy
Suze	Switzerland

Anise-based Liqueurs

Anise is the aromatic base of these liqueurs, which are diluted with cold water when served as aperitifs. Anise liqueurs are between 45 and 50 percent alcohol, and they are sugared.

The Service of Anise Aperitifs

Anise aperitifs are served in an aperitif glass without ice. Ice water is served on the side and is added by the guest in the desired amount. When water is added, the transparent yellow liqueur becomes milky and cloudy. Anise aperitifs are drunk very cool, but the liqueur should not be stored in a cold place, or it will discolor and become cloudy.

Popular Anise Liqueurs

Brand	Origin
Pastis 51	France
Pernod	France
Ricard	France
Berger	France
Ouzo	Greece

Fortified Wines

Fortified wines come from southern Europe (Spain, Portugal, Italy, and Greece). They are strong, alcoholic wines, usually with an alcohol content of 16 to 22 percent, obtained by adding brandy. The taste of fortified wines ranges from dry to sweet; the color, from light yellow to dark red brown.

The Service of Fortified Wines

Fortified wines are served in special wine glasses designed for them. Dry fortified wines are served cool, at about 55°F; sweet wines, at a temperature of approximately 60°F.

Popular Fortified Wines

Wine	Origin	Type	Attributes	Recommended for: Aperitif	Recommended for: Dessert	Brand Names
Sherry	Spain	fino	very dry	X		⎰Apitiv
		manzanilla	dry	X		⎱Diez, Harvey's, Osborne
		amontillado	rich, mild	X		Don Zoilo, Dry Sac
		oloroso	sweet	X	X	Mérito,
		oloroso	dry	X		Gonzales Byass
		cream	strong, sweet		X	Sandeman
Malaga	Spain	seco	dry	X		⎰Sandeman, Buxtorf
		Pajarete	mild	X		⎱Gonzales Byass
		dulce color	sweet		X	
		Lagrima	nutmeg taste, sweet	X	X	
Port	Portugal	pale white	dry or sweet	X	X	⎰Sandeman
		ruby	rich, mild	X	X	Dela Force
		tawny	strong, dry sweet	X	X	⎱Ferreira, Kopke, Souza
Madeira	Portugal	Sercial	dry	X		⎰Kopke
		Verdelho	semi-dry	X		Dela Force
		Boal	mild	X		⎱Sandeman
		Malvasia	sweet	X	X	
Marsala	Italy		Sweet	X	X	Cora
Samos	Greece		Sweet		X	

Liquors

Under the collective name liquor are grouped all beverages distilled from fruits, grains, plants, and roots. Brand-name liquors generally contain 40 to 43 percent alcohol; that is, they are 80 to 86 proof.

Liquor Production

Producing Alcohol

For liquor production, the raw materials must first be processed to become alcoholic. The process used depends on the material.

Raw materials that contain sugar, such as fruits, can be fermented directly to produce alcohol.

For starch-based raw materials such as grains, the starch must be converted into sugar before fermentation can occur. This process is called malting (also see the later section on beer in this chapter). The resulting malt sugar is fermented, becoming alcohol and carbon dioxide.

Raw materials that do not contain enough sugar or starch for fermentation such as berries are steeped in alcohol to absorb the bouquet and aroma. This process is called maceration.

Distillation

The interim product produced by fermentation, the raw material that contains alcohol, is called mash, cider, wort, or wine. Distillation, the separation of the alcohol from the fermented raw material, is the next step.

The fermented product, for example, mash, is now heated in a still. Alcohol has a lower boiling point than water, and it therefore evaporates first. These alcohol fumes are caught and directed into a chilled pipe, where the fumes liquefy again because of the cold. This liquid, called the raw spirit, is then distilled again to refine the product and to achieve a higher alcohol concentration.

After distillation all spirits are crystal clear, even those that are enjoyed later as a gold brown beverages, such as whiskey.

Storage

All spirits must mature through storage. Clear spirits are aged in demi-johns or metal tanks. Spirits that are eventually golden brown, such as whiskey and Cognac, obtain their color through aging in oak casks. Because these casks are porous and permeable, some of the spirits evaporate during the sometimes lengthy aging period. The long storage and the loss through evaporation are the main reasons for the high prices of these products.

Refinement

The high alcohol content of the spirits after distillation and storage (approximately 70 percent) make consumption impossible. Therefore, distilled water is blended with the spirits to produce the appropriate alcohol content. Premium spirits such as Cognac, brandy, and Calvados require an additional step. To guarantee standard color and taste quality, the productions of several years are mixed. This process is called "marriage." Whiskey is also refined by mixing grain and malt whiskey. This process is called "blending."

An Overview of Spirit Production

| Raw Material | Production of Alcohol | Distillation | Coloring | Refinement | Spirit |

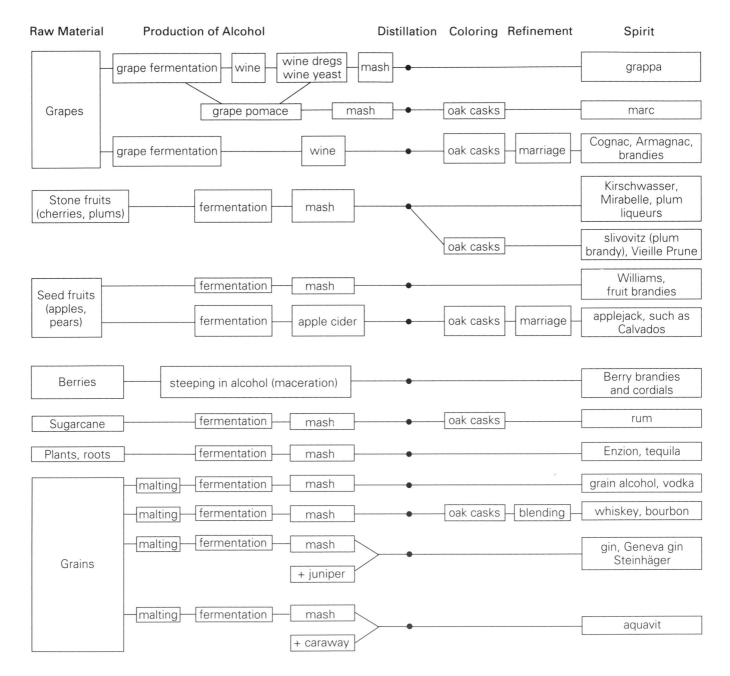

The Service of Liquors

Because of their high alcohol content, all liquors are served in small amounts: 1 fluid ounce for single servings and 2 fluid ounces for double portions. Whiskey is normally served in 1-fluid-ounce shots or is diluted with seltzer, soda, or mineral water if desired. To mention every serving portion has no purpose, since measures differ from country to country, and sometimes even within a country. It is important that shot glasses are of standard measure.

High-proof beverages are recommended as accompaniments (for example, Cognac with coffee or aquavit with beer); they can also be drunk alone. Liquors are often used as ingredients in mixed drinks as well.

Clear liquors are always served cold, whereas the golden brown spirits (aged for several years in oak casks) are served at room temperature, approximately 68°F.

Whiskey is served in several ways.

Whiskey Neat

Connoisseurs prefer premium whiskey served neat — with no dilution or addition — or with a little natural water. The aroma of the oak-aged whiskey can be best appreciated when it is served neat.

Whiskey with Soda, Seltzer, or Mineral Water

A measure of whiskey is poured into a tumbler and then diluted with seltzer, soda, or mineral water, as the guest wishes.

Whiskey on the Rocks

A measure of whiskey is poured into a tumbler and three or four ice cubes are added. This is the most popular way to drink whiskey.

The Age of Liquors

The age of a liquor can rarely be determined exactly for three reasons:

Labels almost never list a year.

Only the years in the cask, not in the bottle, are significant.

Many liquors are mixtures of several years' productions to ensure consistent quality.

Criteria for Cognac

Cognac labels usually contain abbreviations or designations that indicate the age of the brandy. As a member of the service staff, you must know the meanings of these abbreviations.

The legislation that defines Cognac stipulates the following designations:

Description	Minimum Storage Times in Oak Casks
*** (Three-star Cognac) "Cognac" "Cognac authentique"	3 years
"VO" (very old) "VSOP" (very superior old pale) "Reserve"	5 years
"Extra" "Napoléon" "Vieille Réserve"	6 years

The age given is determined by the youngest distillant in the brandy.

Designations for Whiskey

The age of whiskey is indicated with descriptions such as "old whiskey" or "VO" (very old). Every whiskey that is sold must have been aged for at least three years in an oak cask.

In addition to their standard liquors that have been aged for the minimum period, most whiskey producers also sell much older and, therefore, much more expensive whiskeys. The age given, for example, "12 years old," is always based on the youngest distillant in the blend.

Useful Information about Liquors

Spirit	Raw Materials	Glass	Serving Temperature	Common Brands	Country of Origin
Apricot brandy	Apricots		50°F	Barack Palinka Apricotine	Hungary, Switz.
Aquavit	Grain and caraway		33°–35°F	Aalborg, Taffel, Holger	Denmark
Armagnac*	Grapes		65°F	Château Labarthe, Lafontan, Jeanneau, Duc de Maravat, J. de Malliac	France

Spirit	Raw Materials	Glass	Serving Temperature	Common Brands	Country of Origin
Bourbon	Corn and rye		65°F	Four Roses, Jim Beam, Jack Daniels, IW Harper, Old Grand Dad, Old Forester, Old Fitzgerald	U.S.
Calvados*	Apples		65°F	Calvados Busnel, Dauphin, Morin, Père Magloire	France (Normandy)
Canadian whiskey	Corn and rye		65°F	Canadian Club, Seagram's VO, Schenley	Canada
Cognac*	Grapes		65°F	Courvoisier, Bisquit, Hennessy, Martell, Rémy Martin, Otard, Monnet, Roffignac	France
Enzian	Gentian root		50°F	Kindschi, Riemerschmid, Hemmeter, Grundbacher	Switz., Germany, Austria, France
Genever	Grain and juniper		33°–35°F	Bols, Doornkaat	Netherlands, Germany

Spirits	Raw Materials	Glass	Serving Temperature	Common Brands	Country of Origin
Gin	Grain and juniper		50°F	Gordon's, Beefeater, Tanqueray, Gilbey's, Booth, London	Great Britain
Grappa	Grape pomace, wine dregs and yeasts		50°F	Julia, Buton, Contratto, Stock, Tre Castelli, Libarna	Italy, Switz.
Blueberry brandy	Blueberries		50°F	Schladerer, 3 Tannen	Germany
Raspberry brandy	Raspberries		50°F	Schladerer, Bruder	Germany
Irish whiskey	Barley		65°F	Old Bushmills, Tullamore, Paddy, Power's, Jameson	Ireland
Kirschwasser	Cherries		50°F	Zuger Kirsch, Basler Kirsch, Schwarzwälder Kirsch, Basler Dybli, Dettling, General Sutter	Switz., Germany

251

Spirit	Raw Materials	Glass	Serving Temperature	Common Brands	Country of Origin
Grain alcohol	Rye, wheat, barley, oats		33°–35°F	Fürst Bismark, Both Silber, Alte Ernte, Eisweizen	Germany
Marc	Grape pomace		65°F	Marc de Champagne, Marc de Bourgogne, Marc de Dôle	France, Switz.
Mirabelle	Mirabelles (golden plums)		50°F	Schlumberger, Nussbaumer	France (Alsace)
Plum brandy	Plums		50°F	Grundbacher, Bussman, Obi	Switz., France
Prune brandy	Plums (dried)		50°F	Martel & Co., F. Lanz AG, Héritier-Guyot, Morin	
Rum	Sugarcane		65°F	Bacardi, Ronrico, Coruba, Meyer's, Lemon Hart, Negrita	Caribbean islands

Spirit	Raw Materials	Glass	Serving Temperature	Common Brands	Country of Origin
Scotch whisky	Barley and rye		65°F	Ballantine's, Bell's, Black & White, Chivas Regal, Dewar's, Haig, 100 Pipers, Cutty Sark, J&B, Dimple, Johnnie Walker, VAT 69, White Horse	Great Britain, Scotland
Slivovitz	Plums		65°F	Navip, Maraska, Tzuica	Yugoslavia, Romania
Steinhäger	Grains and juniper		33°–35°F	Schinkenhäger, Schlichte	Germany
Tequila	Maguey-agave plant		50°F	Mariachi, Almeca, Cuervo	Mexico
Brandy	Grapes		65°F	Stock, Buton, Eau de Vie, Asbach Uralt, Fundador	Italy, France, Germany, Spain
Williams	Williams pear		50°F	Morand, Le bon père	Switz.

Spirit	Raw Materials	Glass	Serving Temperature	Common Brands	Country of Origin
Vodka	Grains		33°–35°F	Smirnoff, Wyborowa, Moskovskaya, Stolitchnaya, Absolut	Russia, Poland, Sweden

* Recognized internationally as the name of a liquor produced in a particular region. This name is legally protected, and similar liquors not produced in the designated region may not carry it.

Liqueurs

Liqueurs are sweet or bitter, strongly aromatic, and often very alcoholic beverages that are a combination of brandy or pure alcohol, sugar, and flavoring agents. The flavoring agents may be fruits, aromatic plants, or herbs. Liqueurs may be almost any color; practically every color of the spectrum is represented.

Sweet Liqueurs

Like other spirits, liqueurs can be served as an accompaniment to coffee. They are, however, especially popular for mixing. Liqueurs have the same importance in the bar that spices have in the kitchen. Today, clear spirits (for example, gin) usually are mixed together with liqueurs to create aromatic and colorful drinks.

The alcohol content of liqueurs varies from 20 to 55 percent, while the sugar content must be at least 10 percent.

Liqueurs are served only in small portions; the standard measure differs from country to country. In many cases liqueurs are served in small snifters, but establishments often have special liqueur glasses.

	Name	Base
Herb-based Liqueurs	Bénédictine D.O.M.	Sundry herbs
	Bénédictine B.B.	Sundry herbs and Cognac
	Chartreuse vert (green)	Sundry herbs
	Chartreuse jaune (yellow)	Sundry herbs
	Galliano	Sundry herbs
	Goldwasser	Sundry herbs
	Strega	Sundry herbs
Citrus-based Liqueurs	Cointreau	Bitter-orange peel
	Curaçao orange	Curaçao orange
	Curaçao blue	Curaçao orange
	Curaçao red	Curaçao orange
	Curaçao green	Curaçao orange
	Grand Marnier	Orange paste and Cognac
	Mandarine	Mandarin orange
Stone-fruit-based Liqueurs	Apricot brandy	Apricots
	Cherry Heering	Cherries
	Maraschino	Marasca cherries
	Peach brandy	Peaches
	Röteli	Cherries

	Name	Base
Seed-fruit-based Liqueurs	Williamine	Pears
Berry-based Liqueurs	Brombeere	Blackberries
	Cassis	Black currants
	Fraisa	Strawberries
	Sambuca	Elderberries
Cream Liqueurs	Crème de banane	Bananas
	Crème de cacao	Cocoa
	Crème de menthe	Peppermint
	Crème de mokka	Coffee
	Crème de noisette	Hazelnuts
	Crème de vanille	Vanilla
Other Liqueurs	Amaretto	Almonds
	Anisette	Anise
	Drambuie	Scotch whisky and honey
	Eierlikor	Egg powder
	Irish Mist	Irish whiskey and honey
	Kümmell	Caraway seeds
	Lochan Ora	Scotch whisky and honey
	Parfait Amour	Violets
	Suisceri	Cherries and chocolate

Bitter Liqueurs

Bitter liqueurs (also called stomach bitters or bitters for short) are usually drunk as *digestifs,* therefore, after the meal. Bitter liqueurs aid the digestion and help when one has eaten too much or eaten food that is hard to digest. But bitter liqueurs are also drunk for pleasure; even so, as the name indicates, the taste is bitter. Bitter liqueurs are made from herb bases, and therefore are similar in principle to herb liqueurs. The only significant difference is in the composition, because bitter liqueurs have no or very little sugar. The recipes of the best-known brands are kept secret by the producers (often family operations) as precious treasures which are passed on to younger generations and are only known to a very few.

The alcohol content of the different *digestifs* varies between 45 and 49 percent. Therefore, they are, like spirits and liqueurs, served in small portions. They are always served in a shot glass with a glass of ice water on the side.

Common Brands

Boonekamp

Fernet Branca

Jägermeister

Maykamp

Underberg

Mixed Drinks

Mixed drinks can be alcohol free or high in proof. There is an abundance of recipes for both types. Assuming the bartender is skilled, the result is always very attractive. For eye appeal, the composition and presentation of mixed drinks play major roles.

Mixed drinks are equally popular as aperitifs or *digestifs*. But they are also ordered simply as a beverage instead of a ready-made drink.

As a member of the service staff, you should know the most important drinks and how they are prepared, as well as the utensils necessary to prepare them.

The Most Important Mixing Equipment

The Most Important Mixing Equipment

Mixing Glass

For mixed drinks that are only stirred quickly with a barspoon, a mixing glass is used. The beverages mixed in this way must have approximately the same consistency.

Bar Spoon

With a long-handled bar spoon, the beverages in the mixing glass are stirred.

Shaker

Beverages of different consistencies are mixed in a shaker, for instance, light spirits with heavy cream, a liqueur, or syrup.

Strainer

The strainer is held over the mixing glass or the shaker when the drink is poured into the serving glass. It holds back the ice, lemon pits, and so on.

Measuring Cup

Recipes at the bar have to be followed precisely. Therefore, to prepare a drink, a measuring cup is used.

Measuring Glass

This glass has the same purpose as the measuring cup.

Ice Tongs

These are used to handle ice cubes.

Other Bar Equipment

Lemon juicer

Small carving board

Small knife to cut lemons, oranges, and the like

Toothpicks to spear cherries, olives, orange slices, and the like

Alcoholic Mixed Drinks

An in-depth study of all mixed drinks and their recipes would require a book in itself. But, as a server, you should know the most important groups of alcoholic mixed drinks as well as the recipes of the most popular drinks.

Cocktails

Cocktails are mixed drinks that are served in rather small portions. Their alcohol content is clearly noticeable because it is concentrated.

Cocktails are always served in cocktail glasses.

Tall Drinks

Tall drinks are mixed drinks in which the alcohol base is more diluted. The alcohol taste is therefore not as pronounced as in cocktails because the proportion of other ingredients is greater.

Tall drinks are always served in aperitif glasses; examples are sours and fizzes.

The Most Important Mixed Drinks

In the following chart you will find a small selection of classical cocktails and tall drinks and their ingredients.

The abbreviations in the chart are:

ds: dash, a squirt or a few drops

bs: bar spoon

Note that ⅔ fluid ounce is about 4 teaspoons and ⅓ fluid ounce is about 2 teaspoons; 1 fluid ounce is equal to 2 tablespoons or 6 teaspoons, and 1⅓ fluid ounces is equal to 2 tablespoons plus 2 teaspoons.

Classic Cocktails and Tall Drinks

Cocktail	Base Spirit	Aromatic Ingredients	Prepared in	Glass	Garnish or Addition
Alaska	1 fl. oz. gin	⅔ fl. oz. Chartreuse jaune (yellow)	Shaker		
Brandy Alexander	⅔ fl. oz. Cognac	⅔ fl. oz. crème de cacao ⅔ fl. oz. cream	Shaker		
Angel's Face	⅔ fl. oz. gin ⅔ fl. oz. Calvados	⅔ fl. oz. apricot brandy	Shaker		
Daiquiri	1⅓ fl. oz. light rum	⅓ fl. oz. lime juice 1 bs sugar 1 bs grenadine syrup	Shaker		
Gibson	1⅓ fl. oz. gin	⅓ fl. oz. dry vermouth	Mixing glass		1 pearl onion
Manhattan	1 fl. oz. Canadian whiskey	⅓ fl. oz. dry vermouth 1 ds angostura bitters	Mixing glass		1 Maraschino cherry

Cocktail	Base Spirit	Aromatic Ingredients	Prepared in	Glass	Garnish or Addition
Martini (dry)	1⅓ fl. oz. gin	⅓ fl. oz. dry vermouth	Mixing glass		1 olive
Negroni	⅔ fl. oz. gin	⅔ fl. oz. Campari ⅔ fl. oz. Punt e Mes	Mixing glass		1 orange slice
Sidecar	⅔ fl. oz. Cognac	⅔ fl. oz. Cointreau ⅔ fl. oz. lemon juice	Shaker		1 Maraschino cherry
White Lady	⅔ fl. oz. gin	⅔ fl. oz. Cointreau ⅔ fl. oz. lemon juice 2 egg whites	Shaker		1 Maraschino cherry
Screwdriver	1⅙ fl. oz. vodka	2 fl. oz. orange juice	Mixing glass		Ice

Tall Drinks	Base Spirit	Aromatic Ingredients	Prepared in	Glass	Garnish or Addition
Bloody Mary	1⅓ fl. oz. vodka	3½ fl. oz. tomato juice ⅓ fl. oz. lemon juice 3 ds Worcestershire sauce 1 ds Tabasco sauce Salt and pepper	Mixing glass		Celery stalks
Cuba Libre	1⅓ fl. oz. rum	⅔ fl. oz. lime juice	Tumbler		Fill the glass with cola
Gin Fizz	1⅓ fl. oz. gin	2 bs sugar 1⅔ fl. oz. lemon juice	Shaker		Fill the glass with soda
Gin Sour	1⅓ fl. oz. gin	1 bs sugar 1⅓ fl. oz. lemon juice	Shaker		1 lemon slice 1 Maraschino cherry
Omnibus	1 fl. oz. Kirsch	⅔ fl. oz. grenadine syrup	Shaker		Fill the glass with soda
Whiskey Sour	1⅓ fl. oz. bourbon	1 bs sugar 1⅓ fl. oz. lemon juice	Shaker		1 orange slice 2 Maraschino cherries

Punches

The punch is a mixed drink served primarily as an aperitif. Since it is made only for groups, as opposed to individual guests, it is an ideal prelude to a banquet.

A punch is generally made from wine, sparkling wine, sugar, fruits, and liqueur. It is mixed in a glass bowl that is placed in a larger bowl filled with ice. The ice should never be put into the punch itself, since it would dilute the punch and weaken the taste when it melts. It is also important that every bottle of wine used for the punch be of top quality; each should be tasted before adding.

Basic Punch Recipe
(for ten people)

21 ounces fresh fruit, such as strawberries
3.5 ounces sugar
3.5 fluid ounces liqueur, such as Grand Marnier
24 fluid ounces light white wine

Combine the ingredients and let the punch stand for approximately two hours. Just before serving, add another 24 fluid ounces of white wine and half a bottle of sparkling wine. The punch is served in Champagne glasses or in special punch glasses. Teaspoons should be provided for the fruit. The punch is poured into the glasses with a ladle.

Hot Mixed Drinks

Grog and mulled wine are probably the best known hot mixed drinks, and many regional and special house recipes are available. The various recipes differ only in the spices and flavorings used; the basic preparation is essentially the same for all of them.

Because grog and mulled wine are not only mixed hot but drunk hot, they are traditional winter beverages and are age-old remedies for colds.

Grog

Grog is usually prepared with rum, but it can also be made with Cognac, whiskey, or gin. The preparation is simple: in a tea glass, pour a portion of prewarmed rum. Then fill the glass with hot water, add some sugar, and garnish with a wedge of lemon.

The tea glass is presented on a saucer with a teaspoon.

Mulled Wine

Mulled wine is prepared in the following fashion: combine seven to ten fluid ounces of red wine per person with one cinnamon stick, one bay leaf per person, two cloves, sugar, and the zest of a half a lemon. Heat slowly in a pan just to boiling. The wine should not boil under any circumstances.

Strain the mulled wine through a sieve into tea glasses and serve on a saucer with a teaspoon.

Beer

Beer is one of the oldest alcoholic beverages known to man. The German legislation for the brewing of beer, the so-called purity law, was passed in 1516 and is still strictly enforced today.

Beer made its triumphant procession around the world because it is a relatively inexpensive alcoholic beverage, and the alcohol content is low (3 to 6 percent) when compared to other alcoholic beverages. Beer is known as an ideal thirst quencher because it is fizzy and refreshing, tastes tart, and is very easily digested.

Definition

Beer is an alcoholic carbonated beverage that is made from three basic raw materials, barley malt, water, and hops that are fermented with yeast.

Raw Materials for Beer

Malt

Malt is barley grain that has been steeped in water, allowed to germinate, and then dried. In this way the barley malt is prepared for fermentation. Malt dried at a temperature of 185°F is used for the production of light beers, whereas malt lightly roasted at a temperature of 220°F is used to make dark beers.

Hops

The hop plant is a vine, and the flowers of the hop, which resembles a small pine cone, are used to give beer its bitter flavor. Hops also act as a preservative and make the beer's head last longer.

Water

Good brewing water is of the utmost importance to the taste of the beer. The water must be soft and calcium free. In all other respects, it should meet all the requirements of good drinking water.

The Three Main Phases of Beer Production

Brewing

The first phase consists of two major steps: the malting, during which the starch contained in the barley malt is converted into malt sugar, and the cooking, when the malt is concentrated and at the same time seasoned with hops.

Fermentation

During fermentation, the yeast enzymes convert most of the malt sugar into alcohol and carbon dioxide.

Storage

While beer is stored in a cellar, the fermentation process is completed as the remaining malt sugar is converted into alcohol and carbon dioxide. The carbon dioxide cannot escape from the storage tank and therefore remains in the beer, carbonating it and making it easier to digest.

Beer Types

Light or dark beer	Color is determined by the malt. Lightly roasted barley malt makes for a light beer; brown roasted malt, a dark beer.
Light or strong beer	Taste is determined by the wort (the malt sugar solution obtained by brewing) before fermentation. The more concentrated it is, the stronger the taste of the beer.
Top- or bottom-fermented beer	This is a reference to the style of fermentation. Bottom-fermented beer finishes fermenting in the storage cellar. Top-fermenting beer still ferments after bottling. With top-fermenting beer, the yeast stays on the surface; with bottom-fermenting beer, the yeast settles on the bottom of the fermenting keg.

Beer Types

Beer	Bottom- or Top-Fermented	Color	Characteristics
Bock beer	Bottom-fermented	Light and dark	Mild and full
Diet beer	Bottom-fermented	Light	Low calorie, light
Lager beer	Bottom-fermented	Light and dark	Tasty, mild
Light beer	Bottom-fermented	Light	Fizzy and light
Luxury beer	Bottom-fermented	Light	Piquant, tasty
Old beer	Top-fermented	Red brown	Fizzy, tart
Pilsner beer	Bottom-fermented	Light yellow	Slightly bitter, strongly hopped
Special beer	Bottom-fermented	Light and dark	Piquant, tasty
Strong beer	Bottom-fermented	Light and dark	Piquant, full
Wheat beer	Top-fermented	Light	Fizzy, slight yeast taste
Alcohol-free beer	Bottom-fermented	Light	Light and without alcohol

The Service of Beer

Beer can be offered on tap or in bottles. In operations with a substantial turnover, it is most likely offered on tap. A beer tapped fresh from the keg is more appreciated by beer connoisseurs than bottled beers.

But for both types, a scrupulously clean glass is essential. Even the tiniest trace of grease will cause the beloved typical beer head to go flat. Beer glasses should be washed with the least possible amount of detergent and then rinsed in clear cold water.

Beer on Tap

Breweries deliver draft beer to restaurants in metal kegs or in beer containers. The pressure of the trapped carbon dioxide forces the beer to the tap.

The most important prerequisites for the service of draft beer are:

Correct and constant pressure from the CO_2

Proper storage and serving temperatures (about 43° to 50°F)

The cleanliness of the glasses and equipment, which is jeopardized by even the smallest trace of grease

When tapping beer, two steps are followed. These do not require much time and guarantee that the guest receives a proper serving.

Hold the glass at an angle close to the tap and open the tap completely. Fill the glass about three-quarters full, and then set it down.

Wait a bit until the foam has settled, then put the head on the beer, that most important cap of foam. This time the glass is held straight and the tap is only opened a little bit.

With equipment fitted with the so-called Cornelius tap, the lever is pushed all the way back to add the final head.

Bottled Beer

Beer delivered by the brewery in bottles is served to the guest at the table. When serving bottled beer, two steps are followed:

Hold the glass and bottle at an angle, and fill the glass three-quarters full.

Put the glass down and add the head.

 Like all beverages, beer is placed to the right of the guest, and the beer glass is always placed on a clean beer coaster. Be sure that the label of the bottle and the logo on the glass always face the guest.

What Accompanies Beer?

Naturally, beer is often drunk simply to quench thirst. But it also can complement several menu items. Here are a few examples.

Beer goes well with items that are prepared with beer, such as beer-batter specialties or *carbonnade* of beef.

Beer also goes well with dishes with flavored with vinegar, such as different meat and fish specialties preserved in vinegar, for example, herring.

Beer complements cold cuts, charcuterie, and smoked meats.

Beer goes exceptionally well with hot spicy dishes, such as Asian and Mexican specialties.

Mixed Drinks Using Beer

Mixed drinks using beer are also very popular. The best known are:

Amer-Georges	Combine 1 fluid ounce Amer Picon with 2 teaspoons lemon syrup in a beer glass; fill the glass with dark beer.
Beer grenadine	Add 4 teaspoons of grenadine to a beer glass, then fill the glass with light beer.
Beer panache	Combine one part lemonade and two parts lager beer in a beer glass.
Berliner Weisse mit Schuss	To a special broad beer glass, add 4 teaspoons of raspberry syrup. Then fill the glass with *weissbier* (a top-fermented Berlin beer). The thick foam head should extend over the rim of the glass.

Alcohol-free Beverages

The alcohol-free beverages are divided into six categories

Mineral water

Seltzer or club soda

Carbonated soft drinks (soda pop)

Fruit and vegetable juices

Milk and milk drinks

Coffee and tea

Mineral Water

Mineral water, such as Perrier, differs from drinking water because, as the name indicates, it contains minerals. It can but need not contain carbon dioxide, which makes it bubbly. The most important information about the different mineral waters—mineral content and therapeutic value—is always listed on the bottle label.

If not requested otherwise by the guest, mineral water is always served cold, about 45°F. It is always served in a water goblet.

Mineral waters for therapeutic purposes, such as Vichy, Fachinger, and others, are served warm, about 60°F.

Seltzer or Club Soda

Seltzer is a beverage made by carbonating drinking water, used mainly to dilute spirits and aperitifs. If salt and sodium bicarbonate is added, club soda is the result.

Carbonated Soft Drinks

Soda pop and flavored mineral water belong in this category. Flavored mineral water is sweetened with sugar and flavored with fruit juices or plant extracts. Soda pop is made in the same way, but the mineral water is replaced with carbonated drinking water.

Flavored mineral waters and soda pop are served cool, about 45°F. When served from a bottle, they are served in water goblets. When served from a fountain tap, a tumbler is used.

Fruit and Vegetable Juices

Fruit and vegetable juices are either freshly squeezed or are purchased packaged and ready to serve. The most commonly ordered are:

Orange juice

Grapefruit juice

Grape juice

Cranberry juice

Apple juice

Pineapple juice

Tomato juice

Mixed-vegetable juice (e.g., V-8)

Only pure fruit juices can be called juice. When diluted with water, they are called fruit drinks or ades. The water cannot exceed 50 percent of the volume.

Vegetable juices should never be diluted.

Granulated sugar should always be served with fresh-squeezed fruit juices, freshly ground pepper and salt should always accompany vegetable juices. A teaspoon should be provided.

Milk

Cows' milk, commonly called, simply, milk, is a primary source of nourishment, especially for children. Milk is an important nonalcoholic beverage in foodservice. Nevertheless, plain milk is almost never ordered alone; it usually accompanies a meal. Raw milk cannot be served in restaurants; milk must be made germ-free before it can be served.

Ready-to-Drink Milk Is Germ-Free

The milk available commercially is almost or totally germ-free. To achieve this, dairies use two methods, pasteurization and ultra-heat treatment.

Pasteurization

To pasteurize, raw milk is heated to 170°F and then cooled immediately to 40°F. This process kills the pathogenic organisms in raw milk without significantly changing the flavor, odor, or color. The shelf life of pasteurized milk is limited, however, so that all bottles or containers must list the date by which the milk must be sold. Pasteurized milk should be stored cool, at approximately 40°F, and it should be protected from light and odors.

Ultra-Heat-Treated Milk

With this process prewarmed raw milk is placed in a special apparatus in which steam heats the milk to a temperature of 270° to 300°F within seconds, after which the milk is immediately cooled in seconds. Ultra-heat-treated milk is completely germ-free, which allows storage of an unopened package for four months.

To homogenize milk, dairies mechanically break up the fat globules in the milk so they will not rise to the surface. The milk fat (cream) is thus equally distributed throughout the liquid.

Foodservice Operations Can Make Raw Milk Drinkable

If an operation does not purchase commercially available milk, raw milk can be made drinkable by heating it. (Check your local health codes to ensure these procedures are legal in your area.)

Heating in a Pan or Pot

To pasteurize, the milk must be heated to approximately 170° to 180°F and stirred constantly to avoid burning or the formation of a skin on top.

Heating with Steam

For immediate use, milk can be heated with the steam tap on your coffee machine. To prevent the water content of the milk from becoming too high, do not heat more than 16 fluid ounces of milk at once. Milk may not be heated more than once.

The correct method for heating with steam is as follows:

So the condensed water that eventually forms can escape, the steam tap is opened briefly and closed at once.

The steam tube is submerged into a half-filled milk pitcher. The steam tap is opened, and through constant circulation, the milk is heated until a strong foam forms and the milk wells up. The temperature will be approximately 175°F.

The steam tap is closed, the milk pitcher is removed, and then the tap is opened again briefly to allow any milk residue to drip out. The tap is then wiped with a damp cloth.

Cold milk is served in a milk glass; hot milk, in a coffee cup on a saucer with a teaspoon and sugar on the side.

Mixed Milk Drinks

Milk drinks are very popular.

Simple mixed milk drinks should be offered by every operation; they will be drunk readily at any time of the day or the year.

The best-known mixed milk drinks are prepared with the following ingredients:

Chocolate powder
Malt extract, for example, Ovaltine
Various fruit juices
Various fruit syrups

Preparation and Service of Warm Mixed Milk Drinks

Hot Ovaltine or hot chocolate	Steam the milk. Serve in a coffee cup with a saucer and teaspoon, with an individual package of Ovaltine or chocolate powder on the side. (Many operations have special machines that heat the milk/chocolate mixture and produce ready-to-serve hot chocolate.)

Preparation and Service of Cold Mixed Milk Drinks	Cold Ovaltine or cold chocolate milk	Mix cold milk well with Ovaltine or chocolate powder in a shaker or with a stirrer. Serve in a milk glass with a straw.
	Milkshakes	These are popular thirst quenchers on hot days. Combine 5 fluid ounces of milk with 1½ fluid ounces of fruit syrup or juice or other flavoring (chocolate, vanilla, coffee, for example), sugar, and two or three ice cubes or crushed ice. Mix well in a shaker, strain into a milk glass, and serve with a straw.
	Milk frappés	This mixture of milk and ice cream is especially popular with children. For one portion, combine 5 fluid ounces of milk, 1 scoop of ice cream, and if desired, fruit of the appropriate flavor. Mix in a blender so the frappé is thick but creamy.
Three Frappé Recipes	Vanilla frappé	1 scoop vanilla ice cream 5 fluid ounces milk
	Banana frappé	1 scoop vanilla ice cream ½ banana 5 fluid ounces milk
	Chocolate frappé	1 scoop chocolate ice cream 5 fluid ounces milk

Coffee

Coffee beans are grown in Central and South America, Africa, and Asia.

Coffee beans are the seeds inside the red coffee fruit from coffee trees. The flesh of the coffee fruit is removed, and the coffee beans are dried and then sorted by quality.

The consumer country imports the raw coffee and combines and roasts the different types according to their intended use. The mixing and degree of roasting differs from country to country because coffee preferences vary significantly by nationality.

Because the aroma of the coffee diffuses very quickly, coffee roasters sometimes sell the roasted coffee beans, which are then ground by the consumers themselves, or roasters grind the coffee and sell the grounds in vacuum-packed cans or bags.

 Coffee beans and coffee grounds must be kept in airtight containers at all times, or they will lose the aroma that makes coffee so enjoyable.

In foodservice all makes of machines for coffee preparation can be found, but most operations have two types of machines.

The first prepares coffee by pouring hot water over the coffee grounds, which are held in a filter through which the coffee drips into a pot or an urn. This machine can also be used to keep the coffee warm.

This machine can be used to prepare coffee when large quantities are needed, for example, at breakfast. The preparation of coffee with this machine was explained earlier in chapter 9.

Most establishments also have a coffee machine that is used to make single servings of coffee, from regular coffee to espresso to cappuccino. With this machine, coffee is brewed under pressure. The hot water is forced through the coffee grounds, producing the desired foam cap. The operation of this machine is different from make to make and therefore cannot be discussed in detail here.

Regardless of the type of coffee machine, the basic preparation of coffee can be expressed in one sentence:

Hot water, approximately 205°F, is poured over coffee grounds, with or without pressure; one serving of coffee requires between one-quarter and one-half ounce of coffee, depending on the desired strength.

The Service of Coffee

The following list details the most common ways to serve coffee. Depending on the country, as mentioned earlier, coffee preparation styles can be very different.

Black coffee, with sugar	A cup of coffee is served on a saucer with a teaspoon, accompanied by sugar and artificial sweetener.

Regular coffee	A cup of black coffee served on a saucer with a teaspoon accompanied by sugar and coffee cream or milk.
Decaffeinated coffee	Decaffeinated coffee grounds are used to prepare this coffee; otherwise, preparation and service are the same as for regular coffee.
Espresso	A concentrated coffee, brewed under pressure. The amount of coffee grounds used is the same as for regular coffee, but the amount of water is reduced by half. Espresso is served in special small espresso cups with matching saucers, always accompanied by granulated sugar, as well as coffee cream if desired.
Ristretto	Twice as strong as espresso, ristretto is prepared and served in the same way but uses half the amount of water for the same amount of coffee grounds.
Café mélange	A cup of black coffee topped with whipped cream and served in the same way as black coffee, with sugar.
Cappuccino	A cup is filled three-quarters full with black coffee; hot, steamed milk foam is added to fill the cup. A pinch of cocoa powder is sprinkled on top. Cappuccino is served like black coffee, with sugar.

Milk-coffee	A coffee cup is filled with two parts coffee and one part milk; serve like black coffee, with sugar.
A portion of coffee	A portion is two servings of coffee and is served in a small coffee server along with a prewarmed coffee cup, saucer, teaspoon, sugar and artificial sweetener, and a double portion of coffee cream.

Alcoholic Coffee Specialties

Coffee is often enhanced by a shot of liquor or liqueur. The number of recipes for international coffee specialties with alcohol is enormous; listed below are five popular European specialties.

Irish coffee	Into a prewarmed Irish-coffee glass, combine 1.5 fluid ounces of Irish whiskey and 2 to 3 bar spoons of sugar. Stir well, then fill the glass with hot, strong coffee to about three-quarters inch below the rim. Pour lightly whipped cream over the back of a spoon into the glass onto the surface of the drink; it should float on top and should not be mixed with the coffee.
Coffee *luz*	In a coffee glass, mix 2 to 3 sugar cubes with 3.5 fluid ounces of black coffee. Add 1.5 fluid ounces of fruit brandy, and fill with hot water. Serve at once. If the glass has not been tempered to withstand heat, keep a spoon in the glass until it is filled to prevent it from cracking.

283

Rüdesheimer coffee	Combine 3 sugar cubes and 1.5 fluid ounces of warmed Asbach Uralt brandy in a prewarmed coffee cup. Fill with black coffee to three-quarters inch below the rim. Top with whipped cream, and garnish with chocolate shavings.
Coffee corretto	Literally "corrected coffee," this drink is *ristretto* with a dash of grappa.
Café marnissimo	In a prewarmed coffee glass or the original marnissimo coffee cups, combine 4 teaspoons (⅔ fluid ounce) of Grand Marnier and 2 bar spoons of confectioner's sugar. Stir well; fill glass or cup two-thirds full with hot, strong coffee. Pour lightly whipped heavy cream over the back of a spoon onto the surface of the coffee.

Tea

Advice on the correct way to brew tea abounds. But in foodservice tea bags are commonly used, for a variety of sensible reasons, and so the discussion here will be limited to the simplest preparation method.

Tea is generally understood to be black tea, because that type is most frequently drunk. Green tea, which is preferred in some countries, is produced by heating the tea leaves to prevent fermentation; the leaves are steamed and rolled to evaporate the liquid in the leaves. To produce black tea, the tea leaves are allowed to wilt, mechanically rolled tightly, and then fermented. The tea leaves, which turn coppery red after fermentation, are then roasted or dried in hot air, becoming dark brown, almost black; hence the name.

Tea is grown primarily in Asia and Africa. The tea bush reaches a height of approximately thirteen feet when growing wild, but on tea plantations the bushes are grown to a height of about thirty to thirty-five inches. The upper leaves and buds are harvested for tea.

The Flavors of Tea

Unlike coffee, for which one variety is used to prepare many different styles, a number of tea varieties are offered in restaurants and especially in tea-rooms and cafés. The most common are:

Ceylon tea	With a fine, lightly perfumed aroma
Darjeeling tea	From India, with a strong, full aroma
Lapsang Souchong	From China, with a strong smoky aroma
Jasmine tea	From China, with a heavily perfumed, flowery aroma

▶ Tea and tea bags must be stored in airtight containers to protect them from dampness.

The Simplest Method of Tea Preparation

For a cup or tea glass, use 2 grams (1 level teaspoon) of loose tea or one tea bag. For one portion of tea (tea server), use 4 to 5 grams (2 to 2½ teaspoons) of loose tea or two tea bags.

The ideal brewing temperature for tea is the boiling point of water, 212°F. The water should come to a short boil and still be bubbling when poured over the tea.

Tea must steep in the hot water. The best flavor develops after three to five minutes of brewing.

The Service of Tea

Tea is only served in a few ways and always in a thin-walled porcelain cup or a tea glass. When tea bags are used, a small dish should be served on the side for the used bag.

Plain tea	A glass or a cup of tea on a saucer, with a teaspoon and sugar.
Tea with cream	Served like plain tea but accompanied by a portion of milk or coffee cream.
Tea with lemon	Served like plain tea but lemon wedges are served on the side.
Iced tea	Cold tea, ice, a lemon slice, and sugar are combined in a tall stemless glass, which is served on a saucer with an iced-tea spoon and a straw.

Herbal Teas

Herbal teas, unlike black tea, are often domestically produced. Herbal leaves, flowers, fruit, or roots are dried and processed. Many herbal teas and mixtures promise special healing or soothing effects; it is said that for every illness there is an herb to cure it. These special herbal concoctions are rarely served in foodservice establishments. The herbal teas most commonly offered in restaurants are those often found in homes:

Peppermint tea
Rose-hip tea
Lime-blossom tea
Chamomile tea

For foodservice these teas are almost always in tea bags. They are brewed like black tea — placed in a tea glass or cup and steeped in boiling water. Serve on a saucer with a teaspoon and sugar.

17. *The Art of Cooking*

This chapter will introduce you to the world of the kitchen. If you are wondering why, as a member of the service staff, you should be initiated into the art of cooking, the answer is very simple. You must always be able to explain to your guests in a few words how something is prepared. This is a very important skill in acting as an adviser. Please follow us now into the kitchen.

Basic Kitchen Knowledge

With regard to the food, you will find that there are three common questions that your guests will ask:

"How Does It Taste?"

You must know the different tastes and describe the food as appetizingly as possible so that the guest can imagine the food's taste and satisfy a desire for something that is, for example, pungent, spicy, tender, or juicy. This point has already been discussed in chapter 12.

"What Is That?"

Culinary terms should not be a foreign language to you. You should know what a recipe name means, what it means when something is prepared *à la florentine* and what sauce diane is. You will find a glossary of classical cooking terms in chapter 19.

"How Is It Prepared?"

This question will be discussed in this chapter. You will learn the fourteen basic preparation methods so you can always explain to your guests the difference between a grilled or a fried chicken, between poached and sautéed fish.

Knowing the fourteen basic preparation methods is essential. Only when you understand the terms used in the kitchen can you advise your guest properly and make alternative suggestions. In the chapter on sales technique, you learned that, when making suggestions, the methods of preparation should differ to provide variety. This chapter will give you the tools to offer a varied selection.

The Basic Preparation Methods

Blanching (*blanchir*)

Boiling (*bouillir*)

Steaming (*cuire à la vapeur*)

Poaching (*pocher*)

Frying/pan-frying/deep-frying (*frire*)

Sautéing (*sauter*)

Grilling/broiling (*griller*)

Gratinéing (*gratiner*)

Baking (*cuire au four*)

Roasting (*rôtir*)

Braising (*braiser*)

Glazing (*glacer*)

Pot-roasting (*poêler*)

Stewing (*étuver*)

Blanching

Blanching is a cooking or precooking method that involves heating quickly in a large amount of liquid. The technique used depends on the food being cooked: food may be blanched by being placed in cold water that is slowly brought to a boil, by being placed in already boiling water, or by being placed in hot oil (265°F). When blanching in water, the food is brought to the boiling point and then cooked at that temperature for a very short time.

Blanching Is Suitable for:

Potatoes
Vegetables
Meat

Boiling

Boiling means cooking in a large amount of water that has been heated to 212°F. Depending on the food to be cooked, the food is either placed in cold water and heated to a boil or placed in already boiling water. Whether rapidly boiling water or water just below the boiling point is used again depends on the food being cooked.

Boiling Is Suitable for:

Potatoes
Fresh or dried vegetables
Meat
Rice
Pasta

Steaming

Steaming involves heating food with steam produced by boiling liquid below the food. Steaming preserves vitamins, reduces cooking time, and helps the food retain its shape. Steaming can be done in a steamer, a pressure cooker, or a steaming basket in a pot with a heavy lid.

Steaming is always done with very little liquid and without disturbing the food being cooked.

Steaming Is Suitable for:

Vegetables
Potatoes
Rice
Meat
Poultry

Poaching

Poaching is a very gentle cooking process in which food is heated in water, in stock, or in a water bath. The food is not heated above 175°F and is therefore cooked very gently.

Poaching Is Suitable for:

Fish and poultry, in stock
Eggs, sausages, and dumplings, in water
Creams and sauces, in a water bath

Frying

To fry, food is placed in liquid fat (frying fat or oil) and cooked under constant or increasing heat (320° to 355°F).

<u>Frying Is Suitable for</u>:

Potatoes, for example, french fries
Fish and shellfish
Meat, for example, brains, sweetbreads
Chicken
Vegetables, for example, salsify, eggplant, zucchini
Pastries, for example, doughnuts and fritters

Sautéing

To sauté means to pan-fry quickly over high heat. A small amount of fat (such as butter) or oil is heated in a frying pan and then the food is added. The food is cooked at a temperature of 320° to 465°F. Meat and fish are turned; vegetables are tossed.

After removing the food, the remaining drippings can be used as a basis for a sauce by deglazing the pan with wine, or the drippings can be used directly on the cooked food.

<u>Sautéing Is Suitable for</u>:

Poultry parts
Small pieces of fish
Meat in pieces, for example, steaks, cutlets, chops
Potatoes
Various vegetables, for example, beans

Grilling/Broiling

Grilling is done over an open fire on a metal grill; broiling, under an electric or infrared broiler. Depending on the food to be grilled, it is first lightly marinated in oil, seasoned, or basted with a marinade. Meat is first seared with high heat (430° to 480°F), then cooked at a lower heat (300° to 390°F). Searing keeps the meat juicy inside and allows the popular crisp crust to form.

Grilling and Broiling Are Suitable for:

Small to medium pieces of meat, for example, schnitzel, sirloin
    steak, cutlets, chateaubriand
Small fishes or fish steaks, for example, salmon
Shellfish, for example, shrimp
Poultry

Gratinéing

To gratiné means to brown the top of a dish. This procedure is usually the last cooking step before serving. Crumbs (bread, corn flake, potato chip, for example), grated cheese, and dots of butter are some of the toppings sprinkled on the dish to create a crispy brown crust. Such dishes are usually deemed au gratin. High heat (480° to 575°F) from above the food is used to brown it.

Gratinéing Is Suitable for:

Fish
Poultry
Potatoes
Vegetables
Pasta
Cheese dishes

Baking

Baking, done in the oven, is a cooking method using dry heat. When baking, you are cooking without additional liquid or fat, either in molds or on sheet pans or in containers without lids. During baking, heat may be increased or decreased after a certain amount of time, depending on the item being baked.

Baking Is Suitable for:

Potatoes
Dishes with pastry
Pies and cakes
Soufflés

Roasting

Roasting can be done in an oven or on a spit. When roasting in an oven, the food is placed in a roasting pan. It is cooked at a medium temperature without a lid initially, then finished at a lower temperature. The food should be frequently basted with drippings throughout the cooking.

When roasting on a spit, the food is constantly turned to ensure even cooking. The food also must be basted constantly, even more so than in an oven.

Roasting Is Suitable for:

Meat (only tender pieces)
Large fish
Poultry
Game
Potatoes (in the oven)

Braising, Glazing, Pot-Roasting, and Stewing

These four basic preparation methods are all similar. Each is a gentle form of cooking in which the food is covered and heated in liquid. The more tender the food to be cooked, the less heat and liquid required.

Braising Is Suitable for:

Red meat such as pot roast, game stew, lamb ragout
White meat such as veal
Large fish such as salmon, turbot, trout
Vegetables with a low sugar content, such as cabbage, beans,
  lettuce

Glazing Is Suitable for:

White meat, such as veal and poultry
Vegetables with a high sugar content, such as carrots and turnips

Pot-Roasting Is Suitable for:

Tender meat, such as beef and veal
Poultry, such as chicken, turkey
Game birds, such as partridge

Stewing Is Suitable for:

Small pieces of meat
Fruit
Mushrooms
Vegetables with a high water content, such as zucchini and tomatoes

18. *Wine Lexicon*

For the next hundred or so pages, you will take a trip through wine country. On the tour are the major wine-growing areas of Europe: Switzerland, France, Germany, Austria, and Italy. Also included are side trips to Spain, Hungary, Liechtenstein, and the vineyards of California. This tour, of course, can offer only an overview of the many wines; comprehensive knowledge requires many years to acquire. And one does not become a wine connoisseur by reading alone. But with this wine lexicon, you will have a ready reference for the most important wines of a particular country, their taste qualities, the grapes from which they are made, and the foods they best accompany.

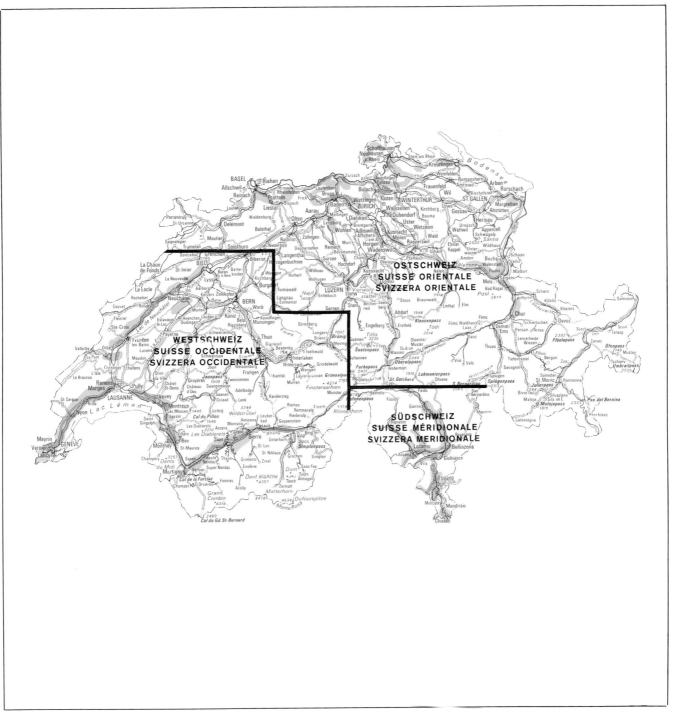

The Wine Appellations of Switzerland

The Swiss wines, like wines that are legally protected with appellations in other countries, naturally are most successful in major markets. The wine appellations of Switzerland are:

Dôle

Only red wines of very good quality from the Valais canton, in south-western Switzerland, can be sold under this name. Dôle is a wine made from Pinot Noir grapes (red burgandy) of very good quality, or from a mixture of Pinot Noir and Gamay grapes of very good quality. The lowest quality of wine that can be designated Dôle is determined in the fall, depending on the sugar content of the grape must.

Salvagnin

These are red wines from the Vaud canton, in western Switzerland, that are made exclusively from Pinot Noir or Gamay grapes or a mixture of the two. Wines that carry this appellation have been judged by a tasting commission and achieved a score of 17 out of 20 points in a taste test.

Dorin

This appellation applies only to white wines from the Vaud canton made exclusively from Chasselas grapes.

Terravin

This appellation is given only to top-quality Dorin wines that have been judged by a tasting commission and achieved a score of 18 out of 20 points in a taste test.

Perlan

This appellation is given to wines from the Geneva canton, in western Switzerland, that are made from Chasselas grapes.

Merlot VITI (Vini Ticinesi)

This appellation applies to red wines made from Merlot grapes. VITI signifies quality red wines made from Merlot in the Ticino canton, in southeastern Switzerland. Criteria for designating such wines are taste tests, sometimes supported by wine analyses.

Winzer-Wy

This appellation is used for top wines from eastern Switzerland. These wines cannot be blended; the grapes must be grown on the premises or bought directly from the grower. The wines must be made and bottled on the premises or in the cellars of a cooperative. They must be judged by a tasting commission and earn at least 18 out of 20 possible points in a taste test.

	Abbreviation	Meaning
Abbreviations in the Following Tables	R	Red wine
	rosé	Rosé wine
	W	White wine
	Sp	Sparkling wine
	D	Dry
	M	Mild
	S	Sweet

	Quality	Meaning
Descriptions in the Following Tables		
	Flowery	Light, reminiscent of flowers
	Strong bouquet	Aromatic
	Fresh	Young, light, and natural
	Fruity	With an aroma of grapes or of fruit in general
	Full-bodied	Full and strong flavor, rich in alcohol
	Balanced	Well-balanced in taste and bouquet
	Light	Relatively low alcohol content
	Heavy	High alcohol content
	Tingling/fizzy	Young, light, and fizzy (CO_2 is present)
	Tart	
	Sweet	

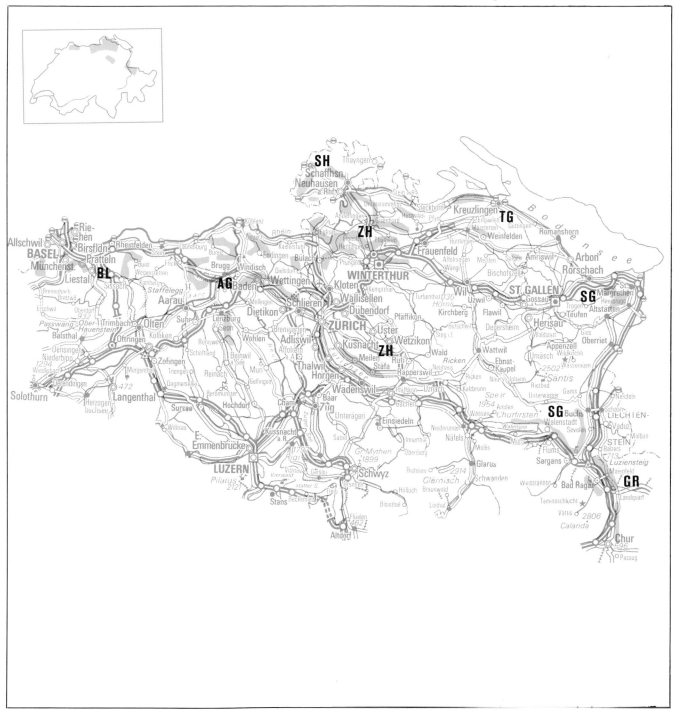

Eastern Switzerland

Wine Name	Wine Type	Taste	Qualities	Grape Varieties	Accompanies
Zurich Canton					
Benkener	R	D	Fruity, fresh	Pinot Noir	Veal, roasted poultry, mushrooms, sausages.
Dachsener	R	D	Fruity, fresh	Pinot Noir	Pasta with rich sauces, snails, ham, veal
Eglisauer	R	D	Flowery, fresh	Pinot Noir	Veal, pork, sausages, grilled poultry
Lattenberger	W	D	Light, fruity	Riesling X Sylvaner	Aperitifs, raw ham, fried freshwater fish
Lattenberger	R	D	Flowery, fresh	Pinot Noir	Veal Zurich style, beef tongue, tripe, liver, veal, pork
Meilener Räuschling	W	D	Light, tart	Räuschling	Aperitifs, freshwater fish, goat and sheep cheeses
Meilener	R	D	Fruity, fresh	Pinot Noir	Veal, pork, grilled kabobs
Ossinger	W	D	Fresh, light, fruity	Riesling X Sylvaner	Aperitifs, poached trout, fried freshwater fish
Rafzer	R	D	Fresh, flowery	Pinot Noir	Veal, pork, crockpot dishes (e.g., cassoulet)
Rafzer	W	D	Fresh, light, fruity	Riesling X Sylvaner	Aperitifs, freshwater fish, simple appetizers
Regensberger	W	D	Light, fruity	Riesling X Sylvaner	Aperitifs, freshwater fish, simple appetizers
Regensberger	R	D	Fresh, flowery	Pinot Noir	Veal, pork, roasted or grilled fowl
Regensberger Pinot Gris (specialty)	W	M	Flowery, full-bodied	Pinot Gris	Terrines, pâtés, smoked eel, smoked salmon, mushrooms, blue cheese

Eastern Switzerland

Wine Name	Wine Type	Taste	Qualities	Grape Varieties	Accompanies
Rudolfinger	R	D	Fresh, fruity	Pinot Noir	Roast veal and pork, fowl
Schiterberger	R	D	Flowery, fruity	Pinot Noir	Irish stew, beef stew, boiled beef, pork
Stammheimer	W	D	Light, fruity	Riesling X Sylvaner	Aperitifs, smoked trout fillet, shrimp cocktail
Stammheimer	R	D	Fresh, flowery	Pinot Noir	Boiled beef, brisket, veal, pork
Sternenhalder	R	D	Fresh, flowery	Pinot Noir	Veal, pork, poultry
Sternenhalder	W	D	Light, fresh, fruity	Riesling X Sylvaner	Aperitifs, freshwater fish
Teufener	R	D	Fresh, flowery	Pinot Noir	Veal Zurich style, liver kabobs, mixed grill
Turmgut (Erlenbach)	R	D	Balanced	Pinot Noir	Tripe, liver, kidneys, veal
Weininger	W	D	Light, fruity	Riesling X Sylvaner	Aperitifs, freshwater fish
Weininger	R	D	Fresh, flowery	Pinot Noir	Veal, pork, crock-cooked dishes
Weininger Räuschling	W	D	Light, tart	Räuschling	Aperitifs, freshwater fish, semi-hard cheeses, goat and sheep cheeses
Worrenberger	R	D	Fruity, full-bodied	Pinot Noir	Noodles, ham soufflé, steak, veal, pork
Worrenberger Gewürztraminer (specialty)	W	M	Full-bodied, strong bouquet	Gewürztraminer	Goose liver, pheasant, asparagus, Munster cheese

In the canton of Zurich, Pinot Noir is called Klevner.

Eastern Switzerland

Wine Name	Wine Type	Taste	Qualities	Grape Varieties	Accompanies
Saint Gall Canton					
Altstätter Forstwein	R	D	Flowery, fruity	Pinot Noir	Appetizers, crock-cooked foods, veal, pork
Balgacher	R	D	Fruity, flowery	Pinot Noir	Veal, roast or grilled poultry, sausages, crock-cooked foods
Bernecker Pinot Gris (specialty)	W	M	Full-bodied, strong bouquet	Pinot Gris	Terrines and pâtés, fish in sauce
Bernecker	R	D	Fruity, flowery	Pinot Noir	Veal, pork, roast or grilled poultry
Buchberger	R	D	Fresh, flowery	Pinot Noir	Veal, pork, cold cuts, sausage specialties
Gonzener Bergwerker	R	D	Full-bodied, fruity	Pinot Noir	Beef, mutton, game birds, blue cheese
Melser	R	D	Fresh, fruity	Pinot Noir	Veal, hearty country-style buffets, bloodwurst, liverwurst
Portaser	R	D	Full-bodied, fruity	Pinot Noir	Beef, mutton, game birds, blue cheese
Walenstadter	R	D	Fresh, flowery	Pinot Noir	Veal, pork, roast or grilled poultry
Graubünden Canton					
Churer Schiller	rose	D	Fruity, fizzy	Pinot Noir and Riesling X Sylvaner	Prosciutto, filled pastries, doughnuts, ham and eggs, poultry
Completer (specialty) Malans	W	D	Fruity, tart	Completer	Aperitifs, freshwater fish

Eastern Switzerland

Wine Name	Wine Type	Taste	Qualities	Grape Varieties	Accompanies
Fläscher	R	D	Balanced, fruity	Pinot Noir	Beef, game, duck, turkey, prosciutto
Jeninser	R	D	Balanced, fruity	Pinot Noir	Beef, pork, poultry in sauce, game, prosciutto
Maienfelder	R	D	Fruity, full-bodied	Pinot Noir	Beef, game, large roast poultry, chicken paprika, pepper steak, blue cheese
Malanser	R	D	Fruity, full-bodied	Pinot Noir	beef, mutton, game birds, blue cheese
Spiegelberger (Trimmis)	R	D	Balanced, fruity	Pinot Noir	Beef, game, goose, duck, turkey
Zizerser	rosé	D	Fruity, fizzy	Pinot Noir	Prosciutto, salami, cold cuts, cheese soufflé, pizza, egg dishes, sausages

Aargau Canton

Wine Name	Wine Type	Taste	Qualities	Grape Varieties	Accompanies
Brestenberger	R	D	Fruity, full-bodied	Pinot Noir	Veal, pork, ham sausages
Böttsteiner	W	D	Light, fruity	Riesling X Sylvaner	Aperitifs, freshwater fish that are sautéed or in a sauce
Döttinger	R	D	Fruity, full-bodied	Pinot Noir	Veal, pork, roast or grilled poultry
Goldwändler	R	D	Full-bodied, balanced	Pinot Noir	Roast veal and pork, poultry in sauce
Herrenberg (Wettingen)	R	D	Balanced	Pinot Noir	Veal, pork, roast or grilled poultry, sausages

Eastern Switzerland

Wine Name	Wine Type	Taste	Qualities	Grape Varieties	Accompanies
Hornusser	W	D	Light, fruity	Riesling X Sylvaner	Aperitifs, freshwater fish
Hornusser	R	D	Fresh, flowery	Pinot Noir	Pork, veal, ham, sausages
Mandacher	R	D	Fresh, fruity	Pinot Noir	Meat, mushroom, or cheese salads, snacks, sausages, stews
Remiger	R	D	Fresh, flowery	Pinot Noir	Stews, sausages, veal, snacks
Schinznacher	W	D	Light, fruity	Riesling X Sylvaner	Aperitifs, freshwater fish
Tegerfelder	W	D	Light, fruity	Riesling X Sylvaner	Aperitifs, freshwater fish
Tegerfelder	R	D	Fresh, flowery	Pinot Noir	Meat or cheese salads, sausages, veal, semi-hard cheeses
Wettinger	R	D	Flowery, fresh	Pinot Noir	Veal, pork, sausages, ham

Thurgau Canton

Wine Name	Wine Type	Taste	Qualities	Grape Varieties	Accompanies
Arenenberger	W	D	Fruity, strong bouquet	Riesling X Sylvaner	Aperitifs, freshwater fish, veal, hard cheeses
Arenenberger	R	D	Fruity, fresh	Pinot Noir	Veal, poultry, grilled kabobs, sausages
Bachtobler	W	D	Light, fruity	Riesling X Sylvaner	Aperitifs, freshwater fish, hard cheeses
Hüttwiler	R	D	Fresh, flowery	Pinot Noir	Veal, pork, sausages, ham
Iselisberger	R	D	Fresh, flowery	Pinot Noir	Veal, pork, poultry, semi-hard cheeses
Iselisberger	W	D	Light, fruity	Riesling X Sylvaner	Aperitifs, freshwater fish, hard cheeses

Eastern Switzerland

Wine Name	Wine Type	Taste	Qualities	Grape Varieties	Accompanies
Karthause Ittingen	R	D	Fresh, flowery	Pinot Noir	Stews, veal, pork
Ottenberger/Bachtobler	R	D	Fresh, flowery	Pinot Noir	Veal, pork, sausages, semi-hard cheeses

Schaffhausen Canton

Wine Name	Wine Type	Taste	Qualities	Grape Varieties	Accompanies
Hallauer	R	D	Flowery, balanced	Pinot Noir	Roast veal and pork, poultry in sauce, Irish stew, semi-hard cheeses, beef stew
Munötler Tokajer (Schaffhausen)	W	M	Full-bodied, strong bouquet	Pinot Gris	Terrines, pâtés, poached fish in sauce
Osterfinger	R	D	Fresh, flowery	Pinot Noir	Roast veal and pork, roasted or grilled poultry, semi-hard cheeses
Trasadinger	R	D	Fresh, flowery	Pinot Noir	Stews, veal, pork, light roasts, semi-hard cheeses
Wilchinger	R	D	Flowery, balanced	Pinot Noir	Partridge, quail, snipe, veal, pork, brisket, appetizers

Basel Canton

Wine Name	Wine Type	Taste	Qualities	Grape Varieties	Accompanies
Kluser (Aesch)	R	D	Fresh, flowery	Pinot Noir	Veal, pork, stews, semi-hard cheeses
Kluser (Aesch)	W	D	Light, fruity	Riesling X Sylvaner	Aperitifs, freshwater fish, simple appetizers, hard cheeses
Maispracher	R	D	Full-bodied, balanced	Pinot Noir	Partridge, quail, snipe, boiled beef, roast veal and pork

Eastern Switzerland

Wine Name	Wine Type	Taste	Qualities	Grape Varieties	Accompanies
Muttenzer	R	D	Fresh, flowery	Pinot Noir	Veal, pork, sausages, ham
Muttenzer	W	D	Light, fruity	Chasselas	Aperitifs, freshwater fish, simple appetizers, semi-hard cheeses
Pratteler	R	D	Fresh, flowery	Pinot Noir	Veal, pork, roast or grilled poultry, semi-hard cheeses
Schlipf bei Riehen	W	D	Light, fruity	Riesling X Sylvaner	Aperitifs, freshwater fish that is roasted, grilled, or poached in a sauce

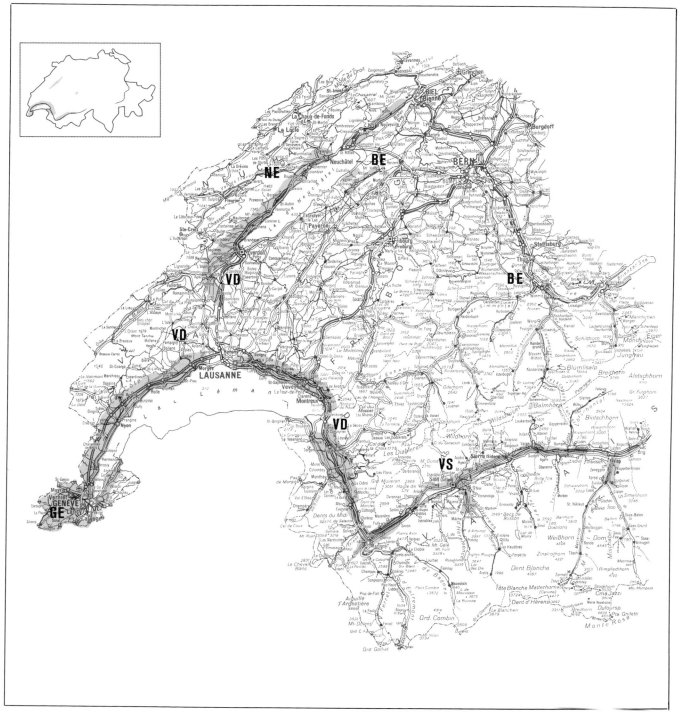

Western Switzerland

Wine Name	Wine Type	Taste	Qualities	Grape Varieties	Accompanies
Bern Canton					
Oberhofener	W	D	Light, fresh, fizzy	Riesling X Sylvaner	Aperitifs, fried freshwater fish, simple appetizers, hard cheeses
Oberhofener	R	D	Fresh, fruity	Pinot Noir	Stews, veal, pork, semi-hard cheeses
Schafiser	W	D	Light, fresh, fizzy	Chasselas	Aperitifs, fried or baked freshwater fish, simple appetizers, hard cheeses
Schafiser	R	D	Fresh, fruity	Pinot Noir	Veal, pork, roast or grilled poultry, semi-hard cheeses
Spiezer	W	D	Light, fresh, fizzy	Riesling X Sylvaner	Aperitifs, fried freshwater fish, simple appetizers, hard cheeses
Spiezer	R	D	Fresh, fruity	Pinot Noir	Veal, stews, roast or grilled poultry, semi-hard cheeses
Twanner	W	D	Light, fresh, fizzy	Chasselas	Aperitifs, roast or fried freshwater fish, asparagus, simple appetizers, hard cheeses
Twanner	R	D	Fresh, fruity	Pinot Noir	Veal, pork, roast or grilled poultry, semi-hard cheeses
Neuchâtel Canton					
Auvernier	W	D	Fizzy, fruity	Chasselas	Aperitifs, vol-au-vent, cold cuts, fried or poached freshwater fish, hard cheeses
Auvernier	R	D	Balanced, full-bodied	Pinot Noir	Red meat (roasted, braised, marinated), delicate game birds (pheasant, quail)
Bouvier Frères Brut	Sp	D	Tingling, tart	Chenin Blanc Sauvignon Semillon	Aperitifs; a dry sparkling wine can be served during the whole meal

Western Switzerland

Wine Name	Wine Type	Taste	Qualities	Grape Varieties	Accompanies
Bouvier Frères Demi-Sec	Sp	S	Tingling, lightly sweet	Chenin Blanc Sauvignon Semillon	Sweets and cakes
Bouvier Frères Extra Dry	Sp	D	Tingling, fresh	Chenin Blanc Sauvignon Semillon	See Bouvier Brut; aperitifs, veal, freshwater and saltwater fish, shellfish
Cortaillod	R	D	Balanced, full-bodied	Pinot Noir	Red-meat roasts, lamb in sauce, game birds, stews, blue cheese
Cressier	W	D	Fizzy, fruity	Chasselas	Aperitifs, fried freshwater fish, cheeses, dried meats
Mauler & Cie Brut	Sp	D	Tingling, tart	Pinot Noir	Can be served during the whole meal
Mauler & Cie Demi-Sec	Sp	S	Tingling, lightly sweet	Pinot Noir	Sweets and cakes
Mauler & Cie Dry	Sp	D	Tingling, fruity	Pinot Noir	See Mauler Brut; aperitifs, veal, freshwater and saltwater fish, shellfish
Neuchâtel	W	D	Fizzy, fruity	Chasselas	Aperitifs, cheese specialties (e.g., fondue), fried freshwater fish
Neuchâtel	R	D	Balanced	Pinot Noir	Beef, delicate game birds, stews, blue cheese
Œil-de-Perdrix	rosé	D	Fruity, fresh	Pinot Noir	Veal, pork, fine cold cuts, luncheon foods

Geneva Canton

Wine Name	Wine Type	Taste	Qualities	Grape Varieties	Accompanies
Aligoté de Genève	W	D	Tart, fruity	Aligoté	Pâtés, fried or roasted freshwater fish, snails; Aligoté with Cassis is Kir (an aperitif)
Chardonnay de Genève	W	D	Strong bouquet, flowery	Chardonnay	Fine terrines, freshwater and saltwater fish, veal, poultry

Western Switzerland

Wine Name	Wine Type	Taste	Qualities	Grape Varieties	Accompanies
Gamay de Genève	R	D	Fresh, fruity	Gamay (Beaujolais)	Veal, cold cuts, country-style buffet, cheeses
Perlan de Mandement	W	D	Fizzy, fruity	Chasselas	Aperitifs, fried or roasted freshwater fish, roast or grilled poultry, cheeses
Perlan Cave de la Souche	W	D	Fizzy, fruity	Chasselas	Aperitifs, fried or roasted freshwater fish, roast or grilled poultry, cheeses
Pinot gris de Genève (Specialty)	W	M	Full-bodied, flowery	Pinot Gris	Fine terrines, pâtés, poached saltwater fish in mousseline sauce, shellfish, snails

Vaud Canton: Bonvillars, Vully, les Côtes de l'Orbe

Wine Name	Wine Type	Taste	Qualities	Grape Varieties	Accompanies
Bonvillars	W	D	Fizzy, fruity	Chasselas	Aperitifs, fried or roasted freshwater fish, brains, sweetbreads, hard cheeses
Côtes de l'Orbe	W	D	Fizzy, fruity	Chasselas	Aperitifs, fried or roasted freshwater fish, brains, sweetbreads, hard cheeses
Salvagnin	R	D	Balanced	Pinot Noir and/or Gamay	Veal, poultry, cold cuts, different cheeses, luncheon foods
Vully	W	D	Fizzy, fruity	Chasselas	Aperitifs, fried or roasted freshwater fish, sweetbreads, hard cheeses

Vaud Canton: La Côte

Wine Name	Wine Type	Taste	Qualities	Grape Varieties	Accompanies
Begnins	W	D	Light, fruity	Chasselas	Aperitifs, freshwater fish, hard cheeses
Féchy	W	D	Balanced	Chasselas	Aperitifs, freshwater fish, veal, poultry, hard cheeses
La Côte	W	D	Fresh, fruity	Chasselas	Aperitifs, freshwater fish, poultry, veal, hard cheeses

Western Switzerland

Wine Name	Wine Type	Taste	Qualities	Grape Varieties	Accompanies
Luins	W	D	Fruity, flowery	Chasselas	Aperitifs, veal, freshwater fish, hard cheeses
Mont-sur-Rolle	W	D	Fruity, flowery	Chasselas	Aperitifs, veal, freshwater fish, asparagus, hard cheeses
Salvagnin	R	D	Balanced	Pinot Noir and/or Gamay	Veal, poultry, cold cuts, different cheeses, luncheon foods
Tartegnin	W	D	Fresh, fruity	Chasselas	Aperitifs, freshwater fish, veal, poultry, hard cheeses
Vinzel	W	D	Fresh, fruity	Chasselas	Aperitifs, freshwater fish, veal, poultry, hard cheeses

Vaud Canton: Lavaux

Wine Name	Wine Type	Taste	Qualities	Grape Varieties	Accompanies
Cully	W	D	Fresh, flowery	Chasselas	Aperitifs, freshwater and saltwater fish, veal, appetizers, hard cheeses
Chardonne	W	D	Fresh, flowery	Chasselas	Aperitifs, freshwater and saltwater fish, veal, hard cheeses
Dézaley	W	D/M	Full-bodied, strong bouquet	Chasselas	Saltwater fish in an exquisite sauce, shellfish, saddle of veal, fine terrines
Epesses	W	D/M	Full-bodied, balanced	Chasselas	Freshwater and saltwater fish, veal, poultry in light sauces
Grandvaux	W	D	Fresh, flowery	Chasselas	Freshwater and saltwater fish, veal, poultry, hard cheeses
Lutry	W	D	Fresh, fruity	Chasselas	Freshwater and saltwater fish, poultry (grilled roasted, baked), veal

Western Switzerland

Wine Name	Wine Type	Taste	Qualities	Grape Varieties	Accompanies
Montreux	W	D	Fresh, flowery	Chasselas	Freshwater and saltwater fish, poultry, veal, hard cheeses
Pully	W	D	Fresh, fruity	Chasselas	Aperitifs, freshwater and saltwater fish, poultry, veal, hard cheeses
Riex	W	D	Fresh, flowery	Chasselas	Freshwater and saltwater fish, poultry, veal, hard cheeses
Rivaz	W	D	Fresh, fruity	Chasselas	Freshwater and saltwater fish, poultry, veal, hard cheeses
Salvagnin	R	D	Balanced	Pinot Noir and/or Gamay	Veal, poultry, cold cuts different cheeses, luncheon foods
St-Saphorin	W	D/M	Balanced, strong bouquet	Chasselas	Freshwater and saltwater fish, shellfish, asparagus, veal, cheese specialties
St. Saphorin	R	D	Balanced	Pinot Noir	Roast meats, poultry in dark sauces, stews
Vevey	W	D	Fresh, fruity	Chasselas	Aperitifs, freshwater fish, grilled or roast poultry, veal, hard cheeses
Villette	W	D	Fresh, flowery	Chasselas	Freshwater and saltwater fish, veal, poultry, asparagus, hard cheeses

Vaud Canton: Chablais

Wine Name	Wine Type	Taste	Qualities	Grape Varieties	Accompanies
Aigle	W	D/M	Full-bodied, strong bouquet	Chasselas	Freshwater and saltwater fish, shellfish, veal in heavy white sauces, poultry in white sauces

Western Switzerland

Wine Name	Wine Type	Taste	Qualities	Grape Varieties	Accompanies
Aigle	R	D	Balanced	Pinot Noir and Gamay	Roast meats, delicate game birds (partridge, quail), poultry
Bex	W	D	Full-bodied, strong bouquet	Chasselas	Freshwater and saltwater fish, veal, cheese dishes (soufflés)
Ollon	W	D	Full-bodied, strong bouquet	Chasselas	Freshwater and saltwater fish, veal, filled pastries, cheese fritters
Salvagnin	R	D	Balanced	Pinot Noir and/or Gamay	Veal, poultry, cold cuts, different cheeses, luncheon foods
Villeneuve	W	D/M	Full-bodied, strong bouquet	Chasselas	Freshwater and saltwater fish, shellfish, asparagus, cheese specialties
Yvorne	W	D/M	Full-bodied, strong bouquet	Chasselas	Fish prepared any style, shellfish, veal and poultry in heavy white sauces
Yvorne	R	D	Balanced	Pinot Noir and Gamay	Roast meats, delicate game birds (partridge, quail)

Valais Canton

Wine Name	Wine Type	Taste	Qualities	Grape Varieties	Accompanies
Amigne	W	D	Strong bouquet, full-bodied	Amigne	Goose liver, fine terrines, sweets, cakes
Arvine	W	D	Strong bouquet, full-bodied	Arvine	Aperitifs, fine terrines and pâtés
Dôle	R	D	Balanced	Pinot Noir and Gamay	Beef, game, mutton, pork, blue cheese, steak tartar
Ermitage	W	M	Full-bodied, flowery	Marsanne Blanche	Aperitifs, terrines, house pâtés, sweets, cakes

Western Switzerland

Wine Name	Wine Type	Taste	Qualities	Grape Varieties	Accompanies
Fendant	W	D	Fresh, fruity	Fendant	Aperitifs, raclette, fondues, cheese platters, air-dried beef, sauerkraut, snails, freshwater fish
Goron	R	D	Balanced, light	Gamay and Pinot Noir	Rustic country buffets, cold cut platters, pâté, sausages, poultry
Heida	W	D	Tart, fruity	Traminer	Aperitifs, cold meat platters, air-dried beef, hard cheeses
Humagne blanc	W	M	Flowery, full-bodied	Humagne	Aperitifs, light, cold appetizers
Humagne rouge	R	D	Balanced, flowery	Humagne	Game birds, game, lamb
Johannisberg	W	D/M	Flowery, full-bodied	Green Sylvaner	Shellfish (oysters), asparagus, veal in heavy cream sauces, cheese soufflés
Malvoisie	W	M/S	Full-bodied, strong bouquet	Pinot Gris	Goose liver, fine terrines, flaming desserts, sweets and cakes
Muscat	W	D	Flowery, full-bodied	Muskat	Aperitifs, saltwater fish in a sauce; a dessert wine
CEil-de-Perdix	rosé	D	Fresh, fruity, flowery	Pinot Noir	Veal, beef, fondue, fine cold cuts, luncheon foods
Pinot Chardonnay	W	D/M	Full-bodied, strong bouquet	Chardonnay	Goose liver, fine terrines and pâtés, saltwater fish in refined sauces, shellfish
Pinot noir	R	D	Full-bodied, balanced	Pinot Noir	Beef, lamb, game birds, game, fiery goulash, soft cheeses
Riesling	W	D	Fresh, fruity	Riesling	Aperitifs, freshwater and saltwater fish, veal

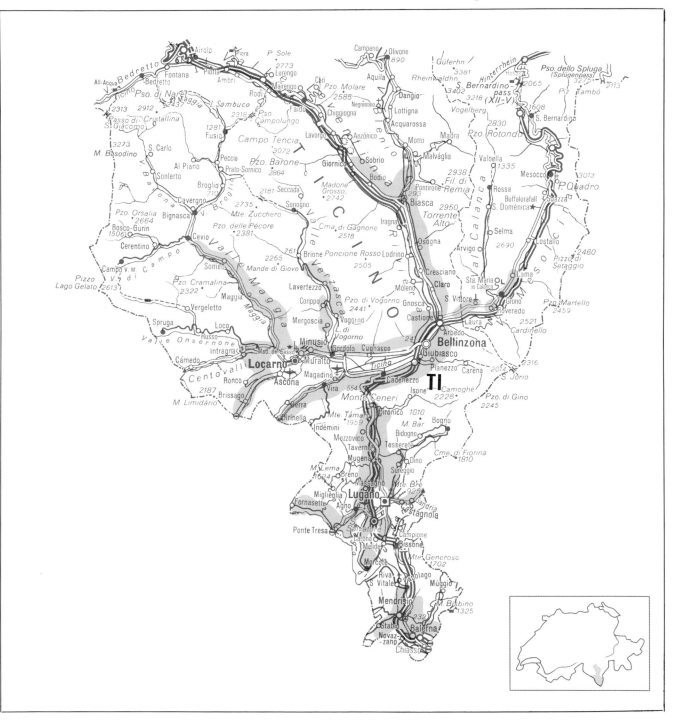

Southern Switzerland

Wine Name	Wine Type	Taste	Qualities	Grape Varieties	Accompanies
Ticino Canton					
Merlot VITI	R	D	Strong bouquet, full-bodied	Merlot	Red- and white-meat roasts, elegant game birds, grilled veal, roast and grilled poultry
Merlot rosato	rosé	D	Light, fruity	Merlot	Aperitifs, risotto, pasta, fresh cheeses
Nostrano	R	D	Fruity, fresh	Bondola	Ticino cold cuts, snacks, cheeses; a table wine

The Appellations of France

French wines are divided into three quality groups.

AC Wines

AC wines are those carrying a designation of origin known as *Appellation d'Origine Contrôlé,* abbreviated AC or AOC.

AC wines are wines of the highest quality that adhere strictly to the production requisites of the Institut national des appellations d'origine (INAO). These requisites stipulate:

- An exactly defined growing area
- The type and blend of grape varieties used
- Care of the vineyard and grafting
- Maximum harvest per acre
- Minimum alcohol content
- Wine production and storage methods
- Official tasting

When, for example, the production of a vineyard exceeds the limit of the maximum harvest per acre, all of the wine from that vineyard loses the right to the designation AC.

VDQS Wines

VDQS wines are of a high quality from a limited growing area, known as *vins délimités de qualité supérieure,* abbreviated VDQS.

VDQS wines are quality wines whose origin and quality are guaranteed because of strict controls. These wines are subject to similar regulations as AC wines, but the rules are not as strict. They include:

- Growing area
- Grape variety
- Minimum alcohol content
- Cultivation and wine production

Country Wines

Country wines, or *vins de pays,* are better-quality table wines and carry a reference to a geographical area, for example Vin de pays de Chablis. When exported to Common Market countries, the wine has to have the additional notation *vin de table,* or table wine.

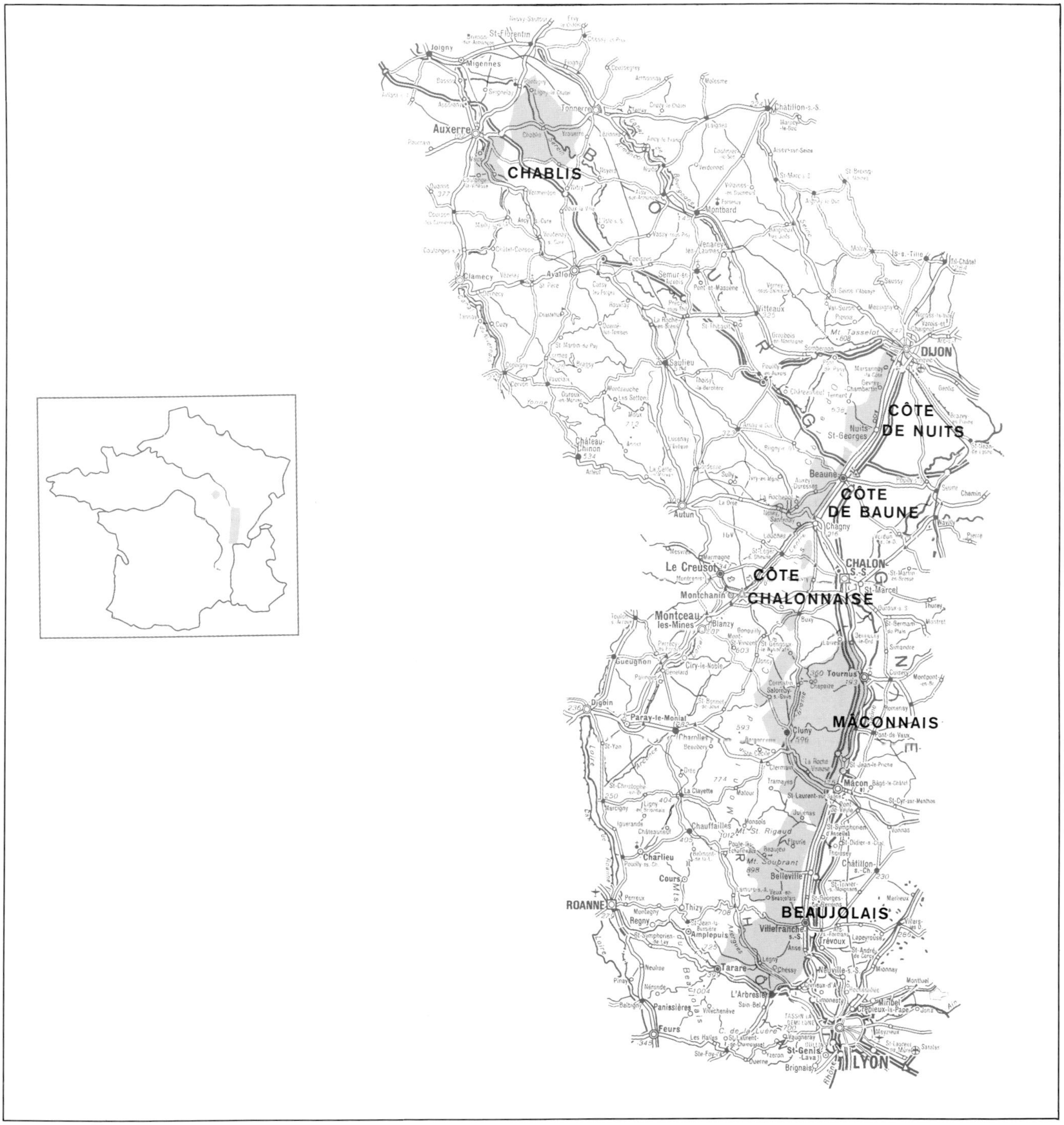

CHABLIS
CÔTE DE NUITS
CÔTE DE BAUNE
CÔTE CHALONNAISE
MÂCONNAIS
BEAUJOLAIS
Auxerre
Tonnerre
Montbard
Avallon
Saulieu
DIJON
Nuits-St-Georges
Beaune
Autun
Le Creusot
CHALON-S.-S.
Tournus
Cluny
Mâcon
Belleville
Villefranche
ROANNE
LYON

Burgundy

Wine Name	Wine Type	Taste	Qualities	Grape Varieties	Accompanies
### Chablis					
Chablis	W	D	Full-bodied, fruity	Chardonnay	Oysters, smoked salmon, grilled shrimps, smoked fillet of trout.
### Côte de Nuits					
Chambolle-Musigny	R	M	Strong, full-bodied, strong bouquet	Pinot Noir	Beef, mutton, game, soft ripened cheeses
Clos Vougeot	R	M	Strong, full-bodied, strong bouquet	Pinot Noir	Beef, mutton, game, soft ripened cheeses
Fixin	R	M	Strong, full-bodied	Pinot Noir	Beef, mutton, game, soft ripened cheeses
Gevrey-Chambertin	R	M	Strong, full-bodied	Pinot Noir	Beef, mutton, game, soft ripened cheeses
Chambertin	R	M	Strong, full-bodied, strong bouquet	Pinot Noir	Beef, mutton, game, soft ripened cheeses
Chambertin-Clos de Bèze	R	M	Strong, full-bodied, strong bouquet	Pinot Noir	Beef, mutton, game, soft ripened cheeses
Mazis-Chambertin	R	M	Strong, full-bodied, strong bouquet	Pinot Noir	Beef, mutton, game, soft ripened cheeses

Burgundy

Wine Name	Wine Type	Taste	Qualities	Grape Varieties	Accompanies
Morey-St-Denis	R	M	Strong, full-bodied, strong bouquet	Pinot Noir	Beef, mutton, game, soft ripened cheeses
Vosne-Romanée	R	M	Strong, full-bodied, strong bouquet	Pinot Noir	Beef, mutton, game, soft ripened cheeses
Romanée-Conti	R	M	Strong, full-bodied, strong bouquet	Pinot Noir	Beef, mutton, game, soft ripened cheeses
La Tâche	R	M	Strong, full-bodied, strong bouquet	Pinot Noir	Beef, mutton, game, soft ripened cheeses
Richebourg	R	M	Strong, full-bodied, strong bouquet	Pinot Noir	Beef, mutton, game, soft ripened cheeses
Romanée-St-Vivant	R	M	Strong, full-bodied, strong bouquet	Pinot Noir	Beef, mutton, game, soft ripened cheeses
Nuits-St-Georges	R	M	Strong, full-bodied, strong bouquet	Pinot Noir	Beef, mutton, game, soft ripened cheeses

Côte de Beaune

Wine Name	Wine Type	Taste	Qualities	Grape Varieties	Accompanies
Aloxe-Corton	R	M	Full-bodied, strong bouquet	Pinot Noir	Warm goose liver as a main course, beef, mutton, saddle of venison
Auxey-Duresses	R	M	Full-bodied, strong bouquet	Pinot Noir	Mutton, venison steak, venison stew, soft ripened cheeses

Burgundy

Wine Name	Wine Type	Taste	Qualities	Grape Varieties	Accompanies
Beaune	R	M	Balanced	Pinot Noir	Beef, lamb, soft ripened cheeses
Bourgogne-Passe-tout-grains	R	M	Balanced	1 part Pinot Noir 2 parts Gamay	Cold cuts, rustic country buffets, air-dried beef, Hungarian goulash
Corton-Charlemagne	W	D/M	Full-bodied, strong bouquet	Chardonnay	Goose liver as an hors d'oeuvre, truffles, grilled halibut, grilled fillet of sole
Meursault	W	D/M	Full-bodied, fruity	Chardonnay	Mussels, sautéed or grilled fillet of sole, oysters
Montrachet	W	D/M	Full-bodied, balanced	Chardonnay	Goose liver as an hors d'oeuvre, truffles, oysters, grilled shrimp, rich appetizers without salads
Pommard	R	M	Full-bodied, balanced	Pinot Noir	Warm goose liver as a main course, mutton, beef, soft ripened cheeses
Santenay	R	M	Full-bodied, strong bouquet	Pinot Noir	*Carbonnade* of beef, steak
Volnay	R	M	Balanced, strong bouquet	Pinot Noir	Beef, game birds, soft ripened cheeses

Côte Chalonnaise

Wine Name	Wine Type	Taste	Qualities	Grape Varieties	Accompanies
Bourgogne-Passe-tout-grains	R	M	Balanced	1 part Pinot Noir 2 parts Gamay	Cold cuts, rustic country buffets, air-dried beef, Hungarian goulash

Burgundy

Wine Name	Wine Type	Taste	Qualities	Grape Varieties	Accompanies
Givry	R	M	Strong bouquet	Pinot Noir	Quail, partridge
Mercurey	R	M	Balanced	Pinot Noir	Quail, partridge, beef
Montagny	W	D	Strong bouquet, fruity	Chardonnay	Rich appetizers, poached fish in classical sauces

Mâconnais

Wine Name	Wine Type	Taste	Qualities	Grape Varieties	Accompanies
Mâcon rouge	R	M	Fresh, fruity	Gamay	Rustic country buffets, semi-hard cheese and goat cheeses, snails, frogs' legs
Mâcon-Villages	W	D	Fresh, fruity	Chardonnay	Sautéed and fried fish, simple appetizers
Pouilly-Fuissé	W	D	Strong bouquet, full-bodied	Chardonnay	Shrimp, smoked eel, smoked salmon

Beaujolais

Wine Name	Wine Type	Taste	Qualities	Grape Varieties	Accompanies
Beaujolais	R	M	Fresh, fruity	Gamay	Veal appetizers, grilled chicken, ham in pastry
Beaujolais-Villages	R	M	Balanced, fruity	Gamay	Pork cutlets, roast pork, chicken in a basket
Fleurie	R	M	Strong bouquet	Gamay	Veal fricassee, beef stews

Burgundy

Wine Name	Wine Type	Taste	Qualities	Grape Varieties	Accompanies
Morgon	R	M	Full-bodied, strong bouquet	Gamay	Venison stew, leg of venison, steak tartare, soft ripened cheeses
Moulin-à-Vent	R	M	Full-bodied, strong bouquet	Gamay	Roast beef, steak marinated in wine

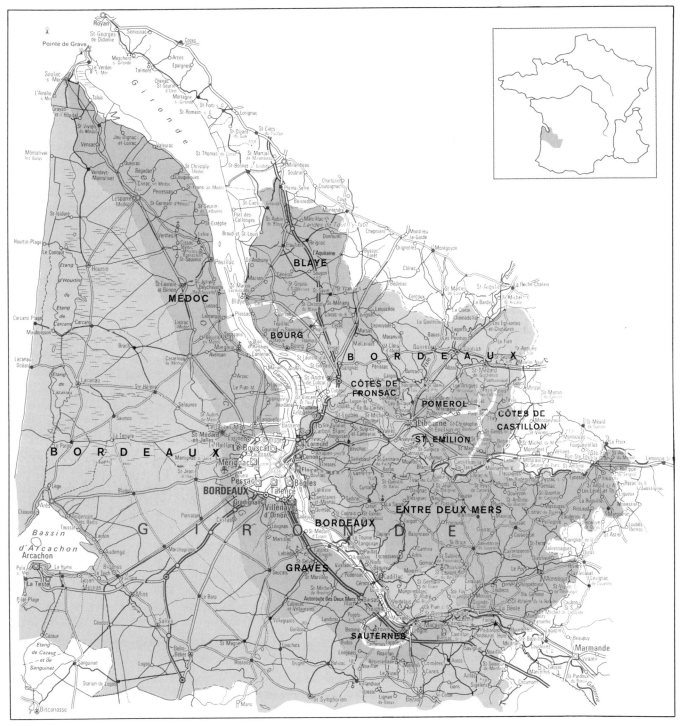

Wine Regions of Bordeaux

Bordeaux

Wine Name	Wine Type	Taste	Qualities	Grape Varieties	Accompanies

Médoc

Wine Name	Wine Type	Taste	Qualities	Grape Varieties	Accompanies
Château Calon-Ségur	R	M	Full-bodied, fruity	Cabernet-Sauvignon, Cabernet Franc, Merlot	Beef, mutton, confit of duck or goose, soft ripened cheeses
Château Chasse-Spleen	R	M	Full-bodied, fruity	Cabernet-Sauvignon, Merlot, Petit Verdot	Quail, partridge, lamb, pork, soft ripened cheeses
Château Cos d'Estournel	R	M	Full-bodied, fruity	Cabernet-Sauvignon, Cabernet Franc, Merlot	Beef, mutton, game, confit of duck or goose, soft ripened cheeses
Château Giscours	R	M	Full-bodied, strong bouquet	Cabernet-Sauvignon, Petit Verdot, Merlot, Cabernet Franc	Beef, mutton, confit of duck or goose, soft ripened cheeses
Château Gruaud-Larose	R	M	Balanced	Cabernet-Sauvignon, Petit Verdot, Merlot, Cabernet Franc	Veal, lamb, cassoulets, soft ripened cheeses
Château Léoville-Poyferré	R	M	Balanced	Cabernet-Sauvignon, Merlot, Cabernet Franc	Veal, lamb, cassoulets, soft ripened cheeses
Château Lynch-Bagnes	R	M	Full-bodied, strong bouquet	Cabernet-Sauvignon, Cabernet Franc, Malbec, Petit Verdot	Leg of venison, saddle of venison, beef, mutton, soft ripened cheeses

Bordeaux

Wine Name	Wine Type	Taste	Qualities	Grape Varieties	Accompanies
Château Montrose	R	M	Full-bodied, fruity	Cabernet-Sauvignon, Cabernet Franc, Merlot	Beef, mutton, game, confit of duck or goose, soft ripened cheeses
Château Mouton-Rothschild	R	M	Full-bodied, strong bouquet	Cabernet-Sauvignon, Cabernet Franc, Merlot	Beef, leg of venison, saddle of venison, mutton, soft ripened cheeses
Château Palmer	R	M	Full-bodied, strong bouquet	Cabernet-Sauvignon, Petit Verdot, Merlot, Cabernet Franc	Beef, mutton, confit of duck or goose, soft ripened cheeses
Château Poujeaux	R	M	Full-bodied, fruity	Cabernet-Sauvignon, Merlot, Petit Verdot	Quail, partridge, lamb, veal, pork, soft ripened cheeses

Côtes de Bourg

Wine Name	Wine Type	Taste	Qualities	Grape Varieties	Accompanies
Château de Barbe	R	M	Fresh, fruity	Cabernet-Sauvignon, Cabernet Franc, Petit Verdot	Rich meat platters, hearty meat dishes

Pomerol

Wine Name	Wine Type	Taste	Qualities	Grape Varieties	Accompanies
Château La Conseillante	R	M	Full-bodied, strong bouquet	Merlot, Cabernet Franc, Malbec	Lamb, veal, pork, soft ripened cheeses
Château l'Evangile	R	M	Full-bodied, strong bouquet	Merlot, Cabernet Franc	Lamb, veal, pork, soft ripened cheeses

Bordeaux

Wine Name	Wine Type	Taste	Qualities	Grape Varieties	Accompanies
Château Petit-Village	R	M	Full-bodied, strong bouquet	Merlot, Cabernet Franc, Malbec	Confit of duck or goose, cassoulets, lamb, soft ripened cheeses
Château Pétrus	R	M	Full-bodied, strong bouquet	Merlot, Cabernet Franc	Confit of duck or goose, cassoulets, lamb, soft ripened cheeses
Vieux-Château Certan	R	M	Full-bodied, strong bouquet	Merlot, Malbec, Cabernet Franc, Cabernet-Sauvignon	Lamb, veal, pork, soft ripened cheeses

St-Emilion

Wine Name	Wine Type	Taste	Qualities	Grape Varieties	Accompanies
Château l'Angélus	R	M	Full-bodied, strong bouquet	Merlot, Cabernet Franc	Veal, pork, game, lamb, soft ripened cheeses
Château Ausone	R	M	Full-bodied, strong bouquet	Merlot, Cabernet Franc, Cabernet-Sauvignon	Beef, game, lamb, soft ripened cheeses
Château Canon	R	M	Full-bodied, strong bouquet	Merlot, Cabernet Franc, Cabernet-Sauvignon	Beef, pork, game, lamb, soft ripened cheeses
Château Cheval Blanc	R	M	Full-bodied, strong bouquet	Cabernet Franc, Merlot	Beef, saddle of veal, game, lamb, soft ripened cheeses
Château Soutard	R	M	Strong bouquet, full-bodied	Merlot, Cabernet Franc, Cabernet-Sauvignon	Lamb, game birds, veal, pork, soft ripened cheeses

Bordeaux

Wine Name	Wine Type	Taste	Qualities	Grape Varieties	Accompanies
Entre-deux-Mers					
Château Mylord	W	D	Light, fruity	Sauvignon	Oysters, mussels, shellfish, snails, frogs' legs, bouillabaisse
Graves					
Château Ferrande	W	D	Fresh, flowerey	Sauvignon	Oysters, mussels, shellfish, goose liver
Château Fieuzal	R	M	Balanced	Cabernet-Sauvignon, Merlot, Malbec, Petit Verdot	Pâtés, veal, game, pork, lamb, soft ripened cheeses
Château La Garde	R	M	Balanced	Cabernet-Sauvignon, Cabernet Franc, Merlot	Pâtés, beef, game, lamb, soft ripened cheeses
Château Laville .	W	D	Strong bouquet	Sauvignon, Sémillon	Oysters, mussels, shellfish, goose liver
Château La Tuilerie	W	D	Fresh, fruity	Sauvignon	Oysters, mussels, shellfish, goose liver
Sauternes					
Château Suduiraut	W	S	Strong, full-bodied, strong bouquet	Sauvignon, Sémillon, Muscadelle	Halibut in sauce, cold goose liver as an hors d'oeuvre, flambéed desserts, Roquefort with ripe pears

Bordeaux

Wine Name	Wine Type	Taste	Qualities	Grape Varieties	Accompanies
Château d'Yquem	W	S	Strong, full-bodied, strong bouquet	Sauvignon, Sémillon, Muscadelle	Delicate fish prepared in sauce, cold goose liver as an hors d'oeuvre, Roquefort with ripe pears

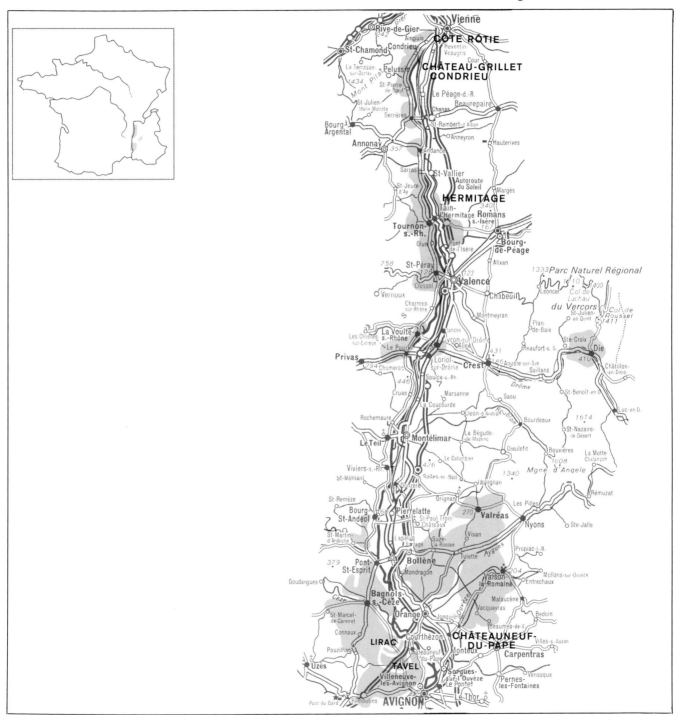

Côtes du Rhône, North and South

Wine Name	Wine Type	Taste	Qualities	Grape Varieties	Accompanies
Château Grillet	W	M	Strong bouquet, full-bodied	Viognier	Oysters, mussels, shellfish
Châteauneuf-du-Pape	R	M	Strong, full-bodied, strong bouquet	Grenache, Cinsault, Syrah, Mourvèdre	Game, venison stew, steak tartare, beef, mutton, soft ripened cheeses
Condrieu	W	M	Strong bouquet	Viognier	Oysters, mussels, shellfish, smoked eel and salmon
Côte Rôtie	R	M	Strong, full-bodied, strong bouquet	Syrah	Game, beef, mutton, soft ripened cheeses
Croze-Hermitage	R	M	Balanced, full-bodied	Syrah	Quail, partridge, beef, mutton, soft ripened cheeses
Hermitage	W	M	Strong bouquet	Marsanne blanche	Appetizers, oysters, mussels, shellfish, veal, poultry
Lirac	rosé	M	Light, fruity	Grenache, Cinsault, Mourvèdre	Bouillabaisse, veal fricassees, meat stews
St-Péray	Sp	D	Fizzy, tingling	Marsanne, Roussette	Oysters, mussels, shellfish, grilled saltwater fish
Tavel	rosé	D	Fresh, fruity	Grenache, Cinsault, Mourvèdre	Bouillabaisse, veal fricassees, meat stews

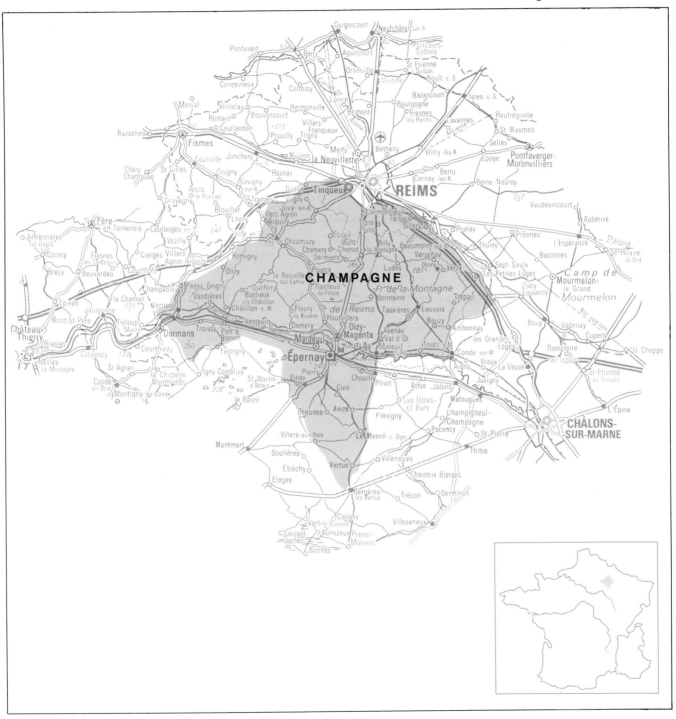

Champagne

Wine Name	Wine Type	Taste	Qualities	Grape Varieties	Accompanies
Champagne Blanc de Blanc (white)	Sp	D	Fizzy, tingling	Chardonnay	Aperitifs, rich hors d'oeuvre, goose liver
Champagne brut (white and pink)	Sp	D	Fizzy, tingling	Pinot Noir, Pinot Meunier, Chardonnay	All foods
Champagne sec (white and pink)	Sp	D	Fizzy, tingling	Pinot Noir, Pinot Meunier, Chardonnay	All foods
Champagne demi-sec (white and pink)	Sp	S	Fizzy, tingling	Pinot Noir, Pinot Meunier, Chardonnay	Desserts, flambéed sweets, dry pastries
Champagne doux (white)	Sp	S	Fizzy, tingling	Pinot Noir, Pinot Meunier, Chardonnay	Desserts, flambéed sweets, dry pastries
Pinot Chardonnay	W	D	Fruity	Pinot Blanc	Oysters, mussels, fish, shellfish

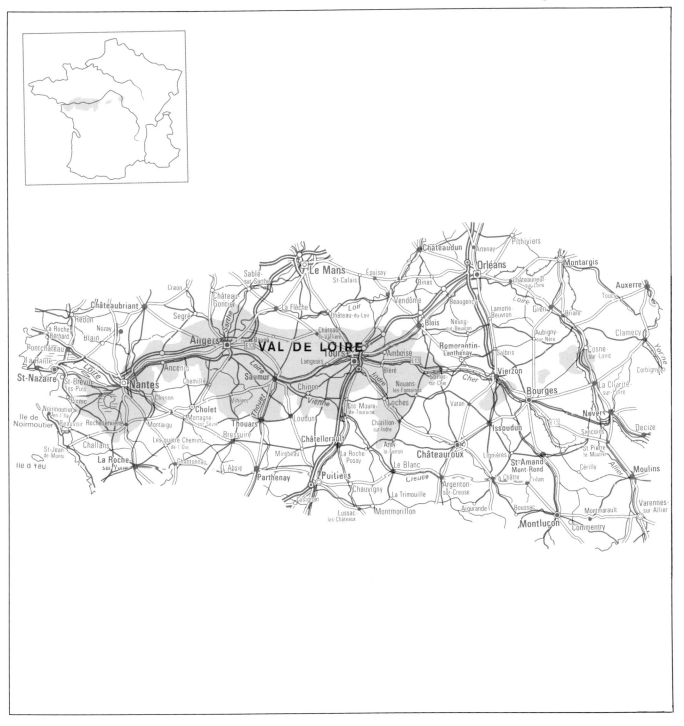

Val de Loire

Wine Name	Wine Type	Taste	Qualities	Grape Varieties	Accompanies
Anjou	rosé	S	Fresh, fruity	Groslot, Cot, Gamay	Goose liver, desserts
Pouilly-Fumé	W	D/M	Strong bouquet, full-bodied	Sauvignon	Mussels, oysters, shellfish, appetizers, grilled and poached fish
Rosé de Cabernet	rosé	D	Light, flowery	Cabernet Franc	Veal, pork, duck à l'orange
Sancerre	R	M	Balanced	Pinot Noir	Beef, mutton, soft ripened cheeses
Saumur	W	D	Light, fruity	Chenin de la Loire	Mussels, oysters, shellfish, appetizers, grilled and poached fish
Vouvray	Sp	D	Fizzy, tingling	Chenin de la Loire	Mussels, oysters, shellfish, appetizers, grilled fish

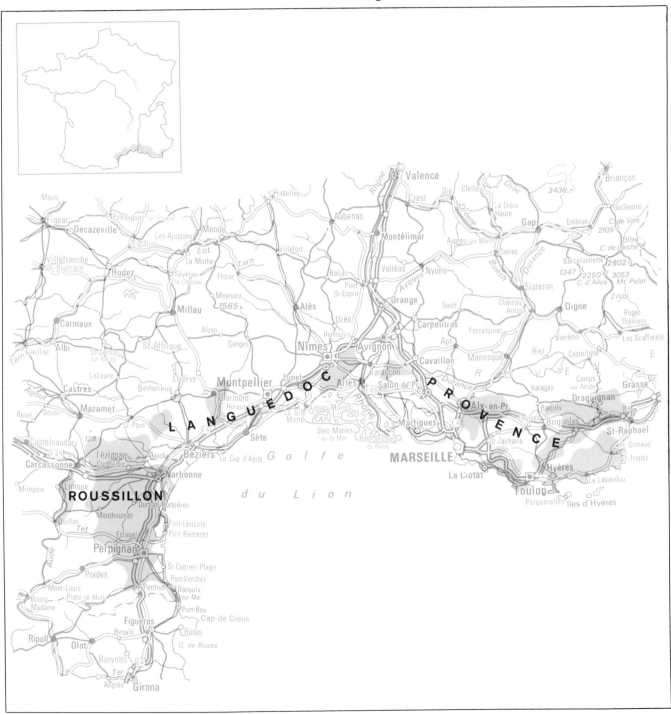

Provence

Wine Name	Wine Type	Taste	Qualities	Grape Varieties	Accompanies
Cassis	rosé	D/M	Fresh, strong bouquet	Carignan, Syrah, Cinsault, Grenache, Mourvèdre	Pork, veal, appetizers, snails, frogs' legs, bouillabaisse
Bandol	rosé	D/M	Fresh, strong bouquet	Carignan, Syrah, Cinsault, Grenache, Mourvèdre	Pork, veal, appetizers, snails, frogs' legs, bouillabaisse
Bellet de Nice	rosé	D/M	Fresh, strong bouquet	Carignan, Syrah, Cinsault, Grenache, Mourvèdre	Pork, veal, appetizers, snails, frogs' legs, bouillabaisse
Palette d'Aix	rosé	D/M	Fresh, strong bouquet	Carignan, Syrah, Cinsault, Grenache, Mourvèdre	Pork, veal, appetizers, snails, frogs' legs, bouillabaisse

Languedoc and Roussillon

Wine Name	Wine Type	Taste	Qualities	Grape Varieties	Accompanies
Banyuls	R	S	Strong bouquet, strong	Grenache Noir	Flambéed desserts
Blanquette de Limoux	Sp	D	Fizzy, tingling	Mauzac	Oysters, mussels, shellfish, appetizers
Cabrières	R	M	Strong bouquet, strong	Carignan, Cinsault, Grenache	Beef, mutton, stews, cassoulets, soft ripened cheeses
Clairette de Bellegarde	W	D	Full-bodied	Clairette	Oysters, mussels, shellfish, smoked salmon and eel, grilled saltwater fish, duck à l'orange
Clairette de Languedoc	W	D	Full-bodied	Clairette	Oysters, mussels, shellfish, smoked salmon and eel, grilled saltwater fish, duck à l'orange
Fitou	R	M	Full-bodied, strong	Carignan, Cinsault, Grenache	Beef, mutton, stews, cassoulets, soft ripened cheeses
Maury	R	S	Strong bouquet, strong	Grenache Noir	Flambéed desserts, fruit, desserts
Minervois	R	M	Balanced, fruity	Carignan, Cinsault, Grenache	Beef, mutton, stews, cassoulets, soft ripened cheeses
Vin de Blanquette	Sp	D	Fizzy, tingling	Mauza	Oysters, mussels, shellfish, appetizers

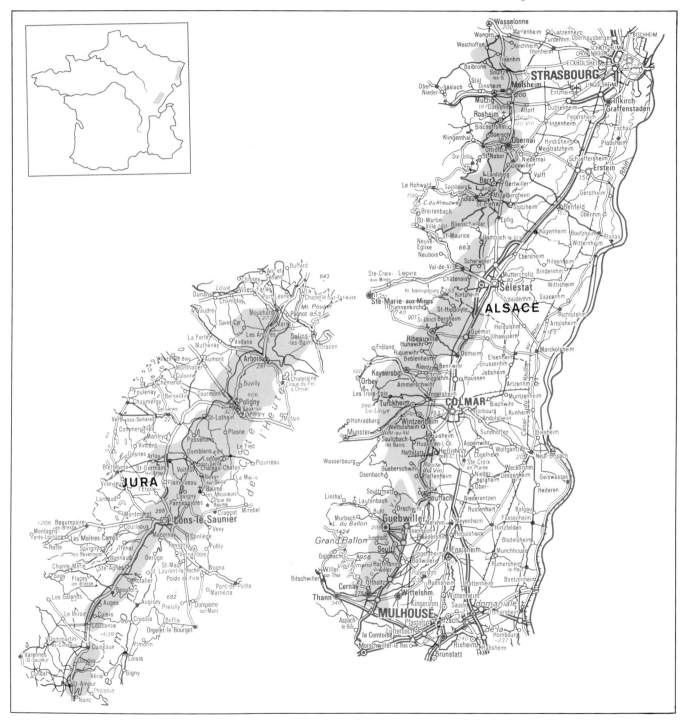

Wine Regions of Alsace and Jura

349

Alsace

Wine Name	Wine Type	Taste	Qualities	Grape Varieties	Accompanies
Gewürztraminer	W	D	Full-bodied, strong bouquet	Gewürztraminer	Goose liver, pheasant, mussels, cheese, asparagus
Muscat	W	D	Strong bouquet, full-bodied	Muscat	Grilled, sautéed, or fried fish
Pinot blanc	W	D	Flowery, full-bodied	Pinot Blanc	Aperitifs, oysters, mussels, fish in sauce, veal in cream sauce, mild cheeses
Riesling	W	D	Balanced, flowery	Riesling	Poached trout, pike in cream sauce, fish stews, perch with almonds, cock in riesling, sauerkraut, asparagus
Silvaner	W	D/M	Fresh, fruity	Sylvaner	Snails Alsace style, freshwater fish, poultry, veal, onion quiche, cheesecake, mild cheeses, asparagus
Tokajer	W	S	Full-bodied, flowery, strong	Pinot Gris	Goose liver, desserts, cakes
Traminer	W	D/M	Full-bodied, strong bouquet	Traminer	Goose liver, duck, quail, partridge, pheasant, mild cheeses, asparagus
Zwicker (Edel)	W	D/M	Fresh, fruity	Mixture of several varieties	Aperitifs, fish dishes

Jura

Wine Name	Wine Type	Taste	Qualities	Grape Varieties	Accompanies
Arbois	W	M	*"Vin jaune"* (yellow wine), full-bodied, strong bouquet	Savagnin	Veal, duck à l'orange
Chateau Chalon	W	M	*"Vin jaune"* (yellow wine), full-bodied, strong bouquet	Savagnin	Veal, duck à l'orange

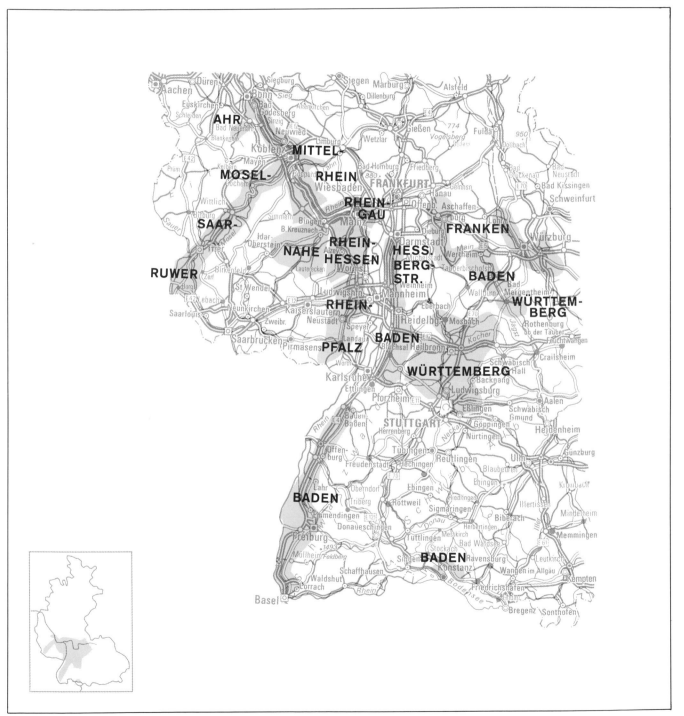

The Appellations of Germany

The wines of West Germany are named for grape varieties and the place of origin.

Deutscher Tafelwein (German Table Wine)

These wines are made exclusively from domestic grapes. Sugaring of the grape must is permitted. Table wines cannot carry the name of a specific vineyard on their labels, only the name of the municipality, growing area, and their subdivisions. At least 75 percent of the grapes must come from the area named on the label.

Landwein (Country Wine)

These table wines are regulated by the state of origin. Their residual sugar content cannot exceed the highest rate allowed for the designation "*halbtrocken*" (semi-dry).

Quality Wines of Specific Growing Areas (QbA-Wines)

These wines can be made only with approved grape varieties. Their place of origin may be one of eleven specific growing areas, as well as names of special sites or areas, communities or villages.

The minimum alcohol content of the wine is specified.

The bottle must carry an official examination number (AP-Nr), which indicates the wine has been officially analyzed and tested for taste and quality. At least 75 percent of the wine must come from the place named on the label.

Quality Wines with Titles

In Germany six different title designations are used. In addition to the stipulations for QbA wines, wines with these titles must meet additional requirements.

Title	Stipulations
Kabinett	Specific growing area Prescribed minimum sugar content of the must No added sugar Appropriate characteristics, based on those established for wines of that origin
Spätlese (late harvest)	Prescribed minimum sugar content of the must No added sugar Grapes must be fully ripe when harvested and can be picked only after the main harvest is completed

Auslese (selected grapes)	Prescribed minimum sugar content of the must
	No added sugar
	Grapes must be fully ripe when harvested and can be picked only after the main harvest is completed
	Wine may be produced only after all sick, unripe, and damaged grapes are removed from the harvest
Trockenbeerenauslese (selected dry grapes)	Only shriveled grapes with noble rot can be used; otherwise, like Auslese
	Minimum sugar content of the must is prescribed
Eiswein (ice wine)	Only very ripe grapes that have been partially frozen may be used
	This title can only be used in combination with another, for example: "Spätlese Eiswein"

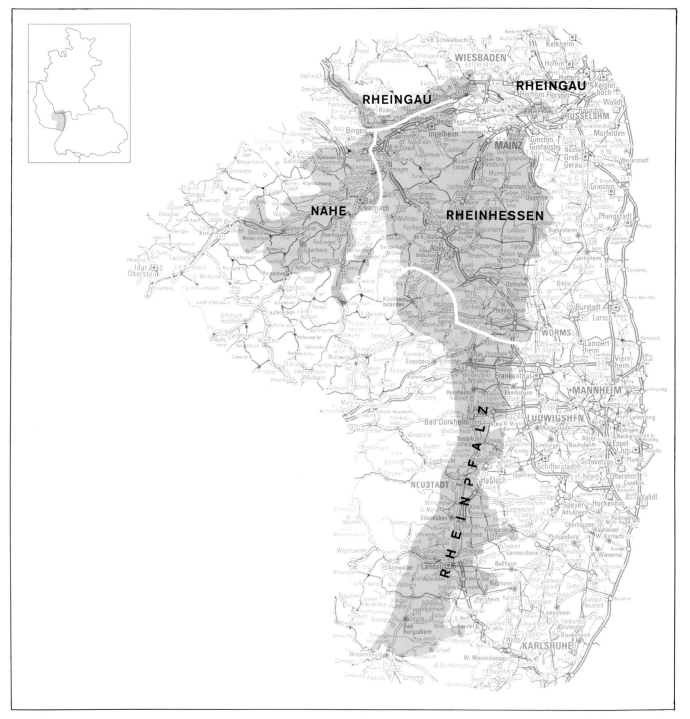

Rheingau

Wine Name	Wine Type	Taste	Qualities	Grape Varieties	Accompanies
Braunberger	W	S	Fruity	Riesling	Aperitifs, freshwater fish, desserts
Hochheimer	W	S	Flowery, full-bodied	Riesling	Aperitifs, asparagus, poultry
Östricher	W	M	Fruity, balanced	Riesling	Aperitifs, goose liver, asparagus
Rüdesheimer	W	S	Fruity, flowery	Riesling	Aperitifs, white meat
Schloss Johannisberg	W	M/S	Flowery, strong bouquet	Sylvaner	Aperitifs, asparagus, shellfish
Winzersekt (halbtrocken — semi-dry)	Sp	D/M	Fizzy, fruity	Riesling	Aperitifs, fish, veal, goose liver, shellfish
Winzersekt (mild)	Sp	M	Fizzy, full-bodied	Riesling	Flambéed desserts, soufflés, cakes
Winzersekt (trocken — dry)	Sp	D	Fizzy, tart	Riesling	Aperitifs, shellfish, fish
Zeller	W	S	Strong bouquet	Riesling	Aperitifs, desserts, freshwater fish

Rheinhessen

Wine Name	Wine Type	Taste	Qualities	Grape Varieties	Accompanies
Binger	W	D	Tart	Scheurebe	Aperitifs, fish, white meat
Niersteiner	W	S	Fruity, light	Riesling X Sylvaner	Aperitifs
Oppenheimer	W	D/M	Flowery, strong bouquet	Scheurebe	Aperitifs, shellfish
Winzersekt (halbtrocken – semi-dry*)*	Sp	D/M	Fizzy, fruity	Riesling	Aperitifs, fish, goose liver, shellfish, veal
Winzersekt (mild)	Sp	M	Fizzy, full-bodied	Riesling	Flambéed desserts, soufflés, cakes
Winzersekt (trocken – dry*)*	Sp	D	Fizzy, tart	Riesling	Aperitifs, shellfish, fish

Rheinpfalz

Wine Name	Wine Type	Taste	Qualities	Grape Varieties	Accompanies
Deidesheimer	W	M/S	Full-bodied, balanced	Riesling	Aperitifs, fish in aromatic sauces
Diedesfelder	W	D	Tart, flowery	Pinot Blanc	Fish, shellfish, kosher meats
Dürkheimer	W	D	Full-bodied, strong bouquet	Gewürztraminer	Goose liver, veal in sauces
Wachenheimer	W	M	Fruity	Riesling	Aperitifs, fish
Kallstadter	W	D	Fruity	Sylvaner	Veal in sauces

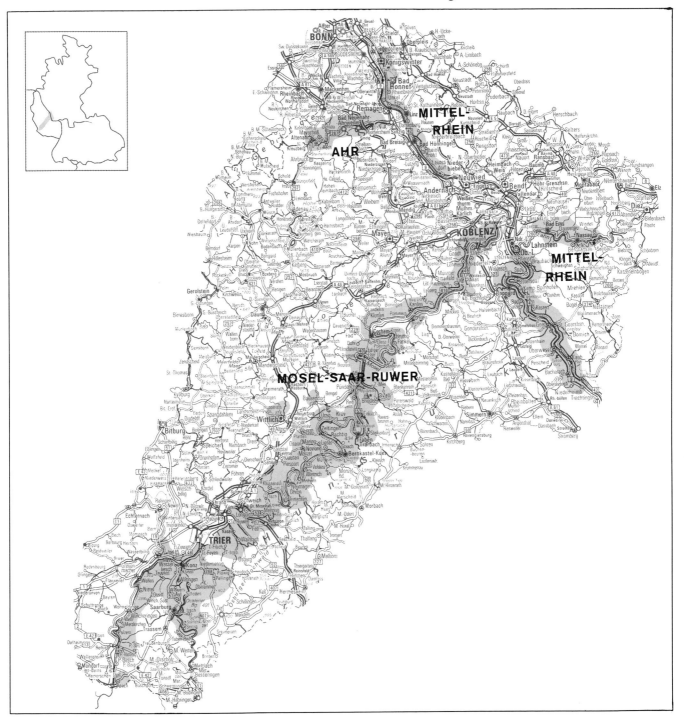

Mosel/Saar/Ruwer

Wine Name	Wine Type	Taste	Qualities	Grape Varieties	Accompanies
Bernkastler	W	S	Strong bouquet, balanced, fruity	Riesling	Aperitifs, desserts, fish
Graacher	W	D/M	Strong bouquet	Riesling	Poultry, shellfish
Mehringer	W	M	Full-bodied, fruity	Riesling	Spicy meat and poultry stews
Piesporter	W	S	Fruity, flowery	Riesling	Aperitifs, desserts, fish
Serriger	W	D	Tart, fresh	Riesling	Fish
Winzersekt (halbtrocken — semi-dry*)*	Sp	D/M	Fizzy, fruity	Riesling	Aperitifs, fish, goose liver, shellfish, veal
Winzersekt (mild)	Sp	M	Fizzy, full-bodied	Riesling	Flambéed desserts, soufflés, cakes

Ahr

Wine Name	Wine Type	Taste	Qualities	Grape Varieties	Accompanies
Marienthaler	R	D	Full-bodied, balanced	Pinot Noir	Beef, pork, poultry, game dishes
Walporzheimer	R	D	Flowery, balanced	Pinot Noir	Beef, pork, poultry, game dishes, sauerbraten

Wine Regions of Franken, Hessiche Bergstrasse, Württemberg, and Baden

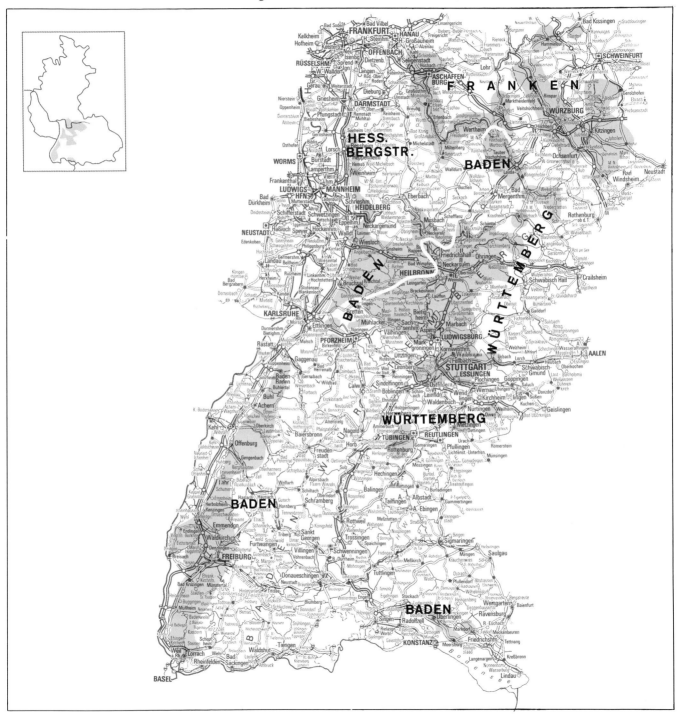

Franken

Wine Name	Wine Type	Taste	Qualities	Grape Varieties	Accompanies
Escherndorfer	W	D/M	Flowery, fruity	Sylvaner	Fish, poultry and veal with cream sauces
Iphöfer	W	S	Full-bodied, strong	Sylvaner	Roasts, desserts
Randersackerer	W	M	Flowery, balanced	Kerner	Veal with cream sauces, asparagus

Hessische Bergstrasse

Wine Name	Wine Type	Taste	Qualities	Grape Varieties	Accompanies
Heppenheimer	W	M	Fruity, flowery	Riesling	Desserts, veal with cream sauces, asparagus

Württemberg

Wine Name	Wine Type	Taste	Qualities	Grape Varieties	Accompanies
Bad Cannstätter	W	D	Strong bouquet	Pinot Noir	Beef, pork, poultry, game dishes, sauerbraten
Heilbronner	R	D	Tart, fruity	Trollinger	Beef, duck, goose, stews
Heilbronner	W	D/M	Fruity, full-bodied	Pinot Gris	Beef, duck, goose, stews, pâtés
Stuttgarter	R	D	Full-bodied, strong	Lemberger	Beef, lamb, game
Stuttgarter	W	D	Flowery	Riesling	Ravioli, pasta, freshwater fish

Baden

Wine Name	Wine Type	Taste	Qualities	Grape Varieties	Accompanies
Durbacher	W	D	Fruity, flowery	Riesling	Pasta, freshwater fish
Kaiserstuhl-Tuniberg	R	D	Strong bouquet, tart	Pinot Noir	Beef, pork
Kaiserstuhl-Tuniberg	W	D/M	Full-bodied, fruity	Riesling X Sylvaner	Freshwater fish, aperitifs
Meersburger	W	D	Flowery, fruity	Riesling X Sylvaner	Freshwater fish, aperitifs

The Appellations of Austria

The wines of Austria are named for the grape variety used or the place of origin.

Wine from Austria

Table-wine-quality wine, exclusively of Austrian origin. This wine must be made exclusively from those grape varieties stipulated by law.

Österreichischer Qualitätswein (Austrian Quality Wine)

The use of the appellation is strictly regulated by law. It can be used only if the wine is made from a quality grape variety stipulated by law, with a minimum must weight (73° Oechsle). In addition, there are stipulations regarding origin and criteria concerning analysis and taste.

Qualitätswein mit Prädikat (Quality Wines with Title)

In Austria six different title designations are used, each of which must fulfill specific requirements.

Title	Designation
Kabinett	Only a quality wine with a specific minimum must weight (84° Oechsle); beyond that, no improvements can be made.
Spätlese (late harvest)	A quality wine from grapes that are only picked after the main harvest of that particular grape variety, fully ripe, with a prescribed minimum must weight (94° Oechsle).
Auslese (selected grapes)	A late harvest exclusively made from carefully selected grapes, with a prescribed minimum must weight (105° Oechsle).
Eiswein (ice wine)	Exclusively made from grapes that were frozen during harvest and pressing, with a prescribed minimum must weight (111° Oechsle).
Beerenauslese (choice grapes)	A selection of overripe grapes with noble rot, the juice of which must have a very specific must weight (127° Oechsle). The wine pressed from such berries is deep golden yellow and very high in natural residual sugar, with a distinct noble-rot bouquet.

Trockenbeerenauslese (dried choice grapes)

A selection of raisinlike shriveled grapes with noble rot, the juice of which must have a specific minimum must weight (156° Oechsle). This is the highest-quality wine. The production of such a wine is only possible in particular climates. It is very labor intensive and risky to produce.

The Austrian Wine Quality Seal with Official Control Number

After application to the ministry of agriculture, the official seal for tested quality wines from Austria is granted. Such wines are analyzed and tested by an officially appointed commission in a blind taste test to ensure they are faultless in appearance, balanced in smell and taste, and typical for the grape variety. For control purposes, the wine quality seal has an official test number.

Lower Austria (Niederösterreich)

Wine Name	Wine Type	Taste	Qualities	Grape Varieties	Accompanies
Dürnsteiner (Wachau)	W	D	Light, fruity	Grüner Veltliner	Fish, shellfish, aperitifs
Gumpoldskirchner Schatzberg	W	M	Light, fruity	Neuburger	Fondues, poultry, veal, pork
Gumpoldskirchner Spiegel	W	D	Flowery, fruity	Rheinriesling	Aperitifs, poultry, fish
Gumpoldskirchner Stocknarrin	W	M/S	Full-bodied, flowery	Spätrot-Rotgipfler	Goose liver, terrines, cakes
Kremser (Krems)	W	M	Flowery, fizzy	Grüner Veltliner	Asparagus, fish, shellfish, goose liver
Malteser (Retz)	W	D	Flowery, fruity	Grüner Veltliner	Veal, pork
Steiner (Krems)	W	D	Full-bodied, fruity	Rheinriesling	Poultry, fish, veal, egg dishes
Weisskirchner (Wachau)	W	D	Fizzy, light	Rheinriesling	Freshwater fish, aperitifs

Burgenland

Wine Name	Wine Type	Taste	Qualities	Grape Varieties	Accompanies
Alter Knabe	R	M	Full-bodied, strong bouquet	Blaufränkisch, St. Laurent	Beef, lamb, game
Grüner Husar	W	M	Light, fruity	Grüner Veltliner	Poultry, veal
Oggauer/Blaufränkisch	R	M	Balanced, full-bodied	Blaufränkisch	Beef, game, cheese
Roter Husar	R	M	Balanced, strong bouquet	Blaufränkisch	Beef, lamb, game
Ruster Baumgarten	R	D	Balanced, full-bodied	Blauburgunder	Beef, lamb, game
Ruster	W	D	Light, flowery	Riesling X Sylvaner	Fish, poultry, terrines
Weisser Husar	W	M	Light, fruity	Riesling X Sylvaner	Poultry, terrines, pâtés, soufflés

Vienna (Wien)

Wine Name	Wine Type	Taste	Qualities	Grape Varieties	Accompanies
Grinzinger	W	D	Fruity, flowery	Grüner Veltliner	Aperitifs, veal, poultry, fish
Wiener Nussberg	W	D	Fruity, strong bouquet	Grüner Veltliner	Aperitifs, veal, poultry, fish

Steiermark

Wine Name	Wine Type	Taste	Qualities	Grape Varieties	Accompanies
Klöcher Berg	W	D	Fruity, flowery	Traminer	Aperitifs, egg dishes, fish
Schilcher	rosé	D	Fizzy, tart	Blauer Wildbacher	Aperitifs, home-style cuisine
Schlossberg	W	S	Full-bodied	Muscat-Sylvaner	Desserts
Sulztal	W	S	Strong bouquet, full-bodied	Traminer	Desserts

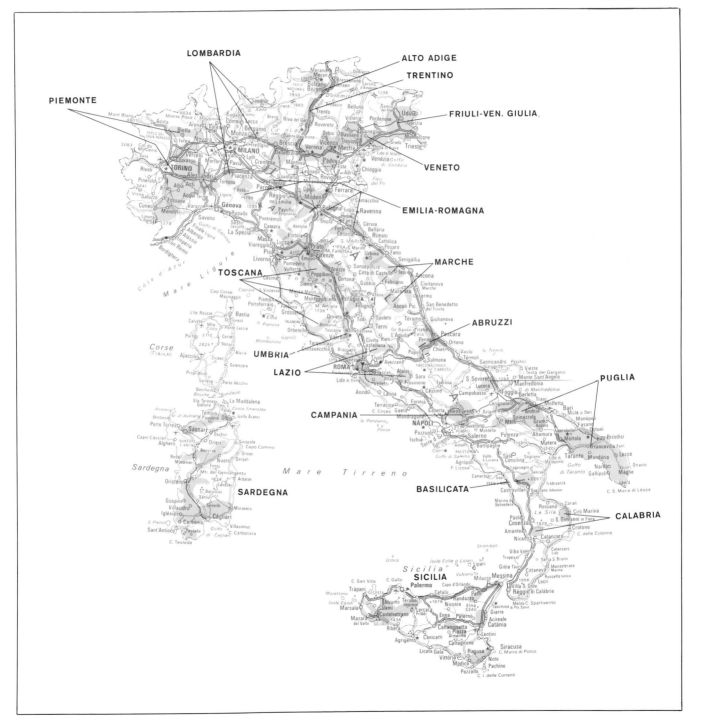

The Appellations of Italy

Italy, the biggest wine producer in the world, usually names its wines for the grape variety used or the place of origin. Italian law recognizes these quality-control categories:

Denominazione semplice (DS)

This class, in which the wine is simply described by place of origin, applies to wines of table-wine quality for which quality criteria are not specified.

Denominazione di origine controllata (DOC)

Wines in this class have a controlled description of origin and must meet certain criteria:

- The growing area is exactly defined.
- The wine production method is prescribed.
- The yield is limited.
- The grape variety and vineyard maintenance are prescribed.

Denominazione di origine controllata e garantita (DOCG)

Wines in this class have controlled and guaranteed descriptions of origin. DOCG is the highest classification, and very few wines are designated as such.

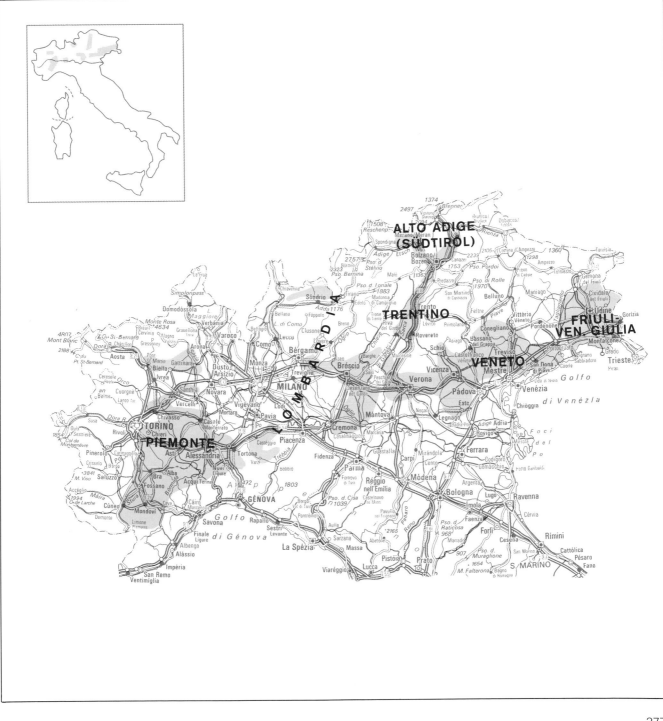

Piedmont (Piemonte)

Wine Name	Wine Type	Taste	Qualities	Grape Varieties	Accompanies
Asti Spumante	Sp	S/M	Fruity, fizzy	Moscato	Desserts, cakes
Barbaresco	R	D	Full-bodied, strong	Nebbiolo	Beef, mutton, game, ripe soft cheeses, e.g., Gorgonzola
Barbera d'Alba	R	D	Full-bodied, tart	Barbera	Beef, mutton, game, ripe soft cheeses, e.g., Gorgonzola
Barbera d'Asti	R	D	Full-bodied, tart	Barbera	Beef, mutton, game, ripe soft cheeses, e.g., Gorgonzola
Barbera del Monferrato	R	D	Fruity, full-bodied	Barbera, Freisa	Beef, boiled beef, raw ham, salami
Barolo	R	D	Full-bodied, balanced, strong	Nebbiolo	Beef, mutton, game, ripe soft cheeses, e.g., Gorgonzola
Boca	R	D	Tart	Nebbiolo, Vespolina, Bonarda	Beef, poultry, pork, ripe soft cheeses, e.g., Gorgonzola
Brachetto d'Acqui	R	M	Strong bouquet, fruity, fizzy	Brachetto, Moscato Nero, Aleatico	Desserts, cakes, *panettone*
Brachetto d'Acqui	rosé	M	Strong bouquet, fruity, fizzy	Brachetto, Moscato Nero, Aleatico	Desserts, cakes, *panettone*

Piedmont (Piemonte)

Wine Name	Wine Type	Taste	Qualities	Grape Varieties	Accompanies
Carema	R	D	Strong bouquet, full-bodied	Nebbiolo, Pugnet-Pientine	Grilled foods, poultry
Dolcetto d'Alba	R	D	Full-bodied, tart	Dolcetto	Grilled foods, veal, ripe soft cheeses, e.g., Gorgonzola
Freisa d'Asti	R	M	Flowery, fruity, fresh	Freisa	Poultry, mutton
Gattinara	R	D	Flowery, tart, strong	Nebbiolo, Bonarda di Gattinara	Roast beef, roast veal, game
Ghemme	R	D	Flowery, tart	Nebbiolo, Vespolina, Bonarda	Roast beef, grilled foods, game
Moscato d'Asti	Sp	S	Fresh, fruity, fizzy	Moscato Bianco	Desserts, cakes
Nebbiolo d'Alba	R	D	Full-bodied, balanced, strong	Nebbiolo	Roast beef, roast veal, game specialties, grilled foods

Veneto

Wine Name	Wine Type	Taste	Qualities	Grape Varieties	Accompanies
Amarone	R	D	Full-bodied, strong, balanced	Corvina Veronese, Rondinella, Molinara	Beef, mutton, grilled foods, soft ripe cheeses, e.g., Gorgonzola
Bardolino	R	D	Flowery, strong bouquet	Corvina Veronese, Rondinella, Molinara, Negrara	Poultry, veal, cheeses
Bianco di Custoza	W	D/M	Flowery, strong bouquet, tart	Trebbiano Toscano, Garganega, Tocai Friulano, Cortese, Malvasia, Riesling	Fish soup, shellfish, veal, risotto
Cabernet	R	D	Full-bodied, tart	Cabernet	Beef, game, soft ripe cheeses, e.g., Gorgonzola
Gambellara	W	D	Fresh, light	Garganega, Trebbiano Soave	Fish, poultry, veal
Merlot	R	D	Strong bouquet, tart	Merlot	Pork, salami, raw ham, poultry
Merlot di Pramaggiore	R	D	Strong bouquet, tart	Merlot	Pork, rabbit, poultry, mutton
Prosecco di Conegliano	W	D	Fruity, tart	Prosecco	Veal, fish, poultry

Veneto

Wine Name	Wine Type	Taste	Qualities	Grape Varieties	Accompanies
Recioto di Gambellara	W	D	Fruity, fizzy	Garganega, Trebbiano Soave	Seafood
Recioto della Valpolicella	R	M	Strong bouquet, full-bodied	Corvina Veronese, Molinara, Rondinella	Beef, mutton, grilled foods, soft ripe cheeses, e.g., Gorgonzola
Soave	W	D	Fresh, light, tart	Garganega	Fish
Valpolicella	R	D	Tart, strong bouquet	Corvina Veronese, Rondinella, Molinara	Pork, poultry, beef, cheeses

Lombardy (Lombardia)

Wine Name	Wine Type	Taste	Qualities	Grape Varieties	Accompanies
Bonarda	R	D	Full-bodied	Bonarda	Beef, risotto, pasta, cheeses
Buttafuoco	R	D	Balanced, strong, tart	Croatina, Uva Rara Vespolina	Grilled foods, roast mutton
Colli morenici mantovani del Garda	R	D	Strong bouquet, tart	Rossanella, Negrara, Rondinella	Pasta, risotto, pizza
Colli morenici mantovani del Garda	W	D	Strong bouquet, tart	Trebbiano Giallo, Garganega	Fish
Grumello (Valtellina)	R	D	Strong bouquet, balanced, tart	Chiavennasca	Game, mushroom dishes, beef, salami, raw ham
Inferno (Valtellina)	R	D	Strong bouquet, balanced, tart	Chiavennasca	Game, mushroom dishes, beef, salami, raw ham
Lugana	W	D	Fresh, balanced	Trebbiano	Fish
Sangue di Giuda	R	D	Full-bodied, tart	Croatina, Uva Rara Vespolina	Grilled foods, roast beef
Sassella (Valtellina)	R	D	Strong bouquet, balanced, tart	Chiavennasca	Game, mushroom dishes, beef, salami, raw ham
Sforzato (Valtellina)	R	D	Strong, balanced	Chiavennasca	Game, mushroom dishes, beef, lamb

Lombardy (Lombardia)

Wine Name	Wine Type	Taste	Qualities	Grape Varieties	Accompanies
Tocai di S. Martino della Battaglia	W	D	Tart	Pinot Gris	Fish soups, fish, shellfish
Valgella (Valtellina)	R	D	Strong bouquet, balanced, tart	Chiavennasca	Game, mushroom dishes, beef, salami, raw ham
Valtellina Superiore	R	D	Strong bouquet, balanced, tart	Chiavennasca	Game, mushroom dishes, beef, salami, raw ham

Alto Adige

Wine Name	Wine Type	Taste	Qualities	Grape Varieties	Accompanies
Kalterersee	R	M	Light, fruity	Vernatsch	Dried meats, poultry, veal
Lagrein Gries	rosé	M	Light, fresh	Lagrein	Poultry, veal, pork
Lagrein dunkel von Gries	R	D	Full-bodied, tart	Lagrein	Game, beef
St. Magdalener	R	M	Full-bodied, balanced	Vernatsch	Cold platters, poultry, veal, cheeses
Südtiroler Blauburgunder	R	M	Fruity, balanced	Pinot Noir	Beef, mutton, game, cheeses
Südtiroler Cabernet	R	D	Full-bodied, strong bouquet	Cabernet	Game, beef
Südtiroler Merlot	R	D	Light, fruity	Merlot	Italian pasta dishes, pizza
Südtiroler Weissburgunder	W	M	Fruity, balanced	Pinot Blanc	Aperitifs, appetizers, fish, cheeses
Südtiroler Gewürztraminer	W	M	Strong bouquet, fruity	Gewürztraminer	Aperitifs, asparagus, shellfish, veal

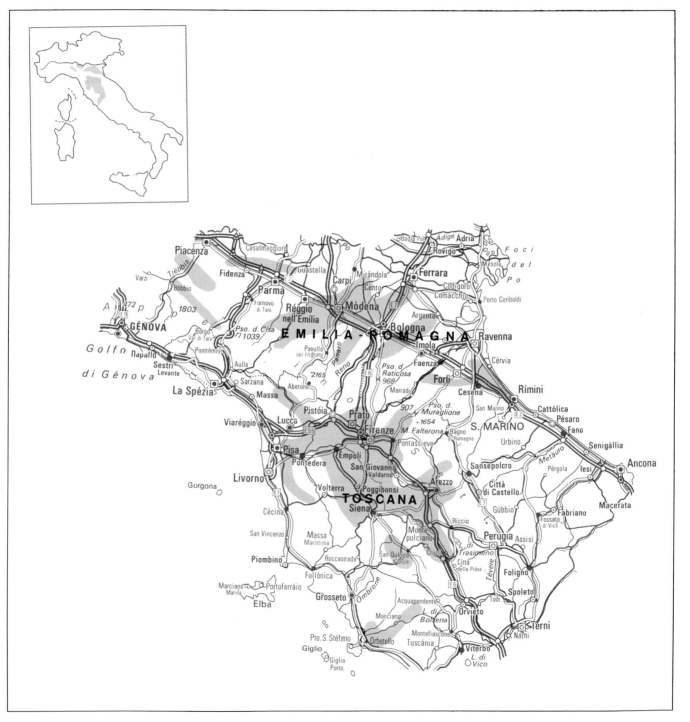

Tuscany (Toscana)

Wine Name	Wine Type	Taste	Qualities	Grape Varieties	Accompanies
Bianco di Pitigliano	W	D	Tart	Trebbiano, Greco, Malvasia	Fish, grilled foods
Brunello di Montalcino	R	D	Full-bodied, tart	Brunello, Sangiovese	Grilled foods, veal, pork
Carmignano	R	D	Flowery, strong bouquet, balanced	Sangiovese, Canaiolo Nero, Trebbiano, Malvasia	Roast beef, game
Chianti	R	D	Flowery, strong bouquet	Sangiovese, Canaiolo Nero, Malvasia, Colorino	Pasta, risotto, pizza, poultry, roast beef, roast veal, roast pork
Parrina	R	D	Strong bouquet, tart	Sangiovese, Canaiolo Nero, Colorino, Trebbiano, Montepulciano	Poultry, veal
Rosso delle Colline Lucchesi	R	D	Tart	Sangiovese, Canaiolo Nero, Colorino, Trebbiano, Malvasia	Poultry, veal
Vernaccia di S. Gimignano	W	D	Fresh, flowery	Vernaccia	Fish
Vino Nobile di Montepulciano	R	D	Flowery, rich	Prugnolo Gentile, Trebbiano, Canaiolo Nero, Malvasia, Mammolo, Pulcincolo	Roast beef, grilled foods, game, rabbit

Emilia-Romagna

Wine Name	Wine Type	Taste	Qualities	Grape Varieties	Accompanies
Albana di Romagna	W	D	Strong bouquet, tart	Albana	Fish
Lambrusco	R	M/S	Fizzy, fruity	Lambrusco	Pasta, pizza, *panettone*
Lambrusco	R	D	Fizzy, strong bouquet	Lambrusco	Pasta, pizza, salami, mortadella, Parma ham, *zampone*
Sangiovese di Romagna	R	D	Balanced, tart	Sangiovese	Beef stew, cheeses, mortadella, Parma ham
Trebbiano di Romagna	W	D	Balanced, tart	Trebbiano	Fish, veal

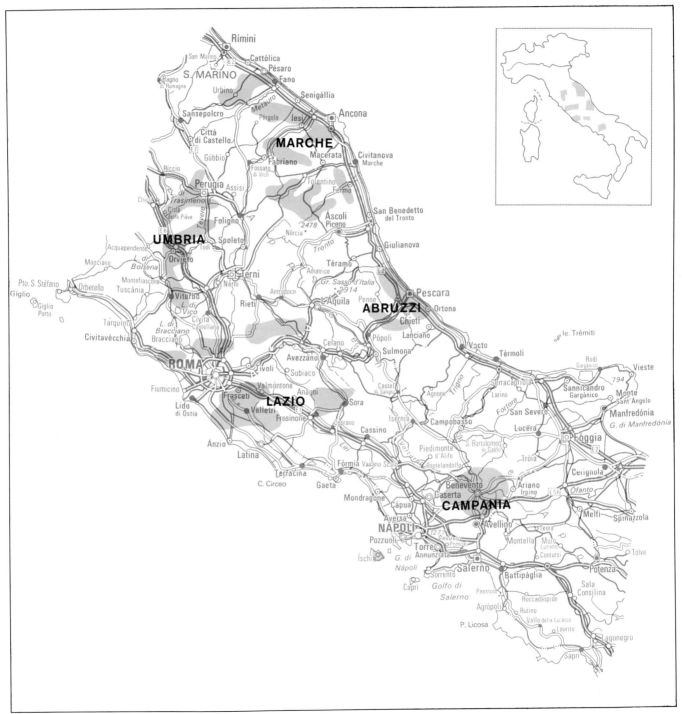

Abruzzi

Wine Name	Wine Type	Taste	Qualities	Grape Varieties	Accompanies
Montepulciano d'Abruzzo	R	D	Fruity, tart, strong bouquet	Montepulciano	Pasta, pizza, pork, salami

Campania

Wine Name	Wine Type	Taste	Qualities	Grape Varieties	Accompanies
Greco di Tufo	W	D	Balanced, tart	Greco	Fish, shellfish, pizza
Ischia bianco	W	D	Balanced, tart	Forastera, Biancolilla, Piedirosso	Fish, aperitifs
Ischia rosso	R	D	Tart	Guarnaccia, Barbera, Piedirosso	Roast beef, roast pork, stews
Lacrima Christi	W	S	Balanced, strong	Fiano, Greco	Desserts, cakes
Lacrima Christi	R	M/S	Fruity, strong bouquet	Aglianico, Piedirosso	Pasta, pizza

Latium (Lazio)

Wine Name	Wine Type	Taste	Qualities	Grape Varieties	Accompanies
Est! Est! Est!	W	D	Balanced	Malvasia, Trebbiano, Rosetto	Fish
Frascati	W	D	Full-bodied, balanced	Malvasia, Trebbiano, Greco	Fish, pasta, pizza, egg dishes

Marches

Wine Name	Wine Type	Taste	Qualities	Grape Varieties	Accompanies
Bianco dei Colli Maceratesi	W	D	Fruity	Malvasia, Trebbiano, Verdicchio, Maceratino	Aperitifs, fish
Rosso conero	R	D	Balanced, tart, strong bouquet	Montepulciano, Sangiovese	Roast veal, roast pork
Sangiovese dei Colli Pesaresi	R	D	Balanced, tart	Sangiovese	Pasta, pizza, roast pork, roast veal, poultry
Verdicchio dei Castelli di Jesi	W	D	Balanced, tart, flowery	Verdicchio	Seafood

Umbria

Wine Name	Wine Type	Taste	Qualities	Grape Varieties	Accompanies
Orvieto	W	D	Flowery, tart	Trebbiano, Verdello, Malvasia, Drupeggio, Grechetto	Fish

Other Wine-producing Countries

In this group are wines from:

Spain

Portugal

Hungary

Liechtenstein

United States (California)

Outside of their country of origin, most of these wines rarely appear on wine lists except in specialty restaurants, not because they are not quality products, but because the amounts exported are too small to warrant an international reputation.

Spain

Wine Name	Wine Type	Taste	Qualities	Grape Varieties	Accompanies
Alella	R	D	Fruity	Garnacha, Tempranillo	Used as an everyday wine, a table wine
Alella	W	D	Fresh, fruity	Garnacha Blanca, Malvasia	Appetizers, aperitifs
Alicante	R	D	Fresh	Garnacha	Used as an everyday wine, a table wine
Jerez (Sherry)	R	S	Strong, full-bodied	Listan, Palomino	Cakes, desserts, aperitifs
Jerez (Sherry)	W	D	Full-bodied	Listan, Palomino	Aperitifs
Jumilla	R	D	Strong, full-bodied	Garnacha	Used as an everyday wine, a table wine
Malaga	R	S	Strong	Pedro Ximenes, Muskateller	Desserts, cakes, aperitifs
Malvasia	W	S	Full-bodied, strong	Malvasia	Cakes, desserts
Moscatel	W	S	Strong, full-bodied	Muskateller	Cakes, desserts
Navarra tinto	R	D	Strong bouquet, full-bodied	Garnacha, Tempranillo, Mazuelo	Beef, game dishes
Panades	W	D	Fruity, tart	Xarel, Macabeo	Aperitifs, seafood
Panades	R	D	Full-bodied	Garnacha	Beef, grilled foods
Priorato	R	D	Full-bodied	Cariñena, Garnacha	Used as an everyday wine, a table wine

Spain

Wine Name	Wine Type	Taste	Qualities	Grape Varieties	Accompanies
Requena	R	D	Fresh, fruity	Cencibel, Bobal, Garnacha	Used as an everyday wine, a table wine
Rioja 3 bandas	R	D	Strong bouquet, balanced	Garnacha Tinto, Tempranillo, Mazuelo, Graciano	Game dishes, lamb, beef
Rioja blanco	W	D	Fresh, fruity	Garnacha Blanca	Appetizer, seafood, asparagus
Rioja rosado	rosé	D/M	Fruity, fresh	Garnacha, Tempranillo, Mazuelo, Graciano,	Fish dishes, veal
Rioja tinto	R	D	Fresh, full-bodied	Garnacha Tinto, Tempranillo, Mazuelo, Graciano,	Cheeses, snacks
Tarragona	R	D	Fresh	Cariñena, Garnacha	Used as an everyday wine, a table wine
Tarragona	W	D	Fresh, fruity	Xarel, Macabeo, Parellada	Appetizers, seafood, asparagus
Valdepeñas	R	D	Fresh, fruity	Garnacha	Used as an everyday wine, a table wine
Valdepeñas	W	D	Full-bodied	Airen, Pardillo, Cirial	Appetizers, cheeses, a table wine
Valencia	R	D	Fresh, flowery	Cencibel, Bobal, Garnacha	Used as an everyday wine, a table wine

Portugal

Wine Name	Wine Type	Taste	Qualities	Grape Varieties	Accompanies
Bucellas	W	D	Fresh, light	Arinto	Appetizers, seafood
Colares	R	D	Tart, strong	Ramisco	Grilled foods
Dão	R	D	Fresh, tart	Tourigo, Bastardo	Everyday wine, a table wine
Dão	W	D	Flowery, fresh	Arinto	Appetizers, seafood
Port	R	S	Strong, full-bodied	Alvarinho, Ramisco	Desserts, cakes, aperitifs
Port	R	M/S	Strong, full-bodied	Alvarinho, Ramisco	Desserts, cakes, aperitifs
Port	W	D	Strong, full-bodied	Alvarinho, Ramisco	Aperitifs
Vinho verde	W	D	Fresh, fruity	Alvarinho	Appetizers, seafood

Hungary

Wine Name	Wine Type	Taste	Qualities	Grape Varieties	Accompanies
Badacsony Kéknyelü	W	D	Full-bodied, tart	Blaustengler	Smoked and cooked fish, veal
Badacsony Szürkebarat	W	M	Full-bodied, strong	Pinot Gris	Veal, desserts, cakes, aperitifs, cheeses
Debrői Harslevelü	W	M/S	Flowery, strong bouquet	Harslevelü	Cold meat platters, desserts, cheeses
Egri Bikaver	R	D	Full-bodied, strong	Kadarka, Blaufränkisch, Medoc Noir	Beef, mutton, game
Tokaj Aszu	W	S	Strong, full-bodied	Harslevelü	Desserts, aperitifs
Tokaj Furmint	W	M/S	Full-bodied, strong bouquet	Furmint	Terrines, pâtés, smoked fish, duck, quail, pheasant, snipe, asparagus, appetizers
Tokaj Szamorodni dry	W	D	Full-bodied, tart, strong	Harslevelü	Aperitifs, duck, game
Tokaj Szamorodni sweet	W	S	Full-bodied	Harslevelü	Aperitifs, desserts

Liechtenstein

Wine Name	Wine Type	Taste	Qualities	Grape Varieties	Accompanies
Beerli	R	D	Full-bodied, balanced, fruity	Pinot Noir	Beef, roast pork, cold meat platters
Süssdruck	R	D	Fresh, fizzy	Pinot Noir	Aperitifs, cold meat platters, appetizers, fish, poultry
Vaduzer Riesling X Sylvaner	W	D	Strong bouquet, fruity, balanced	Riesling X Sylvaner	Aperitifs, fish, appetizers, poultry

United States (California)

Wine Name	Wine Type	Taste	Qualities	Grape Varieties	Accompanies
Cabernet Sauvignon	R	D	Full-bodied, fruity, strong bouquet	Cabernet Sauvignon	Roast beef, game
Chardonnay	W	D	Strong bouquet, full-bodied	Chardonnay	Aperitifs, appetizers, seafood
Gamay	R	M	Flowery, fresh, fruity	Gamay	Poultry, meat platters, cold dishes
Merlot	R	D	Full-bodied, strong	Merlot	Beef, mutton, game
Pinot Noir	R	M	Robust, full-bodied	Pinot Noir	Veal, pork
Zinfandel	R	D	Full-bodied, strong, flowery	Zinfandel	Game, cheese platters

19. Glossary of Culinary Terms

What is fish described on the menu as *Dugléré?* What is *blanquette de veau à l'ancienne?* What is the difference between *sauce allemande* and *sauce aux câpres?* In this chapter you will find out, because it reveals the meaning of the sometimes mysterious jargon used in classical cuisine. The terms are listed first by food category and then alphabetically within each category, so you can find a particular term easily.

French Terminology

All over the world, wherever cooking is considered an art, you will hear French. French is the lingua franca of the kitchen, and the cooking terms derived from it are internationally understood. All the terms that follow are French unless otherwise indicated.

The culinary terms that follow are arranged in food categories and listed alphabetically within these categories. The categories are:

Cold appetizers

Warm appetizers

Soups

Fish dishes

Sauces

Compound butters

Main dishes

Potatoes

Desserts

Term	Meaning
Cold Appetizers	
canapé	Slices of toast cut into different small shapes and topped with various meats, smoked fish, vegetables, cheeses, or eggs, often glazed with aspic.
hors d'oeuvre	Combination of different cold appetizers, such as prosciutto, salami, sardines, tuna, and a variety of salads.
hors d'oeuvre riches	A sumptuous combination of lobster, crayfish, smoked salmon, goose liver, caviar, and the like, elegantly displayed on a large platter or in a variety of small bowls.
pâté	A rich meat, seafood, poultry, or vegetable mixture cooked in pastry and served cold.
pâté de foie gras	Goose-liver *pâté*
pâté de gibier	Cold game *pâté.*
pâté de volaille	Cold poultry pâté
terrine	Meat, poultry, game, or vegetable mixture poached and cooled in a mold lined with bacon or pork strips; sliced and served like a *pâté.* The mold, originally made of earthenware, is called a *terrine;* hence, the name.

Term	Meaning
Warm Appetizers	
beignets de fromage	Cheese fritters.
bouchées Diana	Puff pastry shells with a sauced game and mushroom filling.
bouchées Joinville	Puff pastry shells with a sauced shrimp and mushroom filling.
bouchées à la reine	Puff pastry shells with a sauced poultry and mushroom filling.
cannelloni	(Italian) Small pasta squares, boiled, stuffed with a forcemeat, rolled, and gratinéed with grated Parmesan cheese and tomato sauce.
cromesquis	Meat fritters.
croquettes	Chopped meat, seafood, vegetables, or potatoes that is bound with sauce, crumbed, and fried.
gnocchi parisienne	Dumplings of cream-puff pastry gratinéed with béchamel sauce and grated cheese.
gnocchi piémontaise	Potato dumplings gratinéed with tomato sauce and grated Parmesan cheese.
gnocchi romaine	Semolina dumplings gratinéed with butter and grated Parmesan cheese; tomato sauce is served on the side.
lasagne	(Italian) Wide ribbons of pasta layered with sauce *bolognese,* cheeses, and other fillings, gratinéed with cheese slices.

Term	Meaning
pizza napoletana	(Italian) Light yeast-dough crust covered with mozzarella cheese, tomato sauce, anchovy fillets, capers, olives, and Italian spices (basil and oregano).
quiche lorraine	Custard tart with eggs, cheese, bacon, and onions.
ramequin	A cheese tartlet or slice of bread gratinéed with cheese; also, a small ovenproof dish.
vol-au-vent	Large puff-pastry cases, like *bouchées* but bigger, used to hold savory or sweet fillings.

Soups

bisque d'écrevisses	Crayfish cream soup, refined with cream and crayfish butter and garnished with crayfish tails.
bouillabaisse	French fish soup made from a variety of ocean fish, shellfish, leeks, tomatoes, fennel, garlic, and onions, flavored with saffron.
bouillon	Clear meat broth, made from beef, beef bones, vegetables, and spices.
consommé	Beef broth, flavored with raw chopped meat and vegetables, that is clarified with egg whites and strained.
consommé brunoise	Clarified beef broth garnished with small-diced vegetables.

Term	Meaning
consommé Carmen	Clarified beef broth with tomato puree garnished with green-pepper strips and rice.
consommé Célestine	Clarified beef broth garnished with a julienne of crêpes.
consommé aux diablotins	Clarified beef broth garnished with small cheese canapés seasoned with paprika.
consommé double	Double-strength clarified beef broth—twice the amount of beef is used for the same amount of liquid in the consommé.
consommé hongroise	Clarified beef broth flavored with Madeira and paprika and garnished with tomato cubes.
consommé julienne	Clarified beef broth garnished with a julienne of vegetables.
consommé madrilène	Clarified beef broth flavored with Madeira and Cognac and garnished with tomato cubes.
consommé à la moelle	Clarified beef broth garnished with beef marrow cubes or slices.
consommé Monte Carlo	Clarified beef broth garnished with tiny crêpes stuffed with goose liver.
consommé à l'oeuf	Clarified beef broth garnished with one raw egg yolk per serving.
consommé aux pois frits	Clarified beef broth with pearls of fried batter.
consommé aux pâtés	Clarified beef broth with fine pasta.

Term	Meaning
consommé princesse	Clarified beef broth garnished with molded custard, pearl barley, and a julienne of cooked chicken.
consommé printanière	Clarified beef broth garnished with sliced spring vegetables.
consommé royale	Clarified beef broth garnished with molded custard.
consommé aux vermicelles	Clarified beef broth garnished with vermicelli (fine noodles).
consommé Xavier	Clarified beef broth garnished with egg drops.
crème de . . .	A stock thickened with flour (rice, wheat, or oat), bound with cream and butter or cream and egg yolks, and strained.
crème d'asperges, crème Argenteuil	Cream of asparagus soup garnished with asparagus tips.
crème d'avoine	Cream soup thickened with oat flour instead of wheat flour.
crème aux champignons	Cream of mushroom soup, garnished with mushroom caps.
crème Dubarry	Cream soup of cauliflower stock and white stock, thickened with rice flour, and garnished with tiny florets of cauliflower.
crème portugaise	Tomato cream soup.
crème à la reine	Rice cream soup with chicken stock, garnished with diced chicken meat.
crème de riz	Rice cream soup.

Term	Meaning
Lady Curzon	Turtle soup with whipped cream and egg yolks, sprinkled with curry powder.
minestrone	(Italian) A thick vegetable soup with pasta or rice and tomatoes; grated Parmesan cheese is served separately.
mulligatawny	(Indian) Curry cream soup garnished with rice and strips of cooked chicken.
oxtail clair	Clear broth made from beef tails, garnished with small-diced vegetables and oxtail meat.
oxtail lié	Broth made from beef tails that is thickened with browned flour.
potage	Collective name for soups, especially thick vegetable soups.
potage bâloise	Soup made from browned flour, onions, and beef broth; grated cheese is served separately.
potage Conty	Puree of lentil soup.
potage Crécy	Puree of carrot soup.
potage Dubarry	Puree of cauliflower soup, garnished with tiny florets of cauliflower.
potage Faubonne	Puree of white bean soup.

Term	Meaning
potage florentine	Puree of spinach and potato soup.
potage garbure	Puree of vegetable soup.
potage des Grisons	A Swiss barley soup made with small-diced vegetables, *bündnerfleisch,* and white beans.
potage Lamballe	Puree of green pea soup with tapioca.
potage Parmentier	Puree of potato soup.
potage santé	Puree of potato soup garnished with a julienne of sorrel.
potage St-Germain	Puree of green pea soup garnished with croutons.
potage Victoria	Puree of yellow pea soup garnished with rice.
zuppa pavese	(Italian) Beef broth into which one whole raw egg per serving is placed, topped with a toasted bread sprinkled with grated Parmesan cheese and gratinéed

Term	Meaning

Fish Dishes

Poached Fish

Term	Meaning
à l'ancienne	Coated with white-wine sauce and garnished with pearl onions and mushroom caps.
bonne femme	Coated with white-wine sauce and garnished with mushroom caps and bread croutons.
bordelaise	Coated with bordelaise sauce.
Byron	Coated with red-wine sauce and garnished with mushrooms and truffles.
demi-deuil	Coated with white-wine sauce and garnished with truffles.
Dugléré	Coated with white-wine sauce and garnished with diced tomatoes.
à l'indienne	Coated with a white-wine curry sauce; rice is served separately.
Joinville	Coated with Joinville sauce and garnished with shrimps, truffle slices, and mushrooms.
Marguéry	Coated with white-wine sauce and garnished with shrimp and mussels.
Mornay	Coated with Mornay sauce and gratinéed.

	Term	Meaning
Sautéed Fish	à l'anglaise	Breaded and garnished with lemon.
	Colbert	Breaded and garnished with herb butter (*beurre Colbert*).
	grenobloise	Small-diced peeled lemon, capers, and herbs in foamy butter poured over the fish.
	meunière	Floured and sautéed in butter, garnished with parsley and lemon wedges.
	Murat	Fillet of sole cut in strips, seasoned, rolled in flour, sautéed in butter, and garnished with *pommes parisienne* and artichoke bottoms.
Fried Fish	à l'Orly	Fried in beer batter; tomato sauce is served separately.

Term	Meaning
Sauces	

	Term	Meaning
Brown Sauces	**demi-glace**	The basic brown sauce: brown veal stock flavored with tomato puree and thickened with flour.
Derivations of Demi-glace	bigarade	*Demi-glace* with orange and lemon juice and a julienne of oranges.
	bordelaise	*Demi-glace* with a reduction of red wine, tarragon, and marrow cubes.
	charcutière	Robert sauce with a julienne of pickles, beef tongue, and ham.
	chasseur	*Demi-glace* with mushrooms.
	Diane	Strongly peppered *demi-glace* with cream and truffles.
	diable	*Demi-glace* with a reduction of white wine, shallots, peppercorns, cayenne, and some tomato sauce mixed with butter.
	italienne	*Demi-glace* with tomato sauce, ham, mushrooms, and parsley.
	madère	*Demi-glace* flavored with Madeira wine.
	Périgueux	*Demi-glace* with Madeira wine and truffles.

Term	Meaning
piquante	*Demi-glace* with a white-wine and vinegar reduction, shallots, and cayenne pepper, garnished with chopped parsley, pickles, and tarragon.
poivrade	*Demi-glace* with a white-wine reduction, shallots, and crushed peppercorns.
Robert	*Demi-glace* with a white-wine reduction, chopped onions, mustard, and lemon juice.
zingara	*Demi-glace* with a shallot and white-wine reduction, with tomato sauce, seasoned with paprika, and garnished with truffle and beef tongue.

White Sauces

Term	Meaning
Sauce allemande	A basic white sauce: thickened veal stock (*velouté*), bound with egg yolks and cream.

Derivations of Sauce *Allemande*

Term	Meaning
câpres	*Allemande* sauce with capers.
champignons	*Allemande* sauce with mushrooms.
curry	*Allemande* sauce seasoned with curry and refined with cream.

Term	Meaning
poulette	*Allemande* sauce with mushrooms and chopped parsley.
Sauce suprême	A basic white sauce made from chicken stock refined with cream.

Derivations of Sauce Suprême

Term	Meaning
Albuféra	*Suprême* sauce mixed with meat extract.
estragon	*Suprême* sauce with chopped tarragon.
Toulouse	*Suprême* sauce with truffle essence, lemon juice, and butter.
Sauce au vin blanc	A basic white sauce made with fish stock and refined with egg yolks and cream.

Derivations of Sauce au Vin Blanc

Term	Meaning
Cardinal	Sauce *au vin blanc* refined with lobster butter and truffle essence.
aux crevettes	Sauce *au vin blanc* mixed with shrimp butter and garnished with small shrimp.
diplomate	Sauce *au vin blanc* mixed with lobster butter and garnished with diced lobster meat and truffles.

Term	Meaning
Joinville	Sauce *au vin blanc* with reduced oyster stock, mixed with crayfish and shrimp butter and garnished with truffles.
riche	Sauce *au vin blanc* with lobster butter, truffles, and mushrooms.
Béchamel Sauce	A basic white sauce made with milk thickened with *roux* and flavored with onion.

Derivations of Béchamel Sauce

Term	Meaning
aurore	Béchamel sauce with cream and tomato puree.
crème	Béchamel sauce refined with cream.
Nantua	Béchamel sauce mixed with cream and crayfish butter, garnished with crayfish tails.
Mornay	Béchamel sauce mixed with cream and grated cheese.

	Term	Meaning
Butter Sauces		All butter sauces are made by reducing an acid liquid (such as lemon juice, vinegar, or wine), whisking in egg yolks, and then whisking in melted butter.
	béarnaise	Butter sauce finished with chopped tarragon.
	Choron	Béarnaise sauce with tomato puree.
	hollandaise	Butter sauce with a pinch of cayenne pepper.
	maltaise	Butter sauce with orange juice and a julienne of orange zest.
	mousseline	Butter sauce lightened with whipped cream.
Oil Sauces	**Mayonnaise**	A basic oil sauce made from beaten egg yolks combined with oil and vinegar and seasoned to taste.

	Term	Meaning
Derivations of Mayonnaise	cocktail	Mayonnaise with ketchup, Worchestershire sauce, Cognac, and orange juice.
	rémoulade	Mayonnaise with chopped gherkins, capers, parsley, and anchovies.
	tartar	Mayonnaise with chopped gherkins, hard-boiled eggs, capers, parsley, and onions.
	tyrolienne	Mayonnaise with tomato puree.
	verte	Mayonnaise with a puree of spinach, parsley, and tarragon.
Vinegar Herb Sauce	vinaigrette sauce	Chopped onions and herbs mixed with vinegar and oil.
Cold Specialty Sauces	sauce aux airelles	Lingonberry sauce.
	sauce Cumberland	Red currant jelly, port wine, mustard, orange and lemon juice, garnished with a julienne of lemon and orange peels.

417

Term	Meaning
sauce raifort	Horseradish sauce: whipped cream mixed with grated horseradish.
sauce menthe	Chopped mint leaves boiled with diluted vinegar and sugar, then cooled.

Compound Butters and Butter Preparations

beurre Café de Paris	Herb butter with various spices, anchovy paste, shallots, garlic, lemon juice, parsley, and Cognac.
beurre Colbert	Herb butter with meat extract.
beurre d'écrevisse	Butter mixed with pureed crayfish meat, Cognac, lemon juice, and spices.
beurre fondu	Butter melted in a water bath.
beurre de homard	Like *beurre d'écrevisse* but with lobster meat instead of crayfish meat.
beurre maître d'hôtel	Herb butter with chopped parsley, lemon juice, and spices.
beurre noisette	Butter heated until brown.

Term	Meaning

Main Dishes

Beef

Sautéed Beef
(Sirloin, Tournedos, Round Steak,
Chateaubriand)

à l'américaine	Garnished with a fried egg and bacon bits, accompanied by peas and *demi-glace* with tomatoes.
bordelaise	Garnished with marrow slices and coated with *bordelaise* sauce.
Clamart	Garnished with artichoke bottoms filled with peas.
Dubarry	Garnished with cauliflower.
florentine	Garnished with spinach leaves, with *madère* sauce on the side.
forestiere	Garnished with morels and *madère* sauce, with *pommes parmentier* (potatoes) on the side.
Helder	Garnished with half tomatoes filled with béarnaise sauce, served with *pommes parisienne* (potatoes).
maître d'hôtel	Served with *maître d'hôtel* butter on the meat.
provençale	Garnished with a tomato filled with breadcrumbs, chopped garlic, spices, and parsley.
Rossini	Tournedos topped with a slice of goose liver and truffles, coated with *madère* sauce.

Term	Meaning
filet de boeuf Stroganoff	Cubes of beef filet mignon sautéed, seasoned with paprika, and garnished with pickle strips, mixed with *demi-glace* that has been refined with cream.
tyrolienne	Garnished with deep-fried onion rings and tomato cubes.

Boiled Beef

Term	Meaning
boeuf bouilli à l'alsacienne	Garnished with sauerkraut, bacon slices, and boiled potatoes.
boeuf bouilli flamande	Garnished with carrots, turnips, cabbage, bacon slices, and boiled potatoes; *raifort* sauce and cranberries are served on the side.
langue de boeuf florentine	Boiled beef tongue served on spinach leaves, coated with *madère* sauce.

Braised Beef

Term	Meaning
bourgeoise	Garnished with carrots, small onions, and bacon cubes.
bourguignonne	Garnished with pearl onions, bacon cubes, and mushrooms.
à la mode	Garnished with potatoes, celery, turnips, pearl onions, and calves' feet.

Term	Meaning
carbonnade de boeuf	Braised beef strips in a beer sauce.

Roast Beef
(Filet Mignon, Roasts)

Term	Meaning
à l'andalouse	Garnished with stuffed eggplant, with meat juices served separately.
Dubarry	Garnished with cauliflower, with meat juices served separately.
duchesse	Garnished with *pommes duchesse* (potatoes).
nivernaise	Garnished with glazed pearl onions, potatoes, and turnips, with meat juices served separately.
Tivoli	Garnished with asparagus tips and mushrooms, with meat juices served separately.

Veal

Sautéed Veal
(Chops, Cutlets, Steaks, Chunks)

Term	Meaning
à l'anglaise	Breaded cutlets or chops.
à l'Argenteuil	Garnished with asparagus tips.
bonne femme	Garnished with bacon cubes, pearl onions, carrots, mushrooms, and home-fried potatoes.
côte de veau Pojarsky	Chopped and seasoned veal, shaped into chops, and breaded; garnished with peas and asparagus tips.

421

Term	Meaning
à la crème	Coated with a cream sauce
émincé zurichoise	Veal cut into fine strips, in a cream sauce with mushrooms.
Holstein	Topped with a fried egg and anchovy fillets.
milanaise	Breaded with breadcrumbs and grated cheese, and served with spaghetti with mushrooms and a julienne of ham and beef tongue.
aux morilles	With morels, coated with cream sauce.
napolitaine	Accompanied by spaghetti with tomato sauce.
Nelson	Veal chops covered with onion puree and breaded, served with tomato sauce.
viennoise	Also known as *wiener schnitzel;* breaded cutlets, garnished with a lemon slice topped with a rolled anchovy fillet filled with capers, and a parsley bouquet.
zingara	Coated with *zingara* sauce.

Boiled Veal

blanquette de veau à l'ancienne	Cubes of veal in a white sauce, garnished with pearl onions and mushrooms.

	Term	Meaning
Braised Veal	sauté de veau printanière	Browned veal cubes garnished with carrots, turnips, pearl onions, peas, and celery.
	sauté de veau Marengo	Browned veal cubes garnished with small onions, mushrooms, and heart-shaped bread croutons.
	sauté de veau au curry	Veal stew with curry.
Glazed Veal	chasseur	Garnished with chanterelles and cèpes.
	Dubarry	Garnished with cauliflower
	osso buco	Glazed veal shank garnished with small-diced vegetables and tomato cubes.
Roast Veal (Saddles, Chops, Filets, Loins)	à l'allemande	Garnished with steamed apple slices.
	à l'Argenteuil	Garnished with asparagus tips.

Term	Meaning
flamande	Roasted with braised chicory, garnished with château potatoes.
florentine	Garnished with spinach.

Pork

	Term	Meaning
Sautéed Pork (Chops, Steaks, Cutlets)	bruxelloise	Breaded, and accompanied by brussels sprouts.
	charcutière	Coated with *charcutière* sauce.
	milanaise	Breaded with breadcrumbs and grated cheese; served with spaghetti with mushrooms and a julienne of ham and beef tongue.
	Robert	Coated with *Robert* sauce.
	zingara	Coated with *zingara* sauce.
Roast Pork (Saddles, Chops, Filets, Loins)	à l'allemande	Garnished with steamed apple slices.
	à l'Argenteuil	Garnished with asparagus tips.

Term	Meaning
flamande	Roasted with braised chicory and garnished with château potatoes.
florentine	Garnished with spinach.

Mutton and Lamb

	Term	Meaning
Sautéed Mutton and Lamb (Steaks and Chops)	à l'Argenteuil	Garnished with asparagus tips.
	bergère	Garnished with roasted ham slices, morels, and small glazed onions.
	maréchal	Breaded, topped with truffle slices, and garnished with asparagus tips.
	Nelson	Chops covered with onion puree and breaded; served with tomato sauce.
Braised Mutton and Lamb	navarin	Lamb stew garnished with pearl onions and *pommes parisienne* (potatoes).

	Term	Meaning
Roast Mutton and Lamb (Saddles, Chops, Legs)	bretonne	Roast lamb with dried white beans or wax beans.
	boulangère	Roast leg of lamb with *pommes boulangère* (potatoes).
Boiled Mutton and Lamb	Irish stew	Pieces of lamb (or goat) meat with potatoes, onion slices, and cabbage leaves layered in a pan and boiled (Irish specialty).
	Poultry	
Braised Poultry	poulet Doria	Braised chicken garnished with glazed cucumbers.
	poulet chasseur	Braised chicken garnished with mushrooms.
	chicken curry	Chicken stew with curry sauce.
Roast Chicken	Beaulieu	Roasted or pot-roasted chicken garnished with olives, artichokes, and tomato wedges.

Term	Meaning
bonne femme	Roasted or pot-roasted, garnished with bacon cubes, small onions, and château potatoes.
grand-mère	Pot-roasted and garnished with small onions, mushrooms, bacon cubes, and toasted breadcrumbs.
Demidov	Roasted or pot-roasted, garnished with carrots, turnips, celery, and truffle slices.
bigarade	Roasted duck garnished with orange slices and *bigarade* sauce.

Combination Meat Dishes

bollito misto	An Italian specialty: boiled beef, chicken, beef tongue, veal head, breast of veal, pork sausage, and oxtail, garnished with leeks, carrots, boiled potatoes, and fruit, served with mustard and *verte* sauce on the side.
plat bernois	A Swiss specialty: boiled beef, bacon, smoked pork chops, tongue sausage, and marrow bones, garnished with dried or green leeks, sauerkraut, and boiled potatoes, served with mustard and cranberries on the side.

Term	Meaning
Potatoes	
pommes de terre	The French term for potatoes.
pommes . . .	Potatoes prepared in a certain way. *Pommes de terre* translates literally as "apples of the earth," and *pommes* also means apples. Be careful not to confuse the two.

Boiled Potatoes

Term	Meaning
à l'anglaise	Oval cut with melted butter.
aux fines herbes	Like *pommes à l'anglaise* but with chopped parsley or chives.
maître d'hôtel	Sliced, cooked in milk, and refined with cream.
mousseline	Mashed potatoes refined with cream.
nature	Oval shaped, served plain.
paysanne	Cut into slices and boiled with bacon cubes and chopped onions in broth.
persillées	Like *pommes à l'anglaise* but with chopped parsley.
puree	Mashed potatoes.
en robe de chambre	Cooked and served in their skins.

	Term	Meaning
Baked Potatoes	duchesse	Croquette mixture (see below) piped into rosettes and baked in the oven.
	au four	Baked in the oven unpeeled and served in their skins.
Fried Potatoes	allumettes	Shoestring potatoes.
	Berny	Croquette mixture (see below) that is mixed with chopped truffles, formed into small balls, dipped in egg, coated with chopped almonds, and fried.
	chips	Very thin potato slices (less than $\frac{1}{16}$ inch thick), which can be served hot or cold.
	croquettes	Cooked and mashed potatoes are seasoned and mixed with egg and butter; the mixture is formed into small rolls or balls, breaded, and fried.
	dauphine	Two parts croquette mixture and one part cream-puff pastry (*choux* dough) are mixed and formed into small dumplings.

Term	Meaning
frites	French fries; potatoes cut into sticks about one-half inch wide.
gaufrettes	Sliced with a special fluted tool (a mandoline), into round, waffle-patterned shapes.
mignonnettes	Like *pommes frites* but only half as long.
paille	Straw potatoes; potatoes cut into a fine julienne.
Williams	Croquette mixture (see previous page) that is formed into pear shapes, breaded, and fried.
Pont-Neuf	Steak fries; potato sticks cut twice as thick as *pommes frites*.

Roasted Potatoes
(Roasted in the Oven)

Term	Meaning
boulangère	Potato slices with onions.
château	Oval shaped, like *pommes nature,* but cut smaller, approximately one inch long.
fondantes	Oval shaped, but bigger than *pommes nature,* stewed in the oven.
noisettes	Cut into balls the size of hazelnuts, about one-half inch.
parisienne	Cut into balls twice the size of *pommes noisettes,* about one inch.

	Term	Meaning
Sautéed Potatoes (Sautéed in a Pan)	bernoise	Cooked, peeled, and grated potatoes, sautéed with bacon cubes to a golden yellow.
	lyonnaise	Cooked and peeled potatoes, cut into slices and sautéed with onions.
	sautées	Cooked and peeled potatoes, cut into slices and sautéed.
Gratinéed Potatoes	gratin dauphinois	Potato slices gratinéed with milk, butter, and grated cheese.

Term	Meaning
Desserts	

Cold Desserts

Term	Meaning
blancmange	(British) Almond cream.
cassata	(Italian) An ice-cream cake in which three or four flavors of ice cream (vanilla, strawberry, chocolate) are layered, with pieces of candied fruit and nuts in Italian meringue at the center.
Chantilly	Sweetened whipped cream, flavored with vanilla.
charlotte russe	A Bavarian cream flavored with Kirsch and Maraschino is shaped in a mold lined with ladyfingers; after the cream has set, the dessert is unmolded.
coupe	Ice-cream sundae.
coupe Danemark	An ice-cream sundae of vanilla ice cream and whipped cream, with warm chocolate sauce served on the side.
coupe Helénè	An ice-cream sundae of vanilla ice cream topped with half a stewed pear and whipped cream, with warm chocolate sauce served on the side.
coupe Jacques	Lemon and strawberry ice cream topped with fruit salad, decorated with whipped cream.
coupe Melba	Vanilla ice cream topped with half a poached peach, coated with raspberry puree, and sprinkled with shaved almonds.
coupe Romanov	Vanilla ice cream garnished with fresh strawberries that have been macerated in Kirsch, decorated with whipped cream.

Term	Meaning
coupe Singapour	Pineapple ice cream decorated with pineapple slices, banana slices, and whipped cream.
crème bavaroise	Bavarian cream; a cream made of milk, egg yolks, sugar, gelatin, vanilla, and whipped cream.
crème caramel	Caramel custard.
meringue Chantilly	Meringue shells garnished with whipped cream.
meringues glacées	Meringue shells decorated with ice cream and whipped cream.
parfait glacé	A very light mixture of egg yolks, sugar syrup, and whipped cream, perhaps flavored with liqueur or fruit syrup, which is then frozen.
riz à l'impératrice	Rice pudding with cream and liqueur-macerated candied fruits.
sorbet	Ices; a frozen mixture of sugar syrup, fruit, and water, sometimes refined with sparkling wine or spirits. (Note: *sorbets* are different from sherbets, which contain milk or milk products.)

	Term	Meaning
Warm Desserts	baba au rhum	A cake made from yeast dough with raisins that is soaked in rum syrup and glazed with apricot jam.
	beignets d'ananas	Pineapple fritters; slices of pineapple dipped in frying batter, deep-fried, and sprinkled with cinnamon sugar; fruit sauce is served on the side.

Term	Meaning
beignets de pommes	Apple fritters; apple slices dipped in frying batter, deep-fried, and sprinkled with cinnamon sugar; vanilla sauce is served separately.
crêpes confiture	Thin pancakes filled with jams and jellies.
crêpes normande	Thin pancakes filled with diced apples and raisins with a hint of Calvados.
crêpes Suzette	Thin pancakes in an orange-lemon sauce, flambéed with Grand Marnier, and garnished with vanilla ice cream and whipped cream.
pommes en cage	Whole apples baked in dough.
sabayon	A light wine cream made by beating egg whites, Marsala wine, and sugar over simmering water until foamy; also known by its Italian name, *zabaglione*.
savarin aux fruits	A yeast-dough cake ring soaked in rum syrup and filled with fruit compote.
soufflé au citron	Lemon soufflé.
soufflé mocca	Mocha soufflé.
soufflé Rothschild	Soufflé with fruit.
soufflé Suchard	Chocolate soufflé.

20. *Glossary of Service Terms*

Many culinary terms that you learned in the last chapter are repeated here, because service and kitchen personnel must, of course, speak the same language. Like the culinary terms, the service terms are—with a few exceptions—of French origin. The list includes the most important words and phrases from A to Z.

A

AC	Abbreviation for *Appellation contrôlée;* AC wines are French wines with controlled, guaranteed origins.
à choix	A choice among offerings for example, of fruit, cheese, or hors d'oeuvre.
à discretion	As much as one wants, for example, at a buffet.
à la broche	Roasted on a skewer.
à la carte	An offering from the menu.
à la minute	Quick, prepared to order; used mainly to describe meat dishes that are sautéed, such as sirloin steak.
à la place de	Instead of.
al dente	(Italian) Literally "to the tooth," refers to pasta, risotto, and vegetables that are cooked slightly underdone, so that there is resistance when chewed.
ale	(English) Strong, light English beer.
à part	Served separately.
A.P. Nr.	(German) Abbreviation for *amtliche Prufungsnummer,* the official control number for quality German wines.
à point	Medium-done, describing the degree of cooking for red meat.
assiette	Plate.
assorti(e)s	Assortment, for example, of fruits, cheeses, or hors d'oeuvre.

B

bien cuit	Well done, describing the degree of cooking for red meat.
blanchieren	To blanch.
bleu	Very rare, describing the degree of cooking for red meat.
Bon	(German) Receipt or kitchen voucher, from the cash register or written by hand, to receive food and beverages.
bouchon	Bottle cork or cap.
bouquet	A distinctive and characteristic fragrance, for example, of a wine.
brandy	(English) A spirit distilled from wine.
brigade	(English) A team, for example, the service brigade (all service personnel) or the kitchen brigade (the kitchen personnel).
brochette	Skewer.
brunch	(English) A combination of breakfast and lunch dishes, generally served in the late morning, in place of the two smaller meals.

brut	Very dry, describing the taste of sparkling wines (almost no sugar added).
buffet	A method of serving in which all foods available are placed on the table, and the guests help themselves; service personnel may be on hand to carve.

C

caquelon	Heatproof earthenware container used for the preparation and service of fondue.
carafe	A glass pitcher for the service of open wine; also, a crystal flask for the decanting of old red wines that contain sediment.
carré	The loin or rack of lamb, veal, or pork.
carte des mets	Menu.
carte des vins	Wine list.
carte du jour	Menu of the day.

chambrieren	To bring cool beverages (for example, heavy red wines and aged spirits) slowly and carefully to room temperature (68°F).
château	Vineyard; château-bottled is wine bottled where it was produced, especially in Bordeaux.
chateaubriand	A double cut from the first part of the beef filet, always prepared for two to five persons, it is carved tableside; it is usually grilled and served with *bèarnaise* sauce.
chef de rang	The supervisor of a service station (captain).
choix	Choice, for example, *choix de fromages* is a selection of cheese.
chop	(English) A small cut of meat, for example, lamb or pork, often including part of a rib.
cloche	A cover for a service platter or plate.
cocotte	A round or oval casserole made of heatproof porcelain, copper, or silver.
commis	A young, trained service staff member.
complet	Complete; usage: *menu complet:* the complete menu; *café complet:* coffee with bread, butter, and jam served as a small breakfast.
compote	Stewed or preserved fruit.

contre-filet	Beef loin roasted in one piece.
côte de boeuf	Rib steak.
côtelette	Cutlet.
couvert	Place setting.
crémier	Pitcher for coffee cream or milk.
cuisine	Kitchen, cookery.
cuisse	Leg, shank.
cuvée	The refinement of sparkling wines: wines of different vintage years are blended to achieve consistent quality.

D

darne	A thick slice, or steak, of fish, for example, *darne de salmon* is a salmon steak.
dash	(English) A unit of measure equal to two to three drops, used mainly in bar recipes.
débarasser	To clear.
déjeuner	Lunch.
dekantieren	To decant, that is, to transfer an old red wine from its bottle to a carafe to remove sediment.

demi-sec	Semi-dry, describing the taste of sparkling wines.
dépôt	Sediment in red wine.
dîner	Dinner.
DOC	(Italian) Abbreviation for *Denominazione d'origine controllata;* DOC wines are Italian or Spanish wines of controlled origin.
domaine	Vineyard site.
Dorin	Appellation for white wines from Vaud, Switzerland, made from Chasselas grapes.
doux	Sweet, describing the taste of sparkling wines.

E

émincé	Meat cut into small strips.
entrecôte	Sirloin steak.

entrecôte double	A double sirloin steak, for two people, which is sliced tableside.
entrée	First course; in the United States, the main course.
entremets	Dessert.
escalope	Cutlet, a thin slice of veal or pork.

F

F&B	Abbreviation for food and beverage, used as a short form in the title food-and-beverage manager.
filet/fillet	A slice from the tenderloin of beef, veal, pork, and other meats; also, to remove the bones from fish, and hence, the fish so removed.
finger bowl	(English) A small bowl with water, used to clean the fingers.
frapper	To cool warm beverages in an ice bucket.
fritieren	To deep-fry.

G

Galadîner	Festive banquet.
garçon	Waiter.
garniture	Garnish or accompaniment for meat, poultry, or fish, for example, vegetables, rice, potatoes.
gastronomie	(German) A foodservice establishment; also, fine cuisine.
gigot d'agneau	Leg of lamb.
glasieren	To glaze.

gobelet	(German) A stemless glass used for serving white wines from western Switzerland.
gratinieren	To gratiné, that is, to brown the top of a dish in the oven.
guéridon	Small side table where food is dished out in a restaurant.

H

hors d'oeuvre	Appetizer.

J

jus	The juices from meat, especially roasts.

L

légumier	Vegetable bowl.
lunch	A light meal, served at midday.

M

macédoine	A colorful mixture of small-cut vegetables or fruits.
magnum	(English) A large wine bottle, holding approximately fifty-two ounces.
maître d'hôtel	Headwaiter.
marinieren	To marinate, that is, to steep or soak in a liquid, for example, in a wine or an oil/spice mixture, to season and tenderize.
mazerieren	To macerate, that is, to steep fruits in spirits, to soften and flavor them.
MC	Abbreviation for *Mise en bouteille au Château,* meaning château-bottled, or bottled at the vineyard (see also *château*).
ménage	The collective name for all condiments, seasonings, and spices brought to the table.
menu	The dishes available for or served at a meal; also, a listing of those dishes.
mise en place	Preparation up to the point of usage—the preliminary tasks required to do a job. A perfect *mise en place* is essential in service and cooking.

MO	Abbreviation for *Mise en bouteille à l'origine,* an appellation for French wines bottled at the place of production.
molton	A silence cloth, that is, a soft covering placed on the table under the tablecloth.

N

nappe	Tablecloth.
napperon	A small tablecloth, or overlay, that is placed over the tablecloth or side table to protect the larger cloth and often to enhance the decor.
nature	Natural, plain, pure, ungarnished

P

panaché	Mixed or multicolored, describing fruits, salads, or ice creams.
pâté	A rich meat, game, poultry, seafood, or vegetable mixture cooked in pastry. Do not confuse *pâté* with *pâte,* which means dough or batter.
Perlan	(Swiss) The appellation for white wines of the Geneva canton in Switzerland made from Chasselas grapes.

petit déjeuner	Breakfast.
piccolo	A quarter-bottle of sparkling wine.
plat du jour	Dish of the day.
plateau	Service tray.
pochieren	To poach.
poelieren	To pot-roast or cook gently in the oven in a casserole.
poissonnière	A special container for poaching fish.
premier	The first course of a menu.

R

réchaud	Something that keeps food and plates warm, such as an alcohol burner.
rôtisserie	A restaurant specializing in grilled items; also, a broiling device with a motorized spit for roasting large pieces of meat and poultry.

S

saignant	Rare, describing the degree of cooking for red meat.
saladier	Salad bowl.

Salvagnin	(Swiss) An appellation for red wines from the Vaud canton of Switzerland.
saucière	Sauce boat.
sautieren	To sauté, to pan-fry.
service compris	Indicates the tip is included in the price of the meal.
service station	A specified group of guest tables supervised by a *chef de rang* (captain).
serviette	Napkin.
soigné	Painstaking, careful; used by waitpeople on kitchen orders to indicate the preparation must be perfect, for example, when the guest is very difficult or demanding.
sommelier	Wine steward.
Strohwein	(German) Straw wine, describing selected dry grapes, which are dried on straw mats; the French term is *vin de paille*.
suite, la	The courses that follow in a menu.
supplément	An additional order of food, for example, an addition to a set menu.

T

Terravin	(Swiss) A top-quality Dorin wine.
tranche	Slice.
tumbler	(English) A stemless glass for whiskey.

V

VIP	(English) Abbreviation for very important person; it is noted on the order of a very important guest.
VITI	(Swiss) The appellation for Merlot wines from the Ticini canton in Switzerland.
voiture	A rolling showcase; a service cart on wheels.
Vorlegebesteck	(German) Serving utensils—a large fork and spoon for the service of food.

Z

zeste	Zest, that is, the very thin outer peel of a citrus fruit.

Acknowledgments

Thanks to all the individuals who were consulted in preparing this book:

Hans Jörg Vock, Reinach
Dr. François Diebold, Bern
Dr. Antonio Misale, Zurich
Eberhard Ott,
Hochheim/Mainz
Ing. Georg Victor Eller, Mainz
Hans Reiss, Bern
Adolf Schnider, Bülach
Walter Schudel, Dachsen
Raimond Silvani, Zurich
Klaus-Peter Wiede, Zurich
Walter Trösch, Valbella
Werner von Däniken, Bern
Peter Blattner, Zurich

Thanks to all the institutions and companies that gave their time:

Amt für Volkwirtschaft, Vaduz, Liechtenstein
American Express, Zurich
Bank Americard
Berndorf AG, Lucerne
Bühlmann-Fenner AG, Littau
Carte Blanche
Comestibles G. Bianchi, Zurich
Deutsches Weininstitut, Mainz
Diners Club International
Einrichtungszentrum für das Gastegewerbe, Zurich
Emil Nüesch AG, Balgach
Eurocard Switzerland SA, Zurich
Fäh Glashalle, Rapperswil
Hotel Savoy Baur en Ville, Zurich
Hotel Zürich, Zurich
Information and Propagandastelle für Bieler Weine, Ligerz
Informationsstelle für Ostschweizer Weine, Löhningen
Italienisches Institut für den Aussenhandel, Zurich
Leinenweberei Langenthal, Langenthal
Lükon-Werke AG, Täuffelen
Martel AG, Saint Gall
Mövenpick AG, Zentralverwaltung, Adliswil/Zurich
NCR (Switzerland), Zurich/Wallisellen
Österreichische Handelsdelegation, Zurich
Office des vins genevois, Geneva
Office des vins neuchâtelois, Neuchâtel
Office des vins vaudois, Lausanne
OPAV Propagandastelle für Erzeugnisse der
  Walliser Landwirtschaft, Sitten

Porzellenfabrik Langenthal AG, Langenthal
Reichmuth Albert AG, Zurich
Schuler & Cie, Schwyz
Schweizerische Bierbrauerverein, Zurich
Schweizerische Käseunion AG, Bern
Spring Metallwarenfabrik, Eschlikon
Schweizerische Servicefachlehrer-Vereinigung
Sopexa, Centre d'information de la gastronomie française, Bern
Weinwirtschaftsfond, Vienna

Index

Aargau canton, wine regions of, 309–10

Abbreviations, in wine tables, 304

Abruzzi, wine regions of, 389–90

Active behavior, 157, 158–59

Activity, spheres of, 12–13

Age, of liquors, 248–49

Ahr, wine regions of, 361, 362

À la carte menu, 70, 75, 76

À la carte service, 119, 169
  service styles for, 116
  setting for, 91–93

À la crème, veal, 422

À l'allemande
  pork, 424
  veal, 423

À la mode, beef, 420

À l'américaine, beef, 419

À l'ancienne
  blanquette de veau, 422
  fish, 410

À l'andalouse, beef, 421

À l'anglaise
  fish, 411
  potatoes, 428
  veal, 421

À l'Argenteuil
  mutton and lamb, 425
  pork, 424
  veal, 421, 423

Albuféra sauce, 414

Alcohol, production of, 244

Alcohol burners, cleaning of, 50

Alcohol-free beverages. See Nonalcoholic beverages

Alcoholic beverages, list of, 221

Alcoholic coffee specialties, 283–84

Alcoholic mixed drinks, 261–66

À l'indienne, fish, 410

Allemande sauce, 413–14

Allumettes, potatoes, 429

A l'Orly, fish, 411

Alsace, wine regions of, 349–50

Alternatives, 163–68
  offering of, 163–68

three rules of, 164
  preparation, 166–68
  price, 165–66
  taste, 164–65

Alto Adige, wine regions of, 377, 384

American breakfast, 127–28

Anise-based liqueurs, 241–42

À part menu, 70, 75

À part service, 119
  service styles for, 115, 116
  setting for, 91–93

Aperitif glass, 35

Aperitifs, 239–43

AP-Nr, 355

Appellations, 237
  of Austria, 368–70
  of France, 324–25
  of Germany, 354–56
  of Italy, 376
  of Switzerland, 302–3

Appetite, stimulation of, 161–62

Appetizer(s)
  as additional sale, 169
  cold, 403
  flatware for, 97–99
  warm, 404–5

Appetizing descriptions, 162–63

Apprentice, 14, 15

Aromas, as stimulants to appetite, 162

Arranging food on plate, 112

Art of cooking, 289–97

Ashtrays
  on service table, 86
  setting of, 92

Attentiveness, 158–60

Au four, potatoes, 429

Aurore sauce, 415

Auslese (selected grapes)
  Austrian, 369
  German, 356

Austria, appellations of, 368–70

Austrian wines, 367–73

Aux crevettes sauce, 414

Aux fines herbes, potatoes, 428

Aux morilles, veal, 422

Baba au rhum, 433

Baden, wine regions of, 363, 365

Baked potatoes, 429

Baking (cuire au four), 291, 295–96

Banquet manager, 15

Banquets, 119, 131–39. See also Functions
  assignment of service personnel for, 139
  cheese at, 215
  mise en place for, 138
  preparations for, 136–39
  service styles for, 115, 116, 117

Bar, 59–60
  as distribution and control point, 60, 175–77
  self-service, 60
  service, 60, 178

Bar spoon, 260

Bartender, 15

Basel canton, wine regions of, 311–12

Béarnaise sauce, 416

Beaujolais, 331–32

Beaulieu, chicken, 426

Beef, 419–21
  boiled, 420
  braised, 420–21
  roast, 421
  sautéed, 419–20

Beef fondue, fork for, 30, 97

Beer, 267–73
  accompaniments to, 272
  bottled, 272
  brewing of, 269
  definition of, 267
  fermentation of, 269
  main phases of production of, 268
  mixed drinks using, 273
  raw materials for, 268
  service of, 270–72
  storage of, 269
  on tap, 271
  types of, 269–70

Beerenauslese (choice grapes), 369

Beer glasses, 37

Beer glasses *(cont.)*
  cleaning of, 52
Beer tankard, 38
Beer tulip, 38
Behavior
  active, 157, 158–59
  passive, 157
Beignets, 404, 433–34
Bergère, mutton and lamb, 425
Bern canton, wine regions of, 314
Bernoise, potatoes, 431
Berny, potatoes, 429
Berry-based liqueurs, 257
Beurre, 411, 418
Beverage list, 79–81
Beverages, 219–87. *See also* Drinks
  alcoholic. *See* Alcoholic *entries*
  basics of, 220–21
  breakfast, 125
  nonalcoholic, 274–79
    list of, 221
  pouring of, 112–13
  ready-to-drink, 221
Bigarade sauce, 412
  duck with, 427
Billing form, for credit card, 191
Bisque d'écrevisses, 405
Bitters, 241, 258
Blanching *(blanchir)*, 291, 292
Blancmange, 432
Blanquette de veau à l'ancienne, 422
Block shape arrangement of furniture,
    for banquet, 136
Blush wine, making of, 223
Boat, sauce, 44
Boeuf bouilli, 420
Boiled beef, 420
Boiled mutton and lamb, 426
Boiled potatoes, 428
Boiled veal, 422
Boiling *(bouillir)*, 291, 292
Bollito misto, 427
Bone, meat on, carving of, 200
Boneless meat, carving of, 199
Boning, 196–203
  tools for, 196
Bonne femme
  fish, 410
  poultry, 427
  veal, 421
Bordeaux glass, 32
Bordeaux, wine regions of, 333–38
Bordelaise sauce, 412

beef with, 419
fish with, 410
Bottled beer, 272
Bottled wines. *See* Vintage wines
Bouchées, 404
Bouillabaisse, 405
Bouillon, 405
Bouillon cup, 40
Boulangère, potatoes, 430
  mutton and lamb with, 426
Bourgeoise, beef, 420
Bourguignonne, beef, 420
Bowl(s), 41–42, 44
  finger, 44
  sugar, 49
  vegetable, 42
Braised beef, 420–21
Braised mutton and lamb, 425
Braised poultry, 426
Braised veal, 423
Braising *(braisir)*, 291, 296–97
Bread basket, 49
Bread plate, 40
  placing of, 93
Breakfast, 121–29
  American or English, 127–28
  areas for, 122
  beverages for, 125
  continental, 127
  menu for, 126–29
  mise en place and service for, 123–
    24
Breakfast room, hotel, 123
Bretonne, mutton and lamb, 426
Brewing, of beer, 269
Broiling, 291, 294–95
Brown sauces, 412–13
Brunch, 129
Bruxelloise, pork, 424
Buffet(s), 116–17
  breakfast, 129
  cheese, 215–16
Burgenland, wine regions of, 372
Burgundy, wine regions of, 327–32
Burners, 23
  cleaning of, 50
Butler service, 114–15
Butters, compound, and butter
    preparations, 418
Butter sauces, 416
Byron, fish, 410

Café marnissimo, 284

Café mélange, 282
Cafeteria line, cash register at end of,
    178
Cake fork, 28
Cakes, slicing of, 204
Cake server, 30
California wines, 399
Campania, wine regions of, 389, 390
Canapé, 403
Candle réchauds, 23, 50, 86
Candles, in evening, 103
Cannelloni, 404
Cappuccino, 282
Câpres sauce, 413
Captain, 14, 15
Carafes, 36
  cleaning of, 52
Carbonated soft drinks, 275
Carbonnade de boeuf, 421
Cardinal sauce, 414
Carême, Antonin, 70
Caring, 158, 159
Carrying plates, glassware, flatware
    and other utensils, 107–8
Carts, special. *See* Voitures
Carving, 196–203
  tools for, 196
Cash-free methods of payment, 187–
    91
Cash payment, 184–86
Cash register
  at bar/distribution area, 60, 175–77
  electronic
    guest check from, 186
    with programming, 175, 177
  at end of cafeteria line, 178
  for service bar, 60, 178
  single, near exit, 178
Cassata, 432
Casserole, oval, 42
Ceramic snail dish, 43, 99
Ceylon tea, 286
Chablis, wine regions of, 328
Chairs, checking of, 56
Chambrer, 233
Champagne, 224–25
  wine regions of, 341–42
Champagne glass, 33
Champagne saucer, 33
Champignons sauce, 413
Change, 19
Chantilly, 432, 433
Charcutière sauce, 412

pork with, 424
Charlotte russe, 432
Chasseur sauce, 412
    chicken with, 426
    veal with, 423
Chateaubriand, 419–20
Château, potatoes, 430
Check(s)
    guest. *See* Guest check *entries*
    lunch, 188
    traveler's, 189
Cheese(s)
    as additional sale, 169
    extra-hard, 211
    fresh, 213
    hard, 211
    semi-hard, 212
    semi-soft, 212
    service of, 208–17
    soft, 213
    sour-milk, 213
Cheese fondue
    fork for, 30, 97
    service of, 217
Cheese platter, 214–17
Chicken, roast, 426–27
    carving and boning of, 197–98
Chicken curry, 426
Children, small, 146
Chilling, of wine, 233
China, 39–40
    cleaning of, 50–51
    on service table, 85
    table decoration and, 102
Chips, potato, 429
Chops
    mutton and lamb, 425, 426
    pork, 424
    veal, 421–22, 423–24
Choron sauce, 416
Choux dough, 429
Chunks, veal, 421–22
Citrus-based liqueurs, 256
Clamart, beef, 419
Classical menu structure, 70–71
Cleanliness
    as attentiveness, 159–60
    in working at guest table, 194
Clearing
    of plates, 109
    sequence of, 113
Cloche, 43
Closed container, for sparkling wine, 224

Club soda, 275
Coatroom, 56
Cocktails(s)
    as additional sale, 168
    classic, 262–63
    definition of, 261
    as stimulants to appetite, 161
Cocktail glass, 35
Cocktail sauce, 417
Cocotte, 42
Coffee, 280–84
    as additional sale, 169
    black, with sugar, 281
    breakfast, 125
    decaffeinated, 282
    machines for preparation of, 281
    portion of, 283
    regular, 282
    service of, 281–84
Coffee corretto, 284
Coffee cup, 40
Coffee glass, 36
Coffee *luz,* 283
Coffee server, 44
Coffee specialties, alcoholic, 283–84
Coffee spoon, 29
Cognac, criteria for, 248
Cognac glass, 34
Colbert, fish, 411
Cold appetizers, 403
Cold desserts, 432–33
Cold specialty sauces, 417–18
Combination meat dishes, 427
Commune, as growing area, 236
Complaints, 151–52
Compound butters, 418
Condiments
    for flambéing, 206
    on service table, 85
    for specific foods, 100–101
    in waiters' pantry, 48–49
Consommé, 405–7
Continental breakfast, 127
Control, cost, 171–81
Control point, bar as, 60, 175–77, 178
Control systems, 172–78
Cooking, art of, 289–97
Corkscrew, 19
Cost control, 171–81
Côte Chalonnaise, wine regions of, 330–31
Côte de Beaune, wine regions of, 329–30

Côte de Nuits, wine regions of, 328–29
Côte de veau Pojarsky, 421
Côte de Bourg, wine regions of, 335
Côtes de Rhône, wine regions of, 339–40
Country wine, German, 354
Coupe, 432–33
Courses, main, special flatware for special, 96–97
Cream liqueurs, 257
Creating interest, 160–61
Credit cards, 189–91
Crème bavaroise, 433
Crème caramel, 433
Crème de . . . , 407
Crème sauce, 415
Crêpes, dessert, 434
Cromesquis, 404
Croquettes
    as appetizers, 404
    potato, 404, 429
Cruets, oil and vinegar, 49
Culinary terms
    glossary of, 401–34
    knowledge of, 290
Cup
    bouillon or soup, 40
    coffee, 40
    espresso, 40
    measuring, 260
Curry, chicken, 426
Curry sauce, 413
Cutlets, veal, 421–22

Darjeeling tea, 286
Dauphine, potatoes, 429
Decaffeinated coffee, 282
Decanter, 37
Decanting, 231–32
Decoration, table, 102–3
Deep-frying, 291, 293–94
Delicacies, as stimulants to appetite, 162
Demi-deuil, fish, 410
Demidov, chicken, 427
Demi-glace, 412–13
Denominazione semplice (DS), 376
Denominazione di origine controllata (DOC), 376
Denominazione di origine controllata e garantita (DOCG), 376
Description, appetizing, 162–63

Desserts(s), 432–34
  as additional sale, 169
  cold, 432–33
  warm, 433–34
Dessert silver, placing of, 95
Deutscher Tafelwein (German table wine), 354
Diable sauce, 412
Diane sauce, 412
Digestifs, 258, 259. See also Bitters
Dining room
  cleaning of, 55
  interior of, 56–57
  mise en place in, 55–57
Dinner fork, 28
  placing of, 92
Dinner knife, 27
  placing of, 91
Dinner plate, 40
Diplomate sauce, 414
Dishes, 39–40
  cleaning of, 50–51
Distillation, 245
Distribution point, bar as, 60, 175–77
Dôle, 302
Dorin, 302
Dostoevsky, Fyodor, 142
Drinks. See also Beverages; Liquors; Spirits
  carbonated soft, 275
  mixed. See Mixed drinks
  mixed milk, 278–79
  prepared, 221
  tall
    classic, 264
    definition of, 261
Dubarry
  beef, 419, 421
  veal, 423
Duchesse, potatoes, 429
  beef with, 421
Dugléré, fish, 410

Eiswein (ice wine)
  Austrian, 369
  German, 356
Electric plate warmers, 23
Electronic cash register
  guest check from, 186
  with programming, 175, 177
Emilia-Romagna, wine regions of, 385, 387
Émincé zurichoise, veal, 422

English breakfast, 127–28
En robe de chambre, potatoes, 428
Entrecôte double (double sirloin), carving of, 199
Entre-deux-Mers, wine regions of, 337
Equipment
  for flambéing, 207
  and materials, 17–45
  for mixed drinks, 259, 260
  personal, 18–19
Espresso, 282
Espresso cup, 40
Espresso spoon, 29
Estragon sauce, 414
Eurochecks, 189
Expectations, of guests, 141–43

Facility, first impressions of, 149–50
Fantasy name, for wine, 237
Farewells, to guests, 153
Fermentation, of beer, 269
Field of view, of menu, 76–77
Filet de boeuf Stroganoff, 420
Filet mignon, 421
Filets
  pork, 424
  veal, 423–24
Finger bowl, 44
First impressions, 149–50
Fish
  fried, 411
  poached, 410
  sautéed, 411
  slicing and boning of, 201–3
Fish fork, 28, 96, 99
Fish knife, 27, 96, 99
Fish server, 42
Flamande
  pork, 425
  veal, 424
Flambéing, 205–7
Flatware. See also Silver; Utensils
  for appetizers, 97–99
  carrying of, 107
  cleaning of, 51, 53
  on service table, 85
  special, for special main courses, 96–97
Florentine
  beef, 419, 420
  pork, 425
  veal, 424
Flowers, 56

Focal point, of menu, 76–77
Fondantes, potatoes, 430
Fondue
  beef, fork for, 30, 97
  cheese
    fork for, 30, 97
    service of, 217
Fondue burners, 23
  cleaning of, 50
Food, appetizing description of, 163
Food-and-beverage manager, 15
Forestiere, beef, 419
Fork(s)
  cake, 28
  dinner, 28
    placing of, 92
  fish, 28, 96, 99
  fondue, 30, 97
  lobster, 29, 96
  oyster, 30, 98
  salad, 28
  second, placing of, 94
  snail, 29, 99
Formaggini in oil, 217
Fortified-wine glass, 35
Fortified wines, 242–43
France, appellations of, 324–25
Franken, wine regions of, 363–64
Frappés, 279
French cuisine, classic menu for, 71
French service, 114–15, 118, 119
French terminology, 402
French wines, 323–51
Fried fish, 411
Fried potatoes, 429–30
Frites, potatoes, 430
Fromage frais, 217
Front waiter, 14, 15
Fruit juices, 275–76
  as stimulants to appetite, 161
Frying/pan-frying/deep-frying (frire), 291, 293–94. See also Fried entries
Functions, 131–39. See also Banquets; Special occasion
  assignment of service personnel for, 139
  checklist for, 134
  in-house instructions for, 135
  types of, 132
Furniture, restaurant, 20–22
  arrangement of, for banquet, 136–39

Gas burners, 23
  cleaning of, 50
Gaufrettes, potatoes, 430
Geneva canton, wine regions of, 315–16
German wines, 353–65
Germany, appellations of, 354–56
Germ-free milk, 276–77
Gesture, helpful, as response to complaint, 152
Gift certificates, 188
Glass(es)
  aperitif, 35
  beer, 37, 52
  bordeaux, 32
  champagne, 33
  cocktail, 35
  coffee, 36
  cognac, 34
  fortified-wine, 35
  Irish-coffee, 35
  measuring, 260
  milk, 36
  mixing, 260
  placing of, 92, 96
  red-wine, 32
  Rhine-wine, 33
  rocks, 35
  shot, 34
  sparkling-wine, 33
  for specific liquors, 249–54
  sundae, 36
  tea, 36, 52
  water, 32, 52
  white wine, 32
Glassware, 31–38
  carrying of, 107
  cleaning of, 52–53
  on service table, 85
Glazed veal, 423
glazing (glacer), 291, 297
Glossary
  of culinary terms, 401–34
  of service terms, 435–49
Gnocchi, 404
Grand-mère, chicken, 427
Grape variety, of wine, 234
Gratinéed potatoes (gratin dauphinois), 431
Gratinéing (gratiner), 291, 295
Graubünden canton, wine regions of, 308–9
Graves, wine regions of, 337

Greeting, attentiveness in, 158
Grenobloise, fish, 411
Grill, cleaning of, 55
Grilling/broiling (griller), 291, 294–95
Grog, 266
Guéridon, 21
Guest check
  cash payment with, 185–86
  cash payment without, 184
  from electronic cash register, 186
  handwritten, 185
  immediate payment with, 186
Guest-check printers, cash registers with, 175, 177
Guest mise en place, 83, 87–103
Guests
  categories of, 144–46
  complaints of, 151–52
  expectations of, 141–43
  farewells to, 153
  first impressions of, 149–50
Guest service, 12
Guest table
  rules for service at, 109–10
  working at, 193–217
    basic rules for, 194–95
    carving and boning, 196–203
    flambéing, 205–7
    service of cheese, 208–17
    slicing cakes and pies, 204

Handicapped guests, 145–46
Hand towels, 19, 26
Headwaiter, 14, 15
Helder, beef, 419
Herbal teas, 287
Herb-based liqueurs, 256
Herb sauce, vinegar, 417
Hessiche Bergstrasse, wine regions of, 363, 364
Hollandaise sauce, 416
Holstein, veal, 422
Hops, 268
Hors d'oeuvre, 403
Horseradish sauce, 418
Host/hostess, 15
Hot chocolate, for breakfast, 125
Hotel breakfast room, 123
Hot mixed drinks, 266
House accounts, 188
Hungarian wines, 397

Ice bucket, 45

Iced tea, 287
Iced tea spoon, 29
Ice tongs, 260
Immediate payment, with guest checks, 186
Impregnation, of sparkling wine, 224
Individual table arrangements, for banquet, 137
Interest, creating of, 160–61
Irish coffee, 283
Irish coffee glass, 35
Irish stew, 426
Italian wines, 375–85
Italienne sauce, 412
Italy, appellations of, 376

Jasmine tea, 286
Joinville sauce, 415
  fish with, 410
Juices
  fruit, 275–76
    as stimulants to appetite, 161
  vegetable, 275–76
Jura, wine regions of, 349, 351

Kabinett
  Austrian, 369
  German, 355
Kitchen knowledge, basic, 290
Kitchen orders, and order writing, 179–81
Knife
  dinner, 27
    placing of, 91
  fish, 27, 96, 99
  second, placing of, 94
  small, 27

Labels, wine, 234–38
Lady Curzon, 408
Lamb, 425–26
  boiled, 426
  braised, 425
  carving leg of, 200
  roast, 426
  sautéed, 425
Landwein, 354
Langue de boeuf florentine, 420
Languedoc, wine regions of, 345, 347
Lapsang Souchong, 286
Lasagne, 404
Latium (Lazio), wine regions of, 389, 391

Left of guest, 110
Liechtenstein, wines of, 398
Lights, checking of, 55
Linens, table, 24–26
   on service table, 85
   setting of, 88–89
   table decoration and, 102
Lingonberry sauce, 417
Liqueurs
   anise-based, 241–42
   bitter, 241, 258
   types of, 255–58
Liquid condiments, maintenance of, 49
Liquor(s), 244–54. *See also* Drinks;
   Spirits
   age of, 248–49
   production of, 244–46
   refinement of, 245
   service of, 247
   storage of, 245
   useful information about, 249–54
Lobster fork, 29, 96
Lobster tongs, 29, 96
Loins
   pork, 424
   veal, 423–24
Lombardy (Lombardia), wine regions
   of, 377, 382–83
Lounge, cleaning of, 55–56
Lunch checks, 188
Lyonnaise, potatoes, 431

Maceration, 244
Mâconnais, wine regions of, 331
Madère sauce, 412
Main courses/dishes, 419–27
   special, special flatware for, 96–97
   Maître d'hôtel, 14, 15
Maître d'hôtel butter, 418
   on beef, 419
   on potatoes, 428
Malt, 268
Maltaise sauce, 416
Malting, 244
Managers, banquet and food-and-
   beverage, 15
Marches, wine regions of, 389, 391
Maréchal, mutton and lamb, 425
Marguéry, fish, 410
Matches, 19
Materials, equipment and, 17–45
Mayonnaise, 416–17
Meal tickets, 188

Measuring cup, 260
Measuring glass, 260
Meat
   on bone, carving of, 200
   boneless, carving of, 199
Meat dishes, combination, 427
Médoc, wine regions of, 334–35
Meissen china, 39
Menu(s), 69–81
   a la carte, 70, 75, 76
   a part, 70, 75
   breakfast, 126–29
   classical structure of, 70–71
   composition of, 70
   design of, 75
   focal point and field of view of, 76–
     77
   format of, 75
   for French cuisine, 71
   as sales tool, 76–78
   on service table, 86
   short, 72–74
   in showcase, 56
   table d'hôte, 70, 75, 76
Meringue Chantilly, 433
Meringues glacées, 433
Merlot VITI (Vini Ticinesi), 303
Meunière, fish, 411
Mignonnettes, potatoes, 430
Milanaise
   pork, 424
   veal, 422
Milk, 276–78
   raw, 276, 277
Milk-coffee, 283
Milk drinks, mixed, 278–79
Milk glass, 36
Milk pitcher, 45
Mineral water, 274
Minestrone, 408
Mise en place
   for banquet, 138
   breakfast, 123–24
   for decanting, 231
   definition of, 12
   in dining room, 55–57
   for flambéing, 206–7
   guest, 83, 87–103
   service, 83, 84–86
   in waiters' pantry, 48–54
Mistakes, excusable and inexcusable,
   151–52
Mixed drinks, 259–66

alcoholic, 261
beer in, 273
equipment for, 259, 260
hot, 266
most important, 261–66
Mixed milk drinks, 278–79
Monthly schedules, 64, 65
Mornay sauce, 415
   fish with, 410
Mosel/Saar/Ruwer, wine regions of,
   361–62
Mousseline, potatoes, 428
Mousseline sauce, 416
Mulled wine, 266
Mulligatawny, 408
Murat, fish, 411
Mussels, flatware for, 99
Mustard container, 49
Mutton, 425–26
   boiled, 426
   braised, 425
   roast, 426
   sautéed, 425

Name
   of wine, 234–37
   of wine producer, 238
Nantua sauce, 415
Napkin(s), 25
   as hand towel, 19
   placing of, 91
   wine, 26
Napolitaine, veal, 422
Napperons, 25
Nature, potatoes, 428
Navarin, mutton and lamb, 425
Nelson
   mutton and lamb, 425
   veal, 422
Neuchâtel canton, wine regions of,
   314–15
Newspapers, 56
Niederösterreich, wine regions of, 371
Nivernaise, beef, 421
Noisettes, potatoes, 430
Nonalcoholic beverages, 274–79
   list of, 221

Occasion, special. *See* Special
   occasion
Occasional guests, 144–45
Oil and vinegar cruets, 49
Oil sauces, 416–17

Older guests, 146
Opening, of sparkling wines, 230
Open wines, 225
    service of, 226
Order(s)
    and cleanliness, as attentiveness,
        159–60
    kitchen, and order writing, 179–81
Order pad, 19
    as control system, 173–74
Organization
    of menu, 78
    service, 63–67
    in working at guest table, 194
Osso buco, veal, 423
Österreichischer Qualitätswein
    (Austrian quality wine), 368
Oval casserole, 42
Overlays, 25, 90
Oxtail soup, 408
Oyster, fork, 30, 98

Pad, order, 19
    as control system, 173–74
Paille, potatoes, 430
Pan
    heating milk in, 277
    potatoes sautéed in, 431
Pan-frying, 291, 293–94. *See also*
    Sautéeing
Pantry, waiters', *mise en place* in, 48–
    54
Parfait glacé, 433
Parisienne, potatoes, 430
Parmesan, containers of grated, 49
Passive behavior, 157
Pasteurization, 276
Pastry tongs, 30
Pâté, 403
Payment, method of, 183–91
    cash, 184–86
    cash-free, 187–91
Paysanne, potatoes, 428
Pen, 19
Périgueux sauce, 412
Perlan, 303
Persillées, potatoes, 428
Personal equipment, 18–19
Personal rules, 106–7
Personnel, service, assignment of, for
    function, 139. *See also* Staff
Phone booth, cleaning of, 55

Piedmont (Piemonte), wine regions of,
    377–79
Pies, slicing of, 204
Pie server, 30
Pilsner beer glass, 37
Piquante sauce, 413
Pitcher(s), 36
    cleaning of, 52
    milk, 45
Pizza napoletana, 405
Placemats, 25
Plants, potted, 56
Plat bernois, 427
Plate(s)
    arranging food on, 112
    bread, 40
        placing of, 93
    carrying of, 107, 108
    clearing of, 109
    dinner, 40
    salad, 40
    snail, 43
    soup, 40
Plate service, 116, 118, 119
Plate warmers, electric, 23, 86
Platter(s), 41
    cheese, 214–17
Platter service, 115, 118, 119
Platter warmers, 23
Poached fish, 410
Poached trout (*truite au bleu*), slicing
    and boning of, 201–2
Poaching (*pocher*), 291, 293
Poise, in working at guest table, 195
Poivrade sauce, 413
Pomeral, wine regions of, 335–36
Pommes de terre, 419, 421, 425, 426,
    428–31
Pommes en cage, 434
Pont-Neuf, potatoes, 430
Pork, 424–25
    roast, 424–25
    sautéed, 424
Portuguese wines, 396
Pot, heating milk in, 277
Potage, 408–9
Potatoes, 428–31
    baked, 429
    boiled, 428
    fried, 429–30
    gratinéed, 431
    roasted, 430
    sautéed, 431

Pot-roasting (*poêler*), 291, 296, 297
Poulette sauce, 414
Poultry, 426–27
    braised, 426
    carving and boning of, 197–98
    roast, 426–27
Pouring beverages, 112–13
Preparation
    basic methods of, 291–97
    knowledge of, 290
Preparation alternatives, 166–68
Preparatory work, 12. *See also Mise
    en place*
    in dining room, 55–57
    in waiters' pantry, 47–54
Prepared drinks, 221
Price alternatives, 165–66
Printers, guest-check, cash register
    with, 175, 177
Producer's name, on wine label, 238
Profession, service, 11–15
Programming, electronic cash register
    with, 175, 177
Provençale, beef, 419
Provence, wine regions of, 345–46
Punches, 265
Puree, potato, 428
Purity law, 267

Quality seal with official control
    number, Austrian wine, 370
Quality wine(s)
    Austrian, 368
    German, 354–55
    with titles
        Austrian (Qualitätswein mit
            Prädikat), 368–70
        German, 355–56
Quiche Lorraine, 405

Raclette, 217
Ramequin, 405
Ready-to-drink beverages, 221
Réchauds, 23
    cleaning of, 50
    on service table, 86
Red wine, making of, 223
Red wine glass(es), 32
    cleaning of, 52
Red wine snifter, 33
Regions, wine. *See* Wine regions
Regular guests, 144
Rémoulade sauce, 417

Reservations, 147–48
Restaurant
  breakfast in, 123
  style of, table decoration and, 102
Restaurant furniture, 20–22
  arrangement of, for banquet, 136–39
Restaurant table, 21
Rheingau, wine regions of, 357–58
Rheinhessen, wine regions of, 357, 359
Rheinpfalz, wine regions of, 357, 360
Rhine wine glass, 33
Riche sauce, 415
Right of guest, 110
Ristretto, 282, 284
Riz à l'impératrice, 433
Roast beef, 421
Roast chicken, 426–27
  carving and boning of, 197–98
Roasted potatoes, 430
Roasting (rôtir), 291, 296
Roast mutton and lamb, 426
Roast veal, 423–24
Robert sauce, 413
  pork with, 424
Rocks glass, 35
Room service
  breakfast in, 124
  service style for, 115
Room-service waiter, 15
Rosé, making of, 223
Rossini, beef, 419
Round steak, 419–20
Round table, 21
Roussillon, wine regions of, 345, 347
Rüdesheimer coffee, 284
Rummer, 34

Sabayon, 434
Saddles
  mutton and lamb, 426
  veal, 423–24
Saint-Emilion, wine regions of, 336
Saint Gall canton, wine regions of, 308
Salad fork, 28
Salad plate, 40
Sales, 13
  additional, 168–69
Sales category totals, 176
Sales technique(s), 155–69
  active behavior as, 157, 158–69
  for additional sales, 168–69
  attentiveness as, 158–60

caring as, 158, 159
creating interest as, 160–61
describing appetizingly as, 162–63
offering alternatives as, 163–68
proper approach to, 156–57
stimulating appetite as, 161–62
Sales tool, menu as, 76–78
Sales totals, 175
Salmon, smoked, slicing of, 201
Salt and pepper shakers, 49, 92, 100
Salvagnin, 302
Sauce(s), 412–18
  bechamel, 415
  brown, 412–13
  butter, 416
  cold specialty, 417–18
  in flambéing, 206
  oil, 416–17
  vinegar herb, 417
  white, 413–15
Sauce allemande, 413–14
Sauce au vin blanc, 414–15
Sauce aux airelles, 417
Sauce boat, 44
Sauce Cumberland, 417
Sauce menthe, 418
Sauce raifort, 418
Sauce spoon, 28
Sauce suprême, 414
Sauté de veau, 423
Sautéed beef, 419–20
Sautéed fish, 411
Sautéed mutton and lamb, 425
Sautéed potatoes, 431
Sautéed veal, 421–22
Sautées, potatoes, 431
Sautéing (sauter), 291, 294. See also
  Pan-frying
Sauternes, wine regions of, 337–38
Savarin aux fruits, 434
Schaffhausen canton, wine regions of, 311
Schedules, work, 64–65
Seed-fruit-based liqueurs, 257
Self-service, 116–17, 119
Self-service bars, 60
Seltzer, 275
Seminars, table arrangements for, 137
Server
  cake and pie, 30
  coffee, 44
  fish, 42
  tea, 44

Service
  of beer, 270–72
  breakfast, 123–24
  of cheese, 208–17
  of coffee, 281–84
  guest, 12
  of liquors, 247
  room. See Room service entries
  of tea, 286–87
  wine, 226–33
Service bar, 60
  cash registers for, 178
Service carts. See Voitures
Service hierarchy
  for large establishment, 15
  for medium-sized operation, 14
  specialists in, 15
Service methods, 118–19
Service mise en place, 83, 84–86
Service organization, 63–67
Service personnel, assignment of, for
  function, 139. See also Staff
Service profession, 11–15
Service rules, 106–110
  for carrying, 107–8
  for clearing, 109
  at guest table, 109–10
  personal, 106–7
Service stations, 66–67
Service style(s), 114–17
  French, 114–15, 118, 119
  plate, 116, 118, 119
  platter, 115, 118, 119
  self-service, 116–17, 119
  side-table, 115–16, 119
Service table, 20, 84–86
Service techniques, 111–13
Service terms, glossary of, 435–49
Service trays, on service table, 86
Serving temperatures
  for liquors, 249–54
  for wines, 230
Setting
  of linens, 88–89
  table, basic, 91–93
    extension of, 94–96
Sèvres china, 39
Shaker(s)
  beverage, 260
  salt and pepper, 49, 92, 100
  sugar, 49
Shape, table, table decoration and, 102
Shot glass, 34

Side dishes, as additional sales, 169
Side table, 21
Side-table service, 115–16, 119
Silence cloths, 24, 88
Silver. *See also* Flatware; Utensils
    cleaning of, 51, 53
    dessert, placing of, 95
Sirloin, 419–20
Slicing
    of cakes and pies, 204
    of fish, 201–3
Small knife, 27
Smoked salmon, slicing of, 201
Snacks, as stimulants to appetite, 162
Snail dish, ceramic, 43, 99
Snail forks, 29, 99
Snail plate, 43
Snail tongs, 29, 99
Snifters, 33, 34
Soft drinks, carbonated, 275
Sole, slicing and boning of, 203
Sommelier, 15
Sorbet, 433
Soufflé, dessert, 434
Soup cup, 40
Soup plate, 40
Soups, 405–9
Soup spoon, 28–29
Soup tureen, 43
Spanish wines, 394–95
Sparkling-wine glass, 33
    making of, 224–25
    opening of, 230
Spätlese (late harvest)
    Austrian, 369
    German, 355
Special flatware for special main
        courses, 96–97
Specialists, 15
Special occasion. *See also* Functions
    arrangements for, 133–35
    table decoration for, 102–3
Spheres of activity, 12–13
Spirits. *See also* Drinks; Liquors
    as additional sale, 169
    for flambéing, 207
    production of, 245–46
Spoon
    bar, 260
    coffee, 29
    espresso, 29
    placing of, 94–95
    sauce, 28

soup, 28–29
sundae or iced-tea, 29
Staff, guests' first impression of, 149–
        50. *See also* Service personnel
Stainless steel, cleaning of, 51
Stance, in working at guest table, 195
Stations, service, 66–67
Steak(s)
    beef round, 419–20
    mutton and lamb, 425
    pork, 424
    veal, 421–22
Steam, heating milk with, 277–78
Steaming (*cuire à la vapeur*), 291,
        292–93
Steiermark, wine regions of, 373
Stew, Irish, 426
Stewing (*étuver*), 291, 296, 297
Strainer, 260
Style of restaurant, table decoration
        and, 102
Sugar bowl or shaker, 49
Sundae glass, 36
Sundae spoon, 29
Suprême sauce, 414
Sweet liqueurs, 255
Swiss wines, 301–22
Switzerland
    appellations of, 302–3
    wine region(s) of, 305–22
        eastern, 305–12
        southern, 321–22
        western, 313–20

Table(s)
    checking of, 56
    decoration of, 102–3
    guest. *See* Guest table
    individual arrangements of, for
        banquet, 137
    restaurant, 21
    round, 21
    service, 20, 84–86
    shape of, table decoration and, 102
    side. *See* Side table *entries*
Tablecloth(s), 25
    laying of, 88–89
    removing clean, 89–90
Table d'hôte menu, 70, 75, 76
Table d'hôte service, 118
    service style for, 115
    setting for, 91–93
Table linens. *See* Linens, table

Table setting, basic, 91–93
    extension of, 94–96
Tall drinks
    classic, 264
    definition of, 261
Tankard, beer, 38
Tartar sauce, 417
Taste alternatives, 164–65
Tastes, knowledge of, 290
Tea(s), 285–87
    as breakfast beverage, 125
    flavors of, 286
    herbal, 287
    iced, 287
        spoon for, 29
    service of, 286–87
    simplest method of preparation of,
        286
Tea glass(es), 36
    cleaning of, 52
Tea server, 44
Teaspoon, 28
Temperature(s)
    of dining room, 56
    serving
        for liquors, 249–54
        for wines, 230
Terminology, French, 402
Terms
    culinary
        glossary of, 401–34
        knowledge of, 290
    service, glossary of, 435–49
Terravin, 303
Terrine, 403
Thurgau canton, wine regions of, 310–
        11
Ticino canton, wine regions of, 322
Title(s), quality wines with
    Austrian, 368–70
    German, 355–56
Tivoli, beef, 421
Tongs
    ice, 260
    lobster, 29, 96
    pastry, 30
    snail, 29, 99
Toothpick holder, 49
Toulouse sauce, 414
Tourists, 145
Tournedos, 419–20
Trademark name, for wine, 237
Traveler's checks, 189

Trays, service, on service table, 86
Trockenbeerenauslese (dried choice grapes)
  Austrian, 370
  German, 356
Trout, poached, slicing and boning of, 201–2
Tulip, beer, 38
Tureen, soup, 43
Tuscany, wine regions of, 385–86
Tyrolienne, beef, 420
Tyrolienne sauce, 417

Ultra-heat-treated milk, 277
Umbria, wine regions of, 389, 392
United States, wines of, 399
U-shape arrangement of furniture, for banquet, 136
Utensils, 27–30; see also Flatware; Silver
  carrying of, 107

Valais canton, wine regions of, 319–20
Val de Loire, wine regions of, 343–44
Vaud canton, wine regions of
  Bonvillars, Vully, les Côtes de l'Orbe, 316
  Chablais, 318–19
  La Côte, 316–17
  Lavaux, 317–18
Veal, 421–24
  boiled, 422
  braised, 423
  glazed, 423
  roast, 423–24
  sautéed, 412–22
Vegetable bowl, 42
Vegetable juices, 275–76
Velouté, 413
Veneto, wine regions of, 377, 380–82
Vermicelli, 407
Vermouths, 239–40
Verte sauce, 417
Vienna (Wien), wine regions of, 373
Viennoise, veal, 422
Vinegar herb sauce (vinaigrette sauce), 417
Vineyard, name of, 237
Vintage, on wine label, 238
Vintage wines, 226
  bottle sizes for, 226
  service of, 227–29
Voitures, 22

Warmers, 23
Water
  brewing, 268
  mineral, 274
Water glasses/goblets, 32
  cleaning of, 52
Weekly schedules, 64, 65
Whiskey
  designations for, 249
  service of, 247
White sauces, 413–15
White wine(s)
  making of, 223
  as stimulants to appetite, 161
White-wine glass(es), 32
  cleaning of, 52
Wiener schnitzel, 422
Williams, potatoes, 430
Wine(s), 222–38. See also individual countries
  appellations of. See Appellations
  blush, 223
  country, German, 354
  definition of, 222
  description(s) of
    appetizing, 163
    in tables, 304
  fortified. See Fortified wine entries
  making of, 223–25
    principles of, 222
  methods of selling, 225–26
  mulled, 266
  name of, 234–37
  name of producer of, 238
  open, 225, 226
  quality. See Quality wine(s)
  red. See Red wine entries
  region of production of. See Wine regions
  rosé, 223
  service of, 226–33
  sparkling. See Sparkling wine entries
  vintage. See Vintage wines
  white. See White wine entries
Wine basket, 45
Wine from Austria, 368
Wine glasses, 32
  cleaning of, 52
Wine labels, 234–38
Wine lexicon, 299–399
Wine napkins, 26
Wine regions, 235–37
  of Abruzzi, Campania, Latium,

cleaning of, 50
Vol-au-vent, 405

Waiter
  front, 14, 15
  room-service, 15
Waiters' pantry, mise en place in, 48–54
Warm appetizers, 404–5
Warm desserts, 433–34
  Marches, and Umbria, 389–92
  of Alsace and Jura, 349–51
  of Austria, 371–73
  of Bordeaux, 333–38
  of Burgundy, 327–32
  of Champagne, 341–42
  of Côtes du Rhône, 339–40
  of Franken, Hessiche Bergstrasse, Württemberg, and Baden, 363–65
  of Mosel/Saar/Ruwer and Ahr, 361–62
  of Piedmont, Veneto, Lombardy, and Alto Adige, 377–84
  of Provence, Languedoc, and Roussillon, 345–47
  of Rheingau, Rheinhessen, and Rheinpfalz, 357–60
  of Switzerland, 305–22
  of Tuscany and Emilia-Romanagna, 385–87
  of Val de Loire, 343–44
Wine steward, 15
Wine tables, abbreviations and descriptions in, 304
Wine tumbler, 32
Winzer-Wy, 303
Worcester china, 39
Work, preparatory. See Preparatory work
Working, at guest table. See Guest table, working at
Work schedules, 64–65
Writing of orders, 179–81
Württemberg, wine regions of, 363, 365

Zabaglione, 434
Zingara sauce, 413
  pork with, 424
  veal with, 422
Zuppa pavese, 409
Zurich canton, wine regions of, 306–7